SNOWBOARDING
the world

SNOWBOARDING
the world

BEAR AGUSHI, LUKE BEUCHAT & JUSTIN DRERUP

PRINCIPAL PHOTOGRAPHER NICK CLARK

LANSDOWNE

Published by Lansdowne Publishing Pty Ltd
Level 1, 18 Argyle Street, Sydney NSW 2000, Australia

First published 1999

Front cover: photograph inset far left—Gavin O'Toole.
Photograph pages 2–3 and main photograph pages 4–5—
Gavin O'Toole.

Commissioned by Deborah Nixon
Designer: Arne Falkenmire
Production Manager: Sally Stokes
Project Coordinator: Kate Merrifield
Editor: Barry Gordon

Set in Gill Sans, Garamond and Stone Sans on QuarkXPress
Printed in Singapore by Kyodo Printing Pte Ltd.

National Library of Australia Cataloguing-in-Publication
data:

Agushi, Bear.
    Snowboarding the world.

    Includes index.
    ISBN 1 86302 671 1.

    1. Snowboarding. 2. Snowboards. 3. Snowboarding -
Guidebooks. I. Beuchat, Luke. II. Drerup, Justin.
III. Clark, Nick, 1968-. IV. Title.
    796.9

Disclaimer
The maps in this book are for illustrative purposes only. The
representation of any or all specifically marked lifts, mountain trails, paths or pistes does not necessarily guarantee their
existence. Mountains may change over time. Obey all signs.

Snowboarding is fun but it is also dangerous. Nature is
unpredictable and when combined with the pursuit of snowboarding it can have devastating consequences. The authors
and the publishers take no responsibility for loss of job,
spouse, friend, limb or life from using this guide.

CONTENTS

ACKNOWLEDGMENTS

KEY RESEARCHERS
Bear Agushi – Australia, New Zealand and USA
Luke Beuchat – Austria and Switzerland
Justin Drerup – France and Japan
Daniel Beuchat – Canada

CONTRIBUTORS
Bear Agushi, Luke Beuchat, Justin Drerup, Ashley Bleeker, Brooke Geary, Sam Schroder, Geir Arne Halvosen, Ruskin McLennan, Peter Murphy, Daniel Beuchat, Josh Blandy, Nick Clark.

PHOTOGRAPHERS
Nick Clark, Gavin O'Toole, Tim Zimmerman, Peter Murphy, Alex Guzman, Jeff Potto, Scott Sine, Ben Blankenburg, Paul Morrison, Nossio, Schmiederer, JP Fankhauser, Jeff Webb, Scalp DPPI, Larry Prosor, Mark Maziarz, Alan Klys (3D images).

PROOFREADERS
David Emery, Andrew McNamara, Jan Ritzmann, Anne Beuchat, Michel Beuchat, Josh Blandy

JAPANESE TRANSLATION
Georgie Landy and Yoshie Ishida.

SPECIAL THANKS TO
Snowave Travel, Specialists in snowboard travel to Japan, New Zealand, Canada and USA.
Ph: +61 2 9977 7488
Email:info@snowave.com
Internet: www.snowave.com

Snowbeds Accommodation, the best place to stay in Hakuba, Japan.
Ph: +81 90 2260 8469 Fax: +81 20 261 5242
Email: snowbeds@yahoo.com

The Gliders Paradise, the coolest hostel in the world and the place to stay in Laax, Switzerland.
Ph: +41 81 911 2903

The Alpine Inn, conveniently located in Frisco, Colorado right next to all of Colorado's major resorts.
Ph: +1 970 668 3122 Fax: +1 970 668 2287
Email: alpinein@colorado.net

Renault Eurodrive, the only way to travel around Europe.
Australian Ph: +61 2 9299 3355
Internet: www.eurodrive.renault.com

The guys at: www.boardtheworld.com and www.boardaustralia.com.au

THANKS TO
Lester and Eva at the Alpine Inn, Yoshie and Mitch at Snowbeds, Gusty at the Gliders Paradise, Werner from Querty, the Querty Mobile, all our friends in Utah (Jared, Chris, Scott, Nicole, Travis, Deanna), Lou and Faye, Rob Bak, Ryan Wainwright, Omer Saar, Jeff Christopherson, Cliff Jones, Shane and Dawesy in Whistler, Shane Stephens, Koala for her love and support, Peter Agushi for allowing us to use his house as an office, Paul Beuchat for photo stamping, the girls from Laax, Janaka Peterson from Ground Swell Agencies, Mark Baders from Spy, Kerry Gratwick from Salomon, Steve from Elan, Mike at the Mordy Snowboard Connection, Andy at the Playground Snowboard Shop, the Hot Zone Snowboard School in Gerlos, Roland at the Banana Snowboard School in Davos, Paul Ehrhardt from the Bar Savoia.

Thanks to all the resorts that helped us out. Sandra Brogle from the Davos Tourist Office, Ariane Ehrat from the Weisse Areana in Laax, Nicole and Franco Gilly in St Moritz, Carole Ansermoz in Verbier, Kristina Clement at the Les Grands Montets, Natalie at Les Arcs, Nadège Benaissa at Tignes, Andrea Kostenzer from Mayrhofen Tourist Office, Rosemarie Kummer in Innsbruck, Armin Egger at Lech, Ulrike Jochum at Zürs, Heinrich Wagner in St Anton, Carmen Fender at Solden, Suzanne Hickey in Whistler/Blackcomb, Rob Cote at Norquay, Brian Browning at Resorts of the Canadian Rockies, Chris Burgner from Park City, Kimberly Peterson and Amber Borowski at Snowbird, Dan Malstrom in Brighton, Leigh Pezzicara from Vail Resorts, Rachael Woods at Alpine Meadows, Amy Phalon from Killington, Carrie Meader from the Canyons, Shuuji Yoshikawa at Kijimadaira, Michaela Crump from Mt Buller, Rod Lake from Thredbo, Don Killen at Perisher Blue.

And to everyone else who helped us out, thanks a million. Hope the book does justice to all the work everyone put in.

With thanks to: **O'NEILL**

FOREWORD

Above: *The size of your airs is only limited by your imagination, not the size of the mountain.*

Another snowboard book. Another group of strangers telling you where to go and what to do. The last time you trusted some 'local' fool to take you to the most 'killer' place in the country you followed him on a two-hour hike, twisted your foot climbing a cliff face and lost six kilograms sweating through your 'breathable' jacket. Only to watch the same fool scream out 'We're here, this is it. Watch my style, bros', then launch a backside 90 to heel edge off a mogul. 'Thanks, dude', you say, 'I'd prefer not to drop the 30-foot cliff to rock garden.' But this is not such a book. It is written by three snowboarders who have shared a passion for the progression of snowboarding since its very early beginnings. They have a wealth of experience and have traveled the world in search of epic powder and pipes.

Flashback 1986: A young rider named Justin (Juz to his friends), inspired by the Burton Backhill in the display cabinet in the local sports store, created his first snowboard from plywood and seat belts. Four years later a softly spoken Swiss-born rider, going under the alias of Mouse (although the name Luke appears on his passport), rented his first board from Monsieur Golut in the tiny Swiss resort of Ovronnaz. Half a world away an Albanian Australian, Bear Agushi, committed the first of many questionable insurance claims to buy his first deck. The scene was set.

Despite different backgrounds, ages and moral codes, they came together at university, driven by the same passion – snowboarding – and before many people had even heard of it. This burning desire to snowboard led them to start a tiny university snowboarding club. From these humble beginnings the club grew into the biggest snowboard organisation in the Southern Hemisphere. Through the club they were able to hone their riding skills and gained a reputation as progressive snowboarders. But to reach the next level of riding, they knew they would have to head overseas.

But traveling costs money and credit cards are not limitless. Even hard work won't provide the dollars needed to fulfil the snowboarding dream. So, following overseas trip after overseas trip, Bear, Mouse and Juz became frustrated with the impossibility of financing their desire to snowboard around the world. From this frustration came innovation – an Internet site on the world's snowboarding resorts. Justin's digital skills and his keen eye for a 'breathtaking view', Mouse's inherent talent for organization, time management and saving a dollar, and Bear's shrewd business sense and his nature as a born entertainer all helped to form a formidable business that became known as Board the World. The Board the World website developed such a following that it became one of the world's most popular snowboarding reference tools.

We have been riding around the world with the three guys for some time now. Their knowledge of where to go snowboarding and how to snowboard continues to astound us. Bear, Mouse and Juz are not content to rest on their laurels. They are always striving to increase what they know about snowboarding and push their riding to the limit. More importantly, they are always there to bring the best out of those they ride with.

The bottom line is, if you've been there, so have they, and if you've landed the trick, they've most likely stomped it switch. This book is simply an extension of their passion.

Jan Ritzmann and Andrew McNamara

INTRODUCTION

Above: *The search for endless powder. Adam Dawes lays a solitary turn in the Tahoe backcountry.*

Snowboarding the World. This is every snowboarder's dream. To grab your backpack and your board and head off. Exploring new and amazing mountains. Experiencing new cultures. Meeting new people. Most importantly, snowboarding to your heart's content. Today, the dream is becoming more and more a reality. Travel is a hell of a lot easier. English is becoming more widely spoken. And in a more uncertain world where 'jobs for life' are a thing of the past, snowboarders are saying, 'Screw you guys, I'm going snowboarding.' It is this spontaneity that makes life exciting, makes it worthwhile to get up in the morning. The thought that one day in the near future you will be able to go riding at your favorite hill wearing your favorite beanie with your favorite friends. The thought that when you arrive at your favorite hill you will be able to try some of the latest tricks as seen in the latest Mack Dawg or FLF video release. These are the attitudes from which snowboarding was hatched. The need to be different, to try something new, to break out of the norm. These are also the attitudes evident in most 18-25 year olds. It's not surprising that snowboarding's first big market was this age group. Today, however, snowboarding is not restricted to this age group. Now, everyone from 5 to 85 is snowboarding. And why wouldn't you? It's probably the most fun you can ever have on snow.

IN THE BEGINNING

To see where snowboarding started we have to turn the clock back to 1965. A chemical engineer from Michigan in the USA, Sherman Poppen, was out sledding with his daughter when he saw his daughter coming down the slope standing up. From this sight, Poppen created the Snurfer, a wooden ski with a rope attached to the nose which was held by the rider and used for stability. Poppen licensed the idea and began manufacturing. Over half a million Snurfers were sold between 1966 and 1977.

As the popularity of Snurfers grew, Poppen organised Snurfer competitions. It was through these competitions that Jake Burton Carpenter was introduced to the concept of snowboarding. Jake would turn out to be the owner of the biggest snowboarding manufacturer in the world, Burton Snowboards.

As Jake Burton fell in love with Snurfers he decided to build his own. In 1978 he made 350 production boards. But Jake's boards were faster and more responsive than Poppen's original Snurfers. So began the decline of the Snurfer. Poppen soon lost interest in the Snurfer and sold the company.

As Jake began to build his snowboarding empire on the East Coast of the USA, Tom Sims brought snowboarding to California. Sims, together with Chuck Barfoot, started Sims Skateboards in 1971. Sims and his team helped to redefine the look, feel and culture of skateboarding. In 1977, Sims set Chuck Barfoot to work on designing a Sims Snowboard. It turned out to be a good business decision. As skateboarding went through a recession phase in the early 1980s, Sims switched his focus to snowboarding and, with all the right media contacts, he was able to cement himself as a leading snowboarding manufacturer.

While the 1970s belonged to the manufacturers, the 1980s belonged to competitions and consumers. The 1980s saw the formation of snowboarding teams and the availability of snowboards in ski and skate shops. The early 1980s saw intense competition between the Burton team on the East Coast of the USA and the Sims team on the West Coast. Jake Burton and Tom Sims were not only rivals in business, but also rivals on the racecourse. The 1980s also saw a whole new breed of freestyle riding, led by the likes of Terry Kidwell, Damien Sanders, Dan Donnelly and Craig Kelly. Kelly would go on to be the dominant force in snowboarding throughout the late 1980s and early 1990s. His smooth style and classic airs would reign over the competition scene. By the late 1980s snowboarding was really turning into a business – Burton was selling over 20,000 boards a year and Sims over 10,000.

Backed by media hype, magazines and videos, the early to mid 1990s saw the explosion of snowboarding. With more snowboard companies, more snowboards and more snowboarders, snowboarding became the 'alternative' winter sport – the thing to do if you wanted to be cool. Snowboarding became universal – people were snowboarding in Japan, Europe, the USA, Canada, Australia, New Zealand and South America. Snowboarding had entered the realm of big business.

PRODUCT INNOVATION

With the assistance of ski technology, snowboard product innovation has proceeded in leaps and bounds. Today's snowboards are far easier to ride, control and learn on than Jake Burton's Backhills of the 1980s. Boards are now a high-tech combination of wood, carbon fiber, fiberglass, dampening materials and P-Tex. The snowboards of the new millenium are extremely responsive and turning has become much easier.

Bindings have also seen an enormous amount of development. Strap bindings are now more comfortable and responsive. And the Holy Grail, step-in freestyle bindings, seems close at hand, with most of the major companies releasing some form of step-in. Only time will tell whether riders will prefer step-ins over the tried and tested strap bindings.

Product innovation has made snowboarding much easier to learn and opened up the market to just about anyone who wants to give it a go.

The tables have now turned: where snowboarding companies once turned to the ski companies for innovation, ski companies are now borrowing ideas from snowboarding. Parabolic skis, fat powder skis and twin-tip skis are all concepts that have come out of snowboarding.

Above: *Hangin' out with your friends — that's what snowboarding is all about.*

SNOWBOARDING AND SKIING

Snowboarding has had a profound and lasting effect on skiing. When snowboarding first began, it was not allowed at many resorts, thus it was not a concern for skiers. Today, almost all resorts allow snowboarding. Resorts now see snowboarding as a big part of their market. This has concerned many diehard skiers who still see snowboarding as dangerous. The way to progress forward is not really through conflict but rather through compromise. If both sports are to continue to flourish, skiers and snowboarders need to work together to understand each other's needs. After all, both skiers and snowboarders are out there for the same purpose – to have fun on the snow.

The progression of snowboarding moves has been amazing – from the plain old method air to 360s to 1080 spins. The latest inverted moves, the Frontside and Backside Rodeos, are mind-blowing. Riders are performing these moves off cliffs, cornices and kickers. The progression of snowboarding moves has also pushed skiers.

Although many freestyle skiers may disagree, it seems difficult to argue that freestyle snowboarding has not had an influence. These days skiers are skiing switch and trying rodeos and 1080s. In fact some of the moves performed by the latest batch of freestyle skiers, particularly the Canadian Airforce, is mind-boggling. This progression is really healthy for both sports.

A LIFESTYLE CHOICE

Snowboarding can become a lifestyle. Many people who get involved in snowboarding make it the focal point of their life. They live for that next snowboarding fix – to capture the sensation of riding down the mountain and using the natural terrain to launch an air or slide a log. To feel the butterflies in their stomach as they strap on their board on a powder day. To feel totally stoked after stomping an air. People surround themselves with snowboarding culture. They buy snowboarding clothes. They watch snowboarding videos every night. They read snowboarding magazines. They have snowboarding heroes. They saturate their lives with snowboarding culture. On the street or at work, they look just like you or me. But ask them any question about snowboarding and words will come tumbling out faster than the processing speed of your brain. This is what snowboarding does.

THE SUPERHEROES

A culture is not really complete without its heroes and villains. Over its 30-year history, snowboarding has certainly developed its fair share of stars and mega-stars.

The first snowboarding superstars came from its birthplace, the USA. Riders such as Terry Kidwell, Damien Sanders, Steve Graham and Craig Kelly built up a cult following. These riders created the first image for snowboarding and brought it into the public eye.

Above: *No single rider has revolutionised snowboarding as much as Terje Haakonsen.*

Above: *Pick your line and go for it.*

The late 1980s and early 1990s saw the birth of snowboarding's first bad boy, Shaun Palmer. Palmer had raw talent, which helped him win many competitions. But Palmer was also a loose cannon – rude, crazy and punk. Palmer brought a whole new alternative image to snowboarding.

The mid 1990s belonged to the Scandinavians. Riders like Sebu Kuhlberg, Terje Haakonsen, Johan Olofsson and Daniel Franck stood out. They redefined the meaning of freestyle snowboarding.

In the big mountain arena, the older riders such as Tex Davenport, Dave Hatchett, Tom Burt and Noah Salasnek continued to push limits. These riders were dropping lines in Alaska and other extreme mountains that no one thought it was possible to snowboard. First descents became the standard rather than the exception.

But without a doubt the Michael Jordan of snowboarding is Norwegian superstar, Terje Haakonsen. Terje dominated all major competitions throughout the early to mid 1990s and redefined halfpipe riding. The size and fluidity of his airs were mind-blowing not only to the judges but also to his fellow riders. The strength of his riding could not be faulted.

Now in the new millennium it's the Americans and Canadians who are again taking over the sport they created some 30 years earlier. The skate-influenced styles of riders such as JP Walker, BJ Leines, Jeremy Jones and Mikey LeBlanc are again pushing the limits of what people thought was rideable on a snowboard. Leading this new progressive style of riding is a diminutive rider from Washington, Peter Line. He is pushing limits and inventing new moves such as the Backside Rodeo. Canadian superstar Trevor Andrews is blowing minds with the size of his airs in the pipe. And another Canadian, Mike Michaelchuck, could well be the next Terje of snowboarding. With airs that defy gravity like double backflips in the halfpipe, Michaelchuck is beginning to command a lot of respect from riders worldwide. In Europe, guys like Michi Albin and Guillaume Chastagnol are also pushing the limits.

THE OLYMPICS

The Olympics came and went in 1998. Snowboarding was part of it for the first time, but nothing really changed. Lesser-known rider Gian Simmen took the gold in the halfpipe, with Daniel Franck grabbing silver. Ross Rebagliati tested positive for traces of marijuana and had his gold medal removed. It was subsequently returned. The Olympics exposed snowboarding to a very wide audience and this has been great for the industry. The Olympics brought out into the open the politics behind snowboarding. Who should be the peak body for snowboarding? Should it be the Federation Internationale du Ski (FIS), the peak body for skiing, or should it be the International Snowboarding Federation (ISF), the body that has run snowboarding competitions since the beginning? The ISF still commands a lot of support among the riders and is a genuine snowboarding body. Only time will tell who will win the day. Let's just hope politics does not get in the way of snowboarding.

THE FUTURE?

Looking into the crystal ball, what does the future hold for snowboarding? It seems inevitable that the number of snowboarders will keep growing. Of course, snowboarding will never replace skiing, nor should it, because both are very worthy winter sports. In terms of tricks, three things can be said: more spins, more inverts and more air. New superstars will come and old stars will fade, but the impression left by Terje Haakonsen will never die. Competitions will continue to be brought into the cities to ensure they are closer to the fans and are more visually stunning. Boardercross will more than likely be added to the Winter Olympics program. The ISF will continue to be the peak body for freestyle snowboarding. Halfpipes will begin to appear at almost every mountain as both snowboarders and skiers alike will demand them. Although all these things are just guesses, mere reflections on what may happen to snowboarding in the future, one thing can be said with certainty. People will continue to have fun riding their snowboards so long as there is snow on the mountains.

SNOWBOARDING THE WORLD

Snowboarding the World will not make you a snowboarding superstar like Terje Haakonsen (although you never know). Nor will it teach you the basics of how to turn your snowboard. You'd be better off spending $20 on a lesson. What it will do is give you a flavor of some awesome places to snowboard around the world. We will take you on a tour from the snow-covered gum trees of Australia to the majestic peaks of the Southern Alps of New Zealand. On to the Japan Alps, through the Canadian Rockies and Colorado Rockies, then over to the Rockies of Utah and the Sierras of California. Finally we will tour the king: the mighty Alps of Switzerland, Austria and France. When we have whetted your appetite for snowboarding

Above: *When the snow conditions are bad, consider heading backcountry. Photo—Gavin O'Toole.*

we will send you on a trick-fest splurge. From 360s to Frontside 720 Rodeos – step-by-step photos will show you how to nail some of the toughest moves in snowboarding. Take the book to your local ski hill, study it, then go out and nail the trick. If you're stoked, we'll be even more stoked. If that is not enough, we tell you how to buy a snowboard, how to maintain it and how to win boardercross races on it. Interested in building halfpipes or kickers? Read on. Ever wondered what causes avalanches and how to avoid them? Now you will know. This guide will certainly give you a taste of what snowboarding is all about and give you plenty of good reasons to get out there and go snowboarding.

FROM THE ARMCHAIR

Before you read on and get involved in all of the hype of snowboarding, remember this: snowboarding is about having fun. It is not about whether you have the latest board with the latest graphics. It is not about whether you wear Burton forward lean socks. It is not about whether you wear straps or step-ins. It is not about whether you drink Mountain Dew or 7-Up. Snowboarding is not about whether you wear baggy pants or how low your pants hang. It is not about whether you wear your cap backwards or forwards or even sideways for that matter. It is not about whether you have the same style as JP Walker or Juha Tenkku. It is not about whether your wear mitts or gloves. What snowboarding is about is whether you wear 1980s fluorescent one-piece outfits. No, just kidding. Snowboarding is about fun. It's about having fun with your friends. If you have to wear all the latest gear to feel good and have fun, then that's fine. And if you don't have any of the latest gear but still have fun snowboarding, then that's great. If you remember one thing from this whole book, go out to snowboard for yourself and have some fun doing it. Avoid the hype and be yourself.

Above: *Below an imposing rock, Bear Agushi carves out another turn.*

THE AIR 101 GUIDE

INTRODUCTION

Take a look at the video rack of any reputable snowboard shop. What do you see? You see videos of pros performing the latest freestyle moves. You don't see videos of GS (Giant Slalom) racers banging gates. Or perhaps check out the pages of any snowboard magazine. You will find photos galore of methods, spins and rodeos. This is because freestyle riding is cool. It's cool because it gives riders the chance to be different, to show their individual style. The style of your 360 may be totally different to your friend's. This doesn't make it any better or worse; it's just different. You can go out and boost a move off a kicker or a halfpipe using your own style. However, while the same move may be performed differently, every move has fundamental principles that lie underneath the style with which it is executed. Once you understand these fundamental principles, you can really get into freestyle riding and start applying your own style to the moves in these pages. Who knows – one day, you may even have a move named after you!

The Air 101 section of this book aims to give you a better knowledge and appreciation of the different freestyle moves that can be performed on a snowboard. Ultimately, Air 101 aims to provide you with the necessary understanding so you can stick any of the moves in this book. And of course, it will help you look cool when you tell all your friends what new tricks you can do!

Above: *Some riders can never be stopped. The allure of the moon draws Damo Liddy across a monster road gap.*
Left: *Air 101 here we go, Jef Billo shows how it's done. Photo—Tim Zimmerman.*

This section is split into five general categories:
1. Straight airs off kickers
2. Spins off kickers
3. Inverted airs off kickers
4. Halfpipe airs
5. Rail slides.

Be sure to know your snowboarding terms so you can fully understand the explanations provided. Check the glossary of technical terms at the back of this book.

AIR 101

To be a champion freestyle snowboarder, you must possess the knowledge and ability to combine the two basic elements:
1. Technical skill
2. Style.

A rider must be able to demonstrate these two elements in order to master a new trick or refine an old one.

Technical skill refers to the techniques required to perform the move. We will talk about 'digging your toe edge in …' and 'turning your head …' throughout this section of the book. A rider must know what the trick involves technically and have the skills to carry it out. Of course, acquiring the skills requires practice.

Looking good is all part of being a snowboarder, and it's no use being able to go off a kicker, spin 360, land and ride away if your arms are flying all over the place and you looked as if you were about to eat it halfway through the trick. This is where style comes into play. Each rider has his/her own unique snowboarding style – his/her own way of expressing themselves on a board. Style in snowboarding refers to the finer details of performing the move – how you grabbed the board, how long you held the board for, if you were crouched enough, or if your arms were flapping. Once you have perfected the actual performance of a trick, you should really concentrate on making sure that the trick is done super smooth so it looks as if you could have done it with your eyes closed.

THINK ABOUT THE MOVE …

On a final note, ask any decent rider how they can perform the moves they do and many of them will tell you that the trick is embedded into their subconscious before they do it.

It's always a good idea to picture a move in your head before you try it for the first time. It's no good attempting a trick unless you can sit back from the jump and picture it in your mind step by step, so it feels as if you know exactly what to do without having to think about it.

A further word of advice is not to get too hung up on the move and the consequences of not pulling it off. Too often, riders are dying to try a new trick, but they keep asking themselves what if this happens, and what if that happens, and fail to progress as a result. Just make things clear in your head and go for it when the conditions are right.

Disclaimer: Remember, never try the trick unless you are ready for it and the conditions are appropriate. It's no good trying to get inverted over a 9 m (30 ft) tabletop when the landing is flat and icy! So jump according to the conditions and your own ability.

Opposite: *Jim Rippey jumps his way to victory over a Lake Tahoe backdrop.*
Below: *Not quite Air-101. Bear Agushi finds an inventive way to cross a creek.*

STRAIGHT AIRS OFF KICKERS

INTRODUCTION

The most basic air to do on a snowboard is the 'straight air'. Simply ride off the jump, get yourself in the air, and then land. Well, perhaps it's not quite so simple – that's why we have explained how it's done in full detail on the following pages. But the point here is that the straight air is the first kind of air a rider will be able to do as he/she picks up snowboarding. A straight air doesn't involve a spin or a flip. Your body should remain vertical and your weight centered over your stance.

Straight airs become more complicated as you begin performing them simultaneously with a grab – that is, you air off the jump, grab the board, let go of the board, and then land. There is a plethora of different grabs a rider can do, and each grab will have its own variations according to the rider's personal style. Understanding what each grab involves is crucial, or you will look like a fool when you say, 'Hey, how was that guy's indy?' when in fact it was a method.

Above: *Bear Agushi focusing on his tail grab.*

DIFFERENT TYPES OF GRABS

1) Indy Grab

The indy grab is when you grab the board with your trailing hand on the toe edge of your board. A regular footer would grab with his/her right hand. A goofy footer would grab with his/her left hand. The grab must be between the legs, most often closer to your back foot. For style points, bone out your front leg whilst grabbing (regular footers bone to the right, goofys bone to the left).

Above: *Faye Middleton styling an indy at Grizzly Gulch.*

2) Mute Grab

The mute grab is similar to the Indy grab but performed with the front hand, not the trailing hand. Therefore, a regular footer will use his/her left hand to grab the toe edge of the board, whilst a goofy footer uses his/her right hand. For style points, you can bone your back leg whilst grabbing, or stiffy both legs at the same time as grabbing.

Left: *Mouse Beuchat going old style with a mute grab.*

3) Tail Grab

As the name suggests, this trick is performed by grabbing the tail of your board with your trailing hand (right hand for regular footers, left hand for goofys). For style points, bone out your front leg. For double style points, bone it out forward and to the side a little (regulars bone to the left, goofys to the right). Make sure you grab the very tip of the tail and not the side of the tail, or else you run the risk of looking like a kook.

4) Nose Grab

No points for guessing how this move is performed; it's the direct opposite of the tail grab. That is, regulars use their left hand and grab the nose, goofys use their right hand and grab the nose. It's not really the coolest trick to do off a straight jump, but have it ready to pull out whilst spinning a 360 and you will look like a real hero.

Above: *Peter Coppleson reaching for his nose off a Falls Creek kicker.*

5) Lien/Melon Grab

When in the air, squat down and grab the heel edge of the board with your front hand (left hand for regular, right hand for goofy). The grab is made between the legs. Perfect this grab before going onto the next grab – the method.

Above: *Lou Rogai, Lein at Park City.*

6) Method Grab

Pretty much the same as the melon only you must also bone out your back leg and twist your legs around so the base of your board faces forward (you'd better see the pic to know what we mean). This is the most timeless and stylish grab around and can be varied in a million different ways. Instead of grabbing between the legs, try grabbing the board just in front of your front foot for a stylish variation.

Above: *Mouse Beuchat getting stinky with a stalefish.*

7) Stalefish Grab

This one is quite tricky, as it requires a bit of a body contortion to do it well. Here you've got to grab the board with your trailing hand on your heel edge (right hand for regular, left hand for goofy). However, don't make the mistake of grabbing the board near the tail or else it will look bad. You have to twist your upper body slightly to ensure you grab the heel edge of the deck between your legs. You can even bone out your front or rear leg for bonus style points.

8) Roast Beef

Even more difficult than the stalefish, the roast beef involves a rider grabbing the board with his/her front hand (regulars left, goofys right) on the heel edge of the board, but through the legs. Your arm must come in front of your body and legs and be grabbing the heel edge under your backside.

The list of grabs goes on and on: taipan, Japan air, tindy … you name it. However, gain an understanding of these eight and you can adapt them not only to straight airs, but to spins and flips as well.

Above: *Travis Parker methods for the cameras.*

Above: *Mouse Beuchat cookin' up a roast at Copper Mountain.*

STRAIGHT AIRS MADE EASY

with Brian Resis

LEVEL OF DIFFICULTY: 3 OUT OF 10

1

2

3

There are a number of very basic rules that generally apply to all straight airs to assist you in pulling them off. Make sure you understand them, as they will help you considerably in becoming a straight air master.

Before you can do straight airs with precision and ease, you must first be able to ollie. An ollie is the key ingredient to being a successful snowboarder.

An ollie is the bread and butter of freestyle snowboarding. If you can't do an ollie well, you may as well use your snowboard as firewood. The principles behind an ollie are crucial to almost every freestyle move under the sun.

Step 1 – The Set-up
- Make sure you are well centered over your board and you are riding in a straight line.
- When you are ready to ollie, place most of your weight on your back foot.

Step 2 – The Spring
- Push down hard on your back foot and try to extract as much spring out of the tail of your board as possible.
- At the same time as you are pushing down on your back foot, lift your front foot up.
- Once you have loaded the board up with spring by simultaneously pushing down with your back foot and lifting your front foot, lift your back foot up with the natural spring of the snowboard.

Step 3 – The Air
- You should now be in the air, so enjoy the extra altitude.
- To increase the height of your ollie, bring your legs up higher.

Step 4 – The Landing
- Bring the snowboard nicely down on a flat base.

Welcome to the world of freestyle snowboarding!

Photo sequence—Tim Zimmerman

4

5

1

2

3

4

5

6

7

8

GOLDEN RULES FOR STRAIGHT AIRS

Step 1 – The Approach

- The approach to the kicker is a crucial step to get right.
- Always approach the kicker with your weight centered over your stance.
- Make sure that your body is sideways – hips and shoulders follow the length of the board. Don't open up your shoulders so that they are facing downhill – this will cause your front leg to stiffen and make it harder to stay balanced.

Step 2 – The Take-off

- Probably the most important part of performing any jump.
- As you hit the lip of the kicker, make sure the base of your board is flat. DO NOT take off on an edge.
- As you leave the lip of the jump, make sure you OLLIE. DO NOT jump with both feet at the same time. It is important that you leave the lip whilst doing an ollie because this will keep your weight centered in the air and stop you being kicked back onto your butt (check out the previous sequence to learn how to ollie). Ollieing will also give you height and distance.

Step 3 – In the Air

- So long as you took off from the lip correctly, this step should be pretty straightforward. Your weight should be centered over your stance and you should be in a crouch position. The crouch helps you keep balanced in the air and is also essential when you want to grab the board.
- Remember to keep an eye on your landing and try and hold your arms steady.

Step 4 – The Landing

- *Landing on hardpack* – as you hit the ground, the base of your board should be flat for stability.
- Squat as you hit the ground so your legs can take the impact of the landing and you can remain balanced.
- Don't land on an edge or you'll be in big trouble. Too often, riders learning straight airs will twist their board sideways (frontside) and land on their heel edge and butt simultaneously. This is wrong and only develops bad habits. Point your nose straight downhill as you land and ride out the landing.
- Don't be afraid of landing with a bit of speed – you will be able to slow down after you stick it.
- *Landing in powder* – this takes more practice, as it is much more difficult than landing on hardpack, but it is less scary because the consequences of a fall are not as harsh.
- As you touch down, keep your weight back from center just a little as you hit.
- Bend your back knee and straighten your front leg slightly – this will get your nose above the powder and stop you from nosediving.

REMEMBER: Keep your body sideways, which means don't turn your shoulders downhill.

Photo sequence—Tim Zimmerman

SPINS OFF KICKERS

INTRODUCTION

Every budding freestyle pro must perfect the art of spinning his/her board in the air. Spins are the obvious progression from straight airs and really aren't much more difficult. You simply require a bit of commitment and understanding before you attempt them. The term 'flat spin' means a rotation of the board whilst the rider remains vertical (upright) and does not get inverted.

Spins progress in difficulty, starting at 180 degrees (a half rotation) and increasing by 180 degrees at a time (180, 360, 540, 720 and so on). Of course you can spin in increments of less than 180, say 90, but I highly doubt your body could take the punishment each time you caught an edge on the landing and ate it! Naturally, each additional 180 you add to your spin, the more difficult it becomes. A 720 or 900 is still regarded as a very difficult trick, and the elusive 1080 can often not be performed perfectly by even the top pro riders.

BACKSIDE VS FRONTSIDE SPINS

A snowboarder can spin either clockwise or anti-clockwise. Because a snowboarder can either be regular (left foot forward) or goofy (right foot forward), it is necessary to give a description that can relate to either stance. If you spin 'backside', you are turning your upper body backwards so that your first 90 degrees of the rotation is blind and your back faces down the hill. On the other hand, when you spin 'frontside', you open up your shoulders so that your upper body is facing forwards down the hill during the first 90 degrees of the rotation.

REGULAR FOOTER
When viewed from above:
Backside (B/S) Spin – Clockwise rotation
Frontside (F/S) Spin – Anti-clockwise rotation

Above: *Bear Agushi going to dizzy land with this spin in Brighton.*
Opposite: *Peter Coppleson is a spinning master. Here he displays his skills. Photo—Gavin O'Toole.*

Once you perfect each spin on its own, start adding grabs, as discussed. For example, try a backside 360 indy grab or a frontside 540 roast beef! By adding the grab whilst spinning, you'll look cooler and you also add a degree of difficulty to the trick.

GOOFY FOOTER
When viewed from above:
Backside (B/S) Spin – Anti-clockwise rotation
Frontside (F/S) Spin – Clockwise rotation

Backside Spin

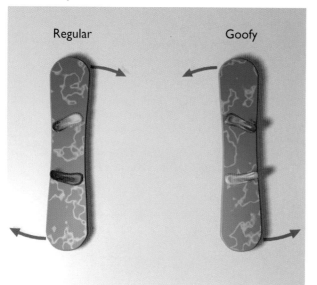

Regular   Goofy

Frontside Spin

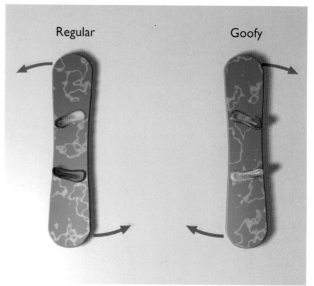

Regular   Goofy

BACKSIDE 180s
with Damo Liddy

LEVEL OF DIFFICULTY: 5 OUT OF 10

Backside 180s are a cool-looking trick that, if done properly, can out-style some of the more technical moves out there. Basically, initiating the backside 180 is very similar to a normal straight air. Follow the steps and give it a go.

GOLDEN RULES FOR BACKSIDE 180s

Step 1 – The Approach
- As for any air, keep your body low on the approach – be bent at the knees, not at the waist.

Step 2 – The Lip
- Take off the lip as you would for a normal straight air. Make sure your base is flat as you leave the lip. DO NOT take off on an edge.
- As you take off the lip you need to start thinking about rotating your body below the waist. The key is to try to ensure that your upper body is rotating at a slower speed than your lower body.
- Make sure when you ollie off the lip that your knees come up into a crouch position and that your weight is kept balanced over your stance.

Step 3 – The Air
- Once you have left the lip of the kicker, try to stay relaxed and concentrate on rotating your board 180 degrees.
- There are two keys to executing this air. First, you need to remain relaxed and let your board drift 180 degrees. If you try to jerk the board it simply won't work.
- Second, you need to try to look at the nose of your board throughout the whole trick. Do not keep rotating your head. This is especially important when you are doing backside 180s off a large kicker. If you look where you are going, you will keep rotating into a 360 or 540. This is the scariest thing about a backside 180 – you never actually see where you are going.
- Adding a grab, such as a method grab, will give you greater stability in the air.

Step 4 – The Landing
- If you are still looking at the nose of your board, you will not have over-rotated.
- As this trick is landed switch, you need to be really comfortable riding switch.
- To ensure you don't over-rotate, spot your landing just beside your front foot (which is now your back foot).
- Make sure you land with a flat base and ride out switch and high five your buddies on the way past.

STYLE MASTER

Once you have sussed out how to do this trick without a grab, start adding in different types of grabs for style points. A stylish-looking grab to do with a backside 180 is a melon or method grab.

Also, the slower the rotation in the air, the more stylish it looks. Keep the spin smooth and slow. Similar to a method, a backside 180 is a great-feeling air, as it gives you that floating sensation.

1

2

3

4

5

6

7

8

9

10

11

BACKSIDE 360s
with Bear Agushi

LEVEL OF DIFFICULTY: 6 OUT OF 10

Simply an extension of the backside 180, a backside 360 is slightly more difficult and a sick move to pull nice and smooth off a big tabletop or kicker. The techniques employed in doing this air are slightly different from those used for a backside 180, so familiarize yourself with them before you give it a go.

GOLDEN RULES FOR BACKSIDE 360s

Step 1 – The Approach
- Keep very low on the approach, with your knees bent. Because you want to spin backside, keep your shoulders and hips pointing slightly forwards – that is, towards the nose of your board.
- Keep your board base flat on the deck; try not to ride in on an edge, yet.

Step 2 – The Lip
- The first shot shows the take-off from the lip of the jump. As you near the lip of the kicker, begin turning off your toe edge much as if you are going to lay down a toe-side turn. Doing this will help as you spin in the air.
- As well as turning off your toe edge as you hit the lip, also rotate your upper body backside, beginning with your head. By turning off your toe edge and spinning your upper body and head backside, you will definitely generate the required amount of rotation for a full 360.
- People who try this trick and stuff up will do so because (a) they don't turn their head and look in the direction that they are spinning; and (b) they don't spin off their toe edge.

Step 3 – The Air
- Keep your head looking in the direction you want to spin. If all has gone well, your knees should be crouched and you will be floating gracefully like a ballerina.

Step 4 – The Landing
- As you come down from your last 90 degrees, you should be able to spot your landing as in shots 6 to 8 at right. This is what makes landing this trick easier than landing a frontside 360.
- A good thing about a 360 is that you will land the same way you took off, which will probably be your preferred stance (for Bear it is goofy). As with all landings, keep your weight centered or just slightly forward of center, depending on how firm the landing is (you usually need to lean back when landing in powder). Preferably, stomp the landing on a flat base so you don't over-spin once you have touched down.

Adding the Grab
Step 3a – The Grab
- Once you have mastered the backside 360 without a grab, it will be time to throw in a stylish grab to raise you to Jedi standard.
- Bear has thrown in an indy grab in this sequence because it is stylish and easy.
- An indy grab is a grab with your trailing arm on your toe edge. Let's say you have spun about 90 degrees (a quarter of a circle). Your knees should be crouched, because your body was crouched on the take-off.
- Put down your trailing arm (left arm for goofy, right arm for regular) and grab your toe edge just in front of your back foot. Don't grab the edge too close to your front foot or else you won't get the bone.
- DO NOT bend down and grab the board – you will lose balance. Bring your knees up and put your arm down for the grab.

Step 3b – The Bone
- You have grabbed the board just in front of your back foot as in the third shot. What makes this move look really stylish is a nice bone with your front leg. Once you have the grab, the bone is the easy part.
- Simply hold the board and straighten out your front leg as in the third and fourth shots. Once you have completed three-quarters of the circle (270 degrees), bring your leg back up as in the sixth shot and prepare for the landing.

REMEMBER: As with any air with a grab, the longer you hold the grab, the more stylish it will look. Notice how Bear has held the grab from the time he leaves the lip of the jump to the very last shot before he touches down on the landing. When you see this trick in real life, the long grab makes the move look much smoother.

1

2

3

4

5

6

7

8

9

10

BACKSIDE 540s & 720s
with Jared Winkler and Chris Coulter

LEVEL OF DIFFICULTY 720: 8.5 OUT OF 10

THE BACKSIDE 540

The backside 540 is an extension of the backside 360, but three things make it more difficult: (1) you are adding an extra 180 to the trick; (2) the landing will be switch; and (3) the last 180 of the trick is blind, meaning it is very difficult to spot the landing. The backside 540 is an awesome move to master and is a perfect stepping stone to doing a misty flip 540 (see inverted airs).

THE BACKSIDE 720

The backside 720 is the follow-up trick to the backside 540, although often, many riders can do the 720 and not the 540 because you land the 720 facing forward and not switch. Two things make the backside 720 harder than the 540: (1) an extra 180 means either more air or a faster spin; and (2) landing an air after two full rotations is difficult due to the momentum of the spinning action.

Follow all the Golden Rules for a backside 360, because the 540 and 720 are done almost the same. Also, check out the following rules.

ADDITIONAL GOLDEN RULES FOR BACKSIDE 540s AND BACKSIDE 720s

Do

- Get extra speed in order to get extra air, OR spin faster off the lip in order to get the extra rotation in before you land.
- Make sure you turn your head backside in order to generate a faster spin and see more of the landing.
- Try to initiate a deeper toe-side turn off the lip in order to spin faster. The deeper the turn off the kicker, the more rotation you will develop.
- The more you want to spin, the harder you will need to throw your head and upper body in a backside motion. Consider throwing your front arm around your body for extra spin.
- As you come in to land, try to look around your back shoulder and see your landing. The more of the landing that you can spot from the air, the better your chance of stomping the trick.
- Follow the same landing principles as for the backside 360, but if you are doing a 540, remember that you will be landing switch.

Don't

- Don't begin turning your head and upper body backside AFTER you have left the lip. Do it as you leave the lip, in conjunction with the toe-side turn.
- Don't panic because you are spinning more quickly or landing switch. Just ride the trick out and chances are you will pull it off first go.

Photo sequence this page—Chris Coulter, backside 720.
Photo sequence opposite—Jared Winkler, backside 540.

1
2
3
4
5
6
7
8

BACKSIDE 540s & 720s

with Jared Winkler and Chris Coulter

LEVEL OF DIFFICULTY 540: 7 OUT OF 10

FRONTSIDE 180s
with Jared Winkler

LEVEL OF DIFFICULTY: 4 OUT OF 10

Whilst not as stylish as a backside 180, frontside 180s are tricks that form the basis of many other better tricks and still look pretty smooth if done well. Follow the steps and give it a go.

GOLDEN RULES FOR FRONTSIDE 180s

Step 1 – The Approach
- As per any air, keep your body low on the approach – be bent at the knees, not at the waist, and maintain a sideways stance as in shot 1 of the sequence.

Step 2 – The Lip
- Take off the lip as you would a normal straight air. Make sure your base is flat as you leave the lip or perhaps even put a little bit of pressure on your toe edge to make it easier.
- Just as you are leaving the lip, begin opening up your shoulders frontside as Jared has done in shot 2 of the sequence.
- Ollie off the lip so that your knees come up into a crouch position and so that your weight is kept balanced over your stance.

Step 3 – The Air
- Begin to open your shoulders a little more as you are in the air. This motion will float your body and board around 180 degrees until you reach the landing.

Step 4 – The Landing
- Probably the hardest part of this trick is the landing, because you are coming in switch.
- As you touch down, keep your weight centered or even slightly forward of center, like Jared in shot 7.
- Stay low as you touch down and squat to stay balanced and absorb the shock.
- If you are landing in powder or deep snow, lean back a little to keep your nose afloat, as Jared has done in shot 8. If you are landing on a firm snow base, lean slightly forward or stay centered, depending on how steep the landing is.

STYLE MASTER

Once you have sussed out how to do this trick without a grab, start adding in different types of grabs for style points. The melon/lien grab that Jared has used is pretty stylish, but you can throw in whatever you like.

1

2

3

4

5

6

7

8

FRONTSIDE 360s
with Jordan Johnston

LEVEL OF DIFFICULTY: 6 OUT OF 10

A rad-looking trick if done well, a frontside 360 is a relatively simple extension of a frontside 180. The principles involved in pulling off this stunt are slightly different from those for the 180, and form the basis of frontside 540s and 720s as well as frontside rodeos.

GOLDEN RULES FOR FRONTSIDE 360s

Step 1 – The Approach
- Keep very low on the approach, with your knees bent. Because you want to spin frontside, keep your shoulders and hips pointing sideways towards your nose and tail. Check out Jordan's stance in photo 1 as he winds up his trailing arm behind him and tucks down super low for maximum spring off the lip.
- It's better to approach the jump with your base flat, although some people like to ride in with a little pressure on their toe edge. See what works for you.

Step 2 – The Lip
- As you hit the lip of the kicker, begin to spring off the toe edge of your board. Don't ollie off the tail or else you will probably flip back on your neck!
- Notice how Jordan has fully extended his body and begun twisting his upper body frontside.
- Look with your head in the direction you want to turn.

Step 3 – The Air
- Keep your head looking in the direction you want to spin. Landing this trick is slightly more difficult than a backside 360 because the last 180 is blind and you can't spot your landing until you have almost completed the whole spin.

Step 4 – The Landing
- It's often good to land this trick a little on your tail as in pictures 8 and 9. This helps absorb the impact and makes the landing more gentle.
- A good thing about a 360 is that you will land the same way you took off, which will probably be your preferred stance. As with all landings, keep your weight centered or just slightly forward of center, depending on how firm the landing is (you usually need to lean back when landing in powder). Preferably, stomp the landing on a flat base so you don't over-spin once you have touched down.

Adding the Grab
- Once you have mastered the frontside 360 without a grab, start adding different grabs for style points.
- In this case, Jordan has added a tail grab, which is probably the most difficult to do for most people.
- Regardless of which grab you do, make sure you suck your knees up to your chest whilst in the air. Never bend forward for the grab – you will miss the grab and lose balance.

A side note: Jordan actually performs this trick switch because he is such a champion. Make sure that when you master the frontside 360, start doing it switch and get that down pat for extra champ status!

5

6

7

8

9

FRONTSIDE 540s & 720s
with Chris Coulter and Jordan Johnston

LEVEL OF DIFFICULTY 720: 8.5 OUT OF 10

THE FRONTSIDE 540

The frontside 540 is an extension of the frontside 360, but two things make it more difficult: (1) you are adding an extra 180 to the trick; and (2) the landing will be switch. One thing that makes the frontside 540 fun is that you can spot your landing for almost the entire last 180 of the spin. The frontside 540 must be mastered if you want to move onto the frontside rodeo flip (see inverted airs).

THE FRONTSIDE 720

The frontside 720 is the follow-up trick to the frontside 540 and is considerably more challenging, mostly because you need to spin very fast and then land your last 180 blind.

Follow all the Golden Rules for a frontside 360 – the 540 and 720 are done almost the same. Also, check out the following rules.

ADDITIONAL GOLDEN RULES FOR FRONTSIDE 540s AND FRONTSIDE 720s

Do

- Get extra speed in order to get extra air, OR spin faster off the lip in order to get the extra rotation in before you land.
- There are two ways to get extra spin off the lip to pull the 540 and 720. One way is to dig your toe edge in deep as you take off the lip. Check out the sequence of Chris doing the 540 and notice that in shot 2, he is coming off a very strong toe edge. By digging in your toe edge, you give your upper body plenty of leverage from which to rotate. The second way to get extra spin is to simply spin your head and upper body much more quickly.
- Always turn your head.
- Suck your knees up as you leave the lip. This will help you maintain balance, speed up the rotation and get the grab.
- Hint for landing the 720: if you are landing on a steep, hard landing, consider spinning the board 630 rather than 720. This will mean that you have to land 90 degrees short and across the slope. If you land this way on your toe edge, you can slide the remaining 90 on the snow and ride out without over-spinning the landing any further. It is a little trick that many pros use – at the end of the day it is cheating, but most people don't even pick up on it.
- Follow the same landing principle as for the backside 360, but if you are doing a 540, remember that you will be landing switch.
- Don't forget the grab for style points.

Don't

- Don't begin turning your head and upper body frontside AFTER you have left the lip. Do it as you leave the lip and at the same time as you dig your toe edge into the snow.
- If you don't spin off your toe edge, you will not get the leverage for the spin.

Photo sequence this page—Jordan Johnston, frontside 720.
Photo sequence opposite—Chris Coulter, frontside 540.

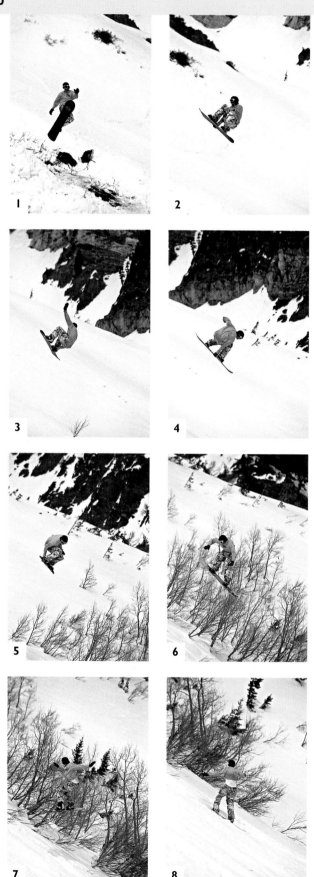

1 2 3 4 5 6 7 8

FRONTSIDE 540s & 720s
with Chris Coulter and Jordan Johnston

LEVEL OF DIFFICULTY 540: 7 OUT OF 10

INVERTED AIRS OFF KICKERS

INTRODUCTION

Snowboarding has progressed rapidly over its brief history, with riders pushing the limits and inventing new tricks. The obvious progression from flat spins is inverted airs. An invert is when a rider flips his/her body so that they go upside down and then land back on their feet. However, the term is used loosely in snowboarding, and can describe certain moves which, technically, are not necessarily fully inverted.

Snowboarders have been doing inverts for years. They started with backflips and frontflips – pretty straightforward stuff! But in recent history, snowboarders have been pulling off inverts with rotations at the same time. There are even moves where the rider will do an invert and then throw in a late spin just before landing. The following is a list of different types of inverts. Learn them and don't confuse them, because mis-labeling tricks is a definite no-no!

Backflip

As with a gymnastics or diving backflip, boost off the kicker and flip your legs in front of you and your head backwards so that you do a complete inverted rotation. There is no spin performed during this trick. For added style points, arch your back or grab the board whilst inverted. Check out the sequence on pages 38-39.

Frontflip

Again, the same as a gymnastics frontflip. Simply boost off the kicker, tuck your head in forwards and let your backside, legs and feet rotate forwards until you land back upright. For style points, throw in a grab. Check out the sequence on page 40.

Misty Flip

One of the very first inverted spin tricks, the misty flip is a combination of the backside 540 with a sideways frontflip. Sounds complicated – well, it is. Just check out the sequence on pages 42-43.

Frontside Rodeo Flip

One of the most revolutionary moves in recent times, the rodeo flip is not a complete inversion, but rather a frontside 540 or 720, spun sideways rather than on a horizontal plane. Instead of being vertical, the rider tilts his/her body whilst spinning so that he/she is on a 45-degree angle with his/her head pointing towards the ground and the base of the board pointing towards the sky. It is usually done with an indy grab at the same time, but throw in any other grab for added coolness. Check out the how-to-do sequence on pages 44-45.

Backside Rodeo Flip

Not to be confused with the 90-roll (see page 49), the rider takes off from his/her heel edge, spins backside and simultaneously flips so that his/her body is virtually horizontal whilst doing a 540 or 720. The rider doesn't actually go completely upside down, and usually grabs melon at the same time. For style points, keep the rotation slow and tight and possibly even vary the grab. Check out the sequence on page 48.

Other Flips

Every rider has his/her own style and consequently, variations of all of the above flips have been created, many without names.

Below: *Chris Coulter goes hugely inverted off a backcountry kicker.*   **Right:** *Gareth Moet with a frontside rodeo over a huge gap in Japan.*

BACKFLIPS

with Jared Winkler

LEVEL OF DIFFICULTY: 6.5 OUT OF 10

Backflips have been around for a long time, but still take spectators' breath away because they can look very stylish and very scary. Quite a basic trick, you only need to get over the fear of getting upside down to pull it off. Together with the frontflip, backflips are the building blocks for all other inverted moves. Learn them first and the others will fall into place.

Backflips should be mastered on a trampoline or diving board before being tried on snow. Our description is brief because you will have little trouble in executing these flips if you can do them off the snow. It's a relatively simple trick that needs more confidence than skill. But be sure to learn it on soft snow, otherwise you risk serious injury.

GOLDEN RULES FOR BACKFLIPS

Step 1 – The Approach
- Keep very low on the approach, with your knees bent.
- Keep your board base flat. Don't ride in on an edge.
- Keep your shoulders open slightly so that they point down the hill rather than sideways.

Step 2 – The Lip
- Ollie as you leave the lip of the jump and begin rotating your head backwards.

Step 3 – The Air
- As you get into the air, arch your back and lay your head backwards so that you can invert your body and spot your landing as in shots 3-5 in the sequence.
- By arching your back as Jared has done, you can slow down the rotation and maintain control by being able to spot your landing for most of the air.
- Be sure to look for your landing, as it makes it much easier to stick the air.

Step 4 – The Landing
- The main tip for landing is not to over-rotate and land on your back or head.
- If you spot your landing while you are in the air, you'll have little problem in stomping this trick.
- Just be sure to keep your weight centered if you are landing on firm snow, or keep your weight slightly on your back foot if you are landing in powder.

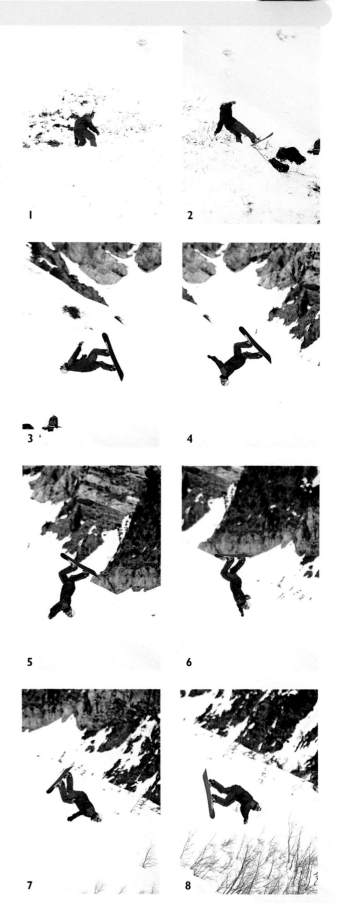

1

2

3

4

5

6

7

8

9   10   11   12

FRONTFLIPS
with Chris Coulter

LEVEL OF DIFFICULTY: 7 OUT OF 10

Much like backflips, frontflips have been around since the beginning of snowboarding. Arguably more difficult to pull off than a backflip because the landing is almost completely blind, most riders find the frontflip less intimidating because they are more comfortable getting their flipping action forwards rather than backwards.

Together with the backflip, the frontflip is a building block for all other inverted moves. Learn them first and the others will fall into place.

GOLDEN RULES FOR FRONTFLIPS
Step 1 – The Approach
- Keep very low on the approach, with your knees bent.
- Keep your board base flat. Don't ride in on an edge.
- Open your shoulders up so that they point down the hill and not sideways.

Step 2 – The Lip
- Pretty self-explanatory: as you hit the lip, roll your body forward.
- Begin by tucking your head into your chest and crouch your waist and legs so you end up in a tight ball.

Step 3 – The Air
- As you roll forward in the air, try to grab your board. Whilst not essential, the grab will win you big style points and help you maintain control of the rotation.
- Try to spot your landing by looking down towards your board as you begin to complete the rotation. It is difficult to spot the landing on a frontflip, but it is made easier because you stand sideways on a snowboard.

Step 4 – The Landing
- The key to landing this trick is to not over-rotate forward when your board touches down.

1

2

3

4

5

6

7

8

9

10

MISTY FLIPS

with Bear Agushi

LEVEL OF DIFFICULTY: 8 OUT OF 10

Misty flips have their origin in their halfpipe equivalent, the McTwist. A combination of a backside 360/540 and a frontflip, the misty flip is a sick-looking move that will always impress spectators. In order to do this trick, make sure you are super confident with backside 360s, backside 540s and frontflips.

GOLDEN RULES FOR MISTY FLIPS

Step 1 – The Approach
- Keep very low on the approach, with your knees bent. Because you want to spin backside, keep your shoulders and hips pointing slightly forwards – that is, towards the nose of your board.
- Keep your board base flat on the deck; try not to ride in on an edge, yet.

Step 2 – The Lip
- Photos 2, 3 and 4 in the sequence are the most important, as they clearly highlight the motion of flipping.
- As you hit the jump, pretend you are doing a backside 360 or 540. That is, begin turning on your toe edge as you leave the lip and rotate your head and upper body backside.
- As you leave the jump and get in the air, frontflip over your toe edge. The action is like a frontflip, only you are front-flipping sideways towards the tail of your board and NOT over the nose of your board. Check out shots 4 to 6.
- The key to this trick is to initiate the spin whilst you are on the lip, and then begin the flip once you have left the lip.

Step 3 – The Air
- This trick is made easier if you try to grab your board on your toe edge as it will force you to flip in the proper direction. Top riders can grab tail or lien to make it look more technical and stylish.
- The difficult aspect of this trick is that it is pretty much totally blind. That is, you can't spot your landing because you are coming in switch, and the flip is disorientating.

Step 4 – The Landing
- Landing this move is tricky, unless you have spun a 720.
- It is a good idea to plant your nose (which is now your tail because you are coming in switch) down on the landing before any other part of the board. This helps absorb much of the brunt of the landing and can make it easier to stomp. However, think about this after you know how to actually initiate the trick.

9

10

11

12

FRONTSIDE RODEO 540s & 720s
with Bear Agushi and Jared Winkler

LEVEL OF DIFFICULTY 540: 8 OUT OF 10

Frontside rodeos are a spectacular-looking move if performed well. The rider doesn't actually flip upside down, but tilts on a 45-degree angle so that their base faces the sky for a moment as they spin either 540 or 720. It is not as difficult a move as it looks. So long as you are comfortable spinning frontside, you should have no problem giving this move a go.

We have shown the trick using two different riders and two different angles so you can fully understand the way it's done.

GOLDEN RULES FOR FRONTSIDE RODEOS
Step 1 – The Approach
- As usual, keep very low on the approach, with your shoulders and hips pointing sideways towards your tip and tail.
- Keep your board base flat. Don't ride in on an edge.

Step 2 – The Lip
- As you hit the lip of the jump, you must dig your toe edge into the lip just as you do when you spin a frontside 360 or 540 etc.
- Begin turning your head frontside (left for regulars, right for goofys like Bear and Jared).
- Open up your shoulders so that they face forward downhill, as Jared does so well in shot 1 of his sequence (opposite).
- Now, the CRITICAL part – as you begin leaving the lip, you have to drop your back shoulder, down the hill towards the nose of your board. Both Jared and Bear really exaggerate this step in their sequences.
- If you check out the first shot of Bear and the second shot of Jared, you will notice how both have turned their hips and shoulders forward. Also, see how they are leaning heavily on their toe edge as they drop their back (left) shoulders.
- It's the dropping of the back shoulder that really gets the inversion happening, while the turning of the shoulders gets the spin going.

Step 3 – The Air and the Grab
- You must make the grab when doing this trick, as it really simplifies the action.

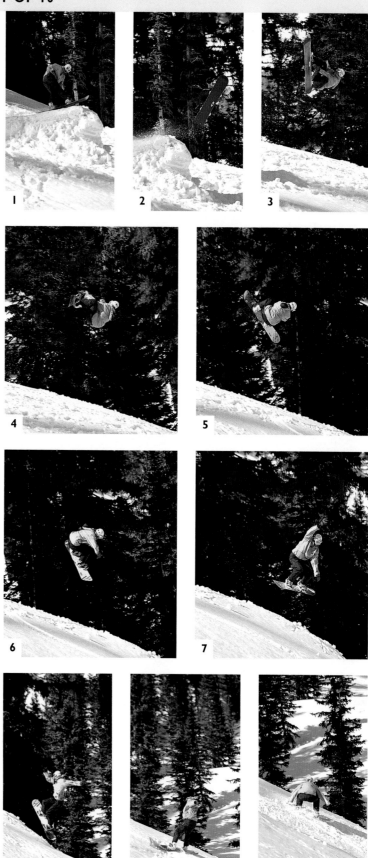

Photo sequence—Bear Agushi, frontside rodeo 720.

FRONTSIDE RODEO 540s & 720s

with Bear Agushi and Jared Winkler

LEVEL OF DIFFICULTY 720: 8.5 OUT OF 10

1

2

3

4

5

6

7

8

9

- The best grab to do when learning frontside rodeos is the indy grab (trailing arm on toe edge). This grab helps you drop your rear shoulder and open up your hips as you leave the kicker.
- Remember to hold the grab as long as possible for style points. If you are spinning only 540, then you will most likely hold the grab almost all the way until you land.
- If you are spinning 720, you will probably have to let go after the 540, as Bear has done in shot 7 (opposite).

Step 4 – The Landing

- If you are doing a rodeo 540, then the landing will be switch. Also, you will be able to spot the landing very early.
- Although the sequence of Bear is a 720, imagine that he is to land on shot 7 after only doing a 540. He has been able to spot his landing all the way from shot 4 through to shot 7. This makes landing a lot easier than landing the 720, which is blind.
- If you are landing the move as a 720, then things get a little more tricky. Because you are spinning an extra 180, the spin will probably be faster than if it were a 540 and therefore controlling the landing will be more difficult. Also, the last 180 is blind so it is a good idea to keep looking over your front shoulder so you can spot the landing.
- Always remember to keep your weight centered if the landing is firm, or slightly back if the snow is soft and deep.

Step 5 – How to get from 540s to 720s

- The key to getting the extra 180 is the take-off.
- You can either: (1) dig more of a toe edge into the lip as you take off; or (2) drop your shoulder more as you leave the lip; or (3) spin your body more strongly as you leave the lip. You can even do a combination of these – we suggest you do until you work out the best way to go from the 540 to the 720.
- Also, you may need a little more hang time in the air, so be prepared to hit the jump with more speed.

Photo sequence—Jared Winkler, frontside rodeo 720.

THE SUPER FLIP
with Jared Winkler

LEVEL OF DIFFICULTY: 8.5 OUT OF 10

There is no real official name for this trick because it doesn't really exist. The trick is a mock of a frontside rodeo that actually looks pretty cool. We have decided to call it the Super Flip because it looks as if the rider is Superman when he/she does it. As far as instruction goes, we have kept it pretty brief because it is basically a frontside rodeo 540, with a very late grab.

GOLDEN RULES FOR SUPER FLIPS

- Make sure you can do a frontside rodeo before trying this trick.
- Hit the kicker with a frontside rodeo 540 in mind, except, as you hit the air, straighten out your body in a Superman fashion.
- Don't go for the grab straight away and don't roll underneath yourself too quickly.
- Try and float for as long as you can in the Superman position. If it helps, wear a cape whilst you're doing it.
- As you begin to roll forward onto your head and back, go for the indy grab and hold it for stability and style.
- Spot your landing as you spin the last 180 and stick it with style.

It's a pretty scary trick because everything happens so late, so make sure you high five your friends for even giving it a go.

46

BACKSIDE RODEOS
with Jared Winkler

LEVEL OF DIFFICULTY: 8.5 OUT OF 10

Yet another revolutionary trick, the backside rodeo is another one of those snowboarding inverts that is not completely inverted. Whether it be a 540 or 720, the techniques to pulling this trick off are the same, it's just that one takes a little extra effort than the other.

Inventor of the Backside Rodeo, Peter Line, says that it is one of the most difficult moves that he can do. Probably about 80% of people who say they can do backside rodeos actually do an easier version of the trick called the 90-roll. Both moves use similar principles and look very similar. Many people can't tell them apart and claim that they can do backside rodeos when in fact they actually do 90-rolls.

The first sequence is of Jared Winkler doing a backside rodeo 540. The second sequence is of Jordan Johnston doing a 90-roll. Both riders are goofy and both are shot from the same angle, so you can get a full appreciation of the difference between these moves and a better understanding of how to pull them off.

GOLDEN RULES FOR BACKSIDE RODEOS AND 90-ROLLS

Step 1 – The Approach
- Of course, keep very low on the approach, with your knees bent.
- Keep your board base flat. Don't ride in on an edge.

Step 2 – The Lip
- These tricks are often referred to as a 'heelside rodeo' because, as you can see by looking at the second shot in each sequence, the rider must take off the lip on his/her heel edge.
- What this means is that just as you are leaving the lip, lean your heel edge into the snow a little.
- As you take off the jump, you must turn your head and shoulders backside as both Jared and Jordan do in shot 3 of their sequences.

1 2 3

4 5 6

7 8 9

10 11 12

90-ROLLS
with Jordon Johnston

LEVEL OF DIFFICULTY: 7.5 OUT OF 10

Step 3 – The Air (pick the difference)

- This is where things get a little different in the two tricks.
- The idea with the backside rodeo is to bring your board around your body in a backside motion. In this way your body DOES NOT perform a complete flip; rather, your body stays quite horizontal to the ground.
- Notice in Jared's sequence (opposite) that from shots 4 through to 9, his body is pretty much horizontal whilst his board faces the camera in shot 4 and moves around the other side of his body by shot 9. He never becomes head down, board up.
- Compare this to Jordan's sequence. From shot 3 onwards, he basically does a backflip off his heel edge, and then spins a late 180 from the sixth shot to the landing. Notice how in shot 4, Jordan is completely upside down.

Step 4 – The Landing

- Whether it be the backside rodeo 540 or the 90-roll, you will be landing switch. This is difficult, especially with the 90-roll, because the landing is pretty much blind and you have to just touch down and hope for the best.
- It is essential that you squat down low as you hit the ground – this will help you keep balance as well as reduce the impact on your body.

2

3

4

5

6

7

8

9

HALFPIPE AIRS

INTRODUCTION

Halfpipe riding, with its origins in the Tahoe City half-pipe back in the '80s, was the first freestyle element of snowboarding to become a competitive discipline. Halfpipe has always been pretty popular, but never more than since it became an Olympic sport in 1998.

Halfpipe riding is very progressive, with new tricks being invented each season. Most riders would have to admit that halfpipe moves are a lot more tricky than kicker airs. The margin for error in riding a pipe is small, and a trick gone wrong can result in pretty bad injuries. But don't be put off. Halfpipe riding is super fun and highly rewarding. Just know your limits and then push them!

FRONTSIDE VS BACKSIDE WALL

In order to understand halfpipe tricks, it's very important to know the difference between your frontside wall and backside wall.

Frontside Wall

When you ride up your frontside wall, the front of your body will be facing INTO the wall with your back facing the opposing wall. You ride up on your frontside wall on your TOE edge. For regular footers, the frontside wall is the right-hand wall of the pipe (looking down the pipe). For goofy footers, the frontside wall will be on the left.

Backside Wall

The backside wall is more intimidating for most riders. When you ride up the backside wall, your back faces into the wall whilst your front faces into the pipe. You approach the backside wall on your HEEL edge. For regular footers, the backside wall is the left-hand wall of the pipe (looking down the pipe). For goofy footers, the backside wall is on the right.

A FEW DEFINITIONS

Flat: When looking down a halfpipe, the flat is the middle section between the walls.

Vert: The vert is the top section of the wall of a halfpipe, which is vertical. The vert stands between the lip of the pipe and the transition.

Transition ('the trannie'): The transition in a pipe is the curved section between the vert of the wall and the flat of the pipe.

Below left: *Andrew Burton loves living his life upside down.*
Below: *Mouse Beuchat putting on a show for the girls.*

FRONTSIDE AIRS

with Jeff Christopherson

LEVEL OF DIFFICULTY: 3 OUT OF 10

A frontside air in a halfpipe is basically a straight air on your frontside wall. Theoretically, you are doing a 180 when you do a frontside air, because you come up the wall pointing out the pipe and then turn back into the pipe when you re-enter and land. But never call it a 180 – people will laugh at you! A frontside air can be done with many of the grabs we listed earlier. Master this air before trying more technical stuff.

GOLDEN RULES FOR FRONTSIDE AIRS

Step 1 – Approaching the Frontside Wall
- Stay very low, with your knees bent and body nice and loose.
- Approach the wall on your toeside edge.
- As you approach the wall on your toe edge, start pumping the transition to maintain speed and balance.

Step 2 – Leaving the Wall
- As you hit the top of the transition, begin opening up your shoulders as in shot 2.
- By shot 3, Jeff has opened up his shoulders even further and is still keeping low as he pumps up the trannie.
- By shots 4 and 5, Jeff has left the lip and has begun focusing on the grab.

Step 3 – Re-entering the Pipe
- If you have initiated this trick properly, you will have no problem landing back in the pipe, hopefully high up on the wall.
- The higher you land on the wall (ie the closer you land to the lip), the more speed you will have for the next hit on your backside wall.
- As you land back in the pipe, remember to keep your weight forward and do NOT stiffen your back leg. In fact, stay low and don't stiffen either leg.
- If you have pulled this off properly, you should be landing back on either your heel edge or a flat base.

GOLDEN RULES FOR HALFPIPE RIDING IN A NUTSHELL
1. Always keep low in the flat and on the transitions.
2. Always pump the wall on your take-off.
3. Never stiffen your legs.
4. Never lean back when you land (try to lean forward, no matter how scary it is).

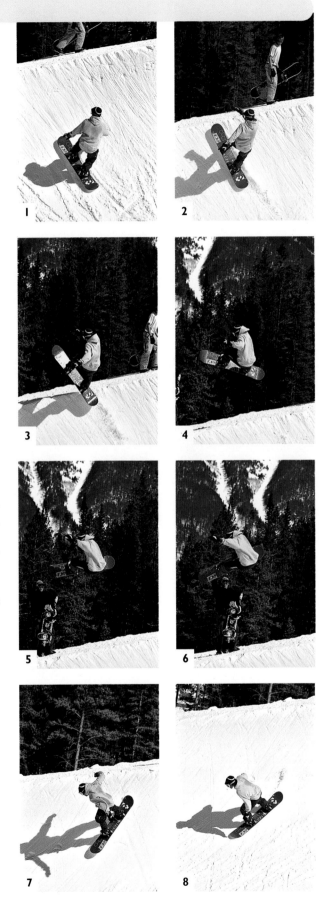

BACKSIDE AIRS
with Andrew Burton

LEVEL OF DIFFICULTY: 3 OUT OF 10

A backside air in the halfpipe is a straight air on your backside wall (as the name implies). Throw in different grabs and you can get heaps of different variations to the air. Master this trick before attempting more technical stuff on the backside wall.

GOLDEN RULES FOR BACKSIDE AIRS

Step 1 – Approaching the Backside Wall
- Keep low and loose. In fact, keep very very low and loose.
- Make sure you approach the wall on a heel edge. Don't wash out and side slide on your approach – you will lose speed.
- As you approach the wall on your heel edge, start pumping the transition to maintain speed and balance.
- Try to hit the wall pretty straight on rather than down the pipe, or you will get less air out of the pipe.
- Push up the wall with your hips whilst staying low.

Step 2 – Leaving the Wall
- As you hit the top of the wall, flatten out the base of your board rather than riding up on your heels. This is shown in shot 2 of the sequence.
- If you stay on your heel edge as you leave the wall, you will have problems keeping balanced and landing back in the pipe. Therefore, NEVER leave the lip on your edge – flatten your base.
- As you flatten the base of your board on the lip, turn your shoulders into the pipe slightly.

Step 3 – Re-entering the Pipe
- If you have remembered to flatten your base as you leave the lip and stay low, you should have no problem in landing back in the pipe.
- But before you do, grab the board on your heel edge and bone out your back leg. This will make you very popular and you'll feel cool.
- The higher you land on the wall (ie the closer you land to the lip), the more speed you will have for the next hit on your frontside wall.
- As you land back in the pipe, remember to keep your weight forward and do NOT stiffen your back leg.
- If you do the trick properly, you will have landed back in the pipe on your toe edge.

GOLDEN RULES FOR HALFPIPE RIDING IN A NUTSHELL
1. Always keep low in the flat and on the transitions.
2. Always pump the wall on your take-off.
3. Never stiffen your legs.
4. Never lean back when you land (try to lean forward, no matter how scary it is).

1   2

3   4

5   6

7   8

9

10

11

AIR TO FAKIES
with Brian Resis

LEVEL OF DIFFICULTY: 6.5 OUT OF 10

Air to fakies are one of those tricks that give you that awesome floating feeling. The trick allows you to drift down the pipe and impress even the most discerning halfpipe fanatic. Although air to fakies are fairly basic, when performed with style and height they are probably one of the best-looking tricks in the pipe. Air to fakies can be performed on the frontside wall (as is shown here) or on the backside wall. As air to fakies are landed switch, you need to be comfortable riding backwards before you attempt them.

GOLDEN RULES FOR AIR TO FAKIES

Step 1 – Approaching the Frontside Wall
- Approach the frontside wall on a toe edge. You want to go straight up the wall as much as possible and flatten your base as you near the lip.
- Keep your shoulders open a little as you pump up the transition.
- Stay very low and loose.

Step 2 – Leaving the Wall
- You should leave the lip with a flat base. Try to minimize the amount of edge you use when you leave the lip. If you use too much toe-side edge, you will not get any height and you will most likely end up doing a backside alley oop.
- Unlike a frontside air, you want to project yourself vertically straight out of the pipe. Ride the wall to the very top and try not to take off too early.
- When you are in the air, stay relaxed. Your momentum will allow you to drift down the pipe. The scary thing about this move is that you will be drifting backwards and will not be able to see where you are going. That's why it's imperative to stay relaxed.
- For extra style, add a grab and try to hold it for as long as possible. Here, Brian has added in a cool method grab to impress his bros.
- This is a very simple move to initiate, but many riders mess it up by leaving the wall way too early. Make sure you ride the wall all the way up and begin your air as you exit the pipe.

Step 3 – Re-entering the Pipe
- This is a tricky air to land because you are re-entering the pipe fakie and landing on a vertical wall. Of course, if you took off too early, you will probably be landing on the flat bottom of the pipe.
- The critical point to remember when trying to land this trick is that you want to land the same way you land a frontside air (but switch). This means you want to land on a slight angle, pointing down the pipe.
- Although you took off by launching vertically straight out of the pipe, you don't want to be landing straight down the pipe. You can see in shot 9 that Brian is slightly angled down the pipe when he lands.
- There are two benefits to landing like this. First, you'll stick more air to fakies and second, you'll be able to maintain speed.

STYLE MASTER

As the air to fakie is a simple move, it is possible to add in a plethora of grabs for extra style points. You can throw in an indy or a tail grab, or maybe even a roast beef. Better still, put in a grab and bone your front leg – this will blow the locals away.

Photo sequence—Tim Zimmerman.

1

2

3

4

5

6

7

8

9

10

FRONTSIDE ALLEY OOPS
with Brian Resis

LEVEL OF DIFFICULTY: 6.5 OUT OF 10

An alley oop can be performed either frontside on the rider's backside wall (as is shown here) or backside on the rider's frontside wall (as is shown in the next sequence). The frontside alley oop is a simple but powerful trick and when performed properly is great to, watch. The alley oop is a 180 that will see the rider hit the wall forward and ride out forward.

GOLDEN RULES FOR FRONTSIDE ALLEY OOPS

Step 1 – Approaching the Backside Wall

* Approach the backside wall on your heel edge quite straight on. Your approach to the wall should be very similar to your approach to the wall when doing a backside air.
* However, you should be thinking frontside 180 rather than backside air as you go up the wall.
* Keep your shoulders open a little as you pump up the transition.
* Stay very low and loose.

Step 2 – Leaving the Wall
* The take-off on this trick is from your heel edge. By leaving the lip on your heel edge, you will initiate the spin more easily. However, the use of your heel edge is only very slight.
* If you use too much heel edge, it will throw you off balance.
* The 180 rotation will come from the slight use of the heel edge, but more importantly, it will come from looking over your leading shoulder, back up the pipe.
* You can see Brian is clearly looking over his leading shoulder in shot 4.
* What makes this trick difficult is it that your momentum is taking you down the pipe, whilst at the same time you are trying to rotate frontside, back up the pipe.
* This is why it is important to minimize the amount of heel edges used to initiate the rotation. Rather, try to think about getting in the air first, before you initiate the rotation.
* Many riders mess this trick up by leaving the wall too early. Make sure you ride the wall all the way to the top.

Step 3 – Re-entering the Pipe

* You want to land with a flat base or a slight amount of toeside edge, as high as possible on the wall.
* You can see here that Brian has landed with a flat base and pumped out of the transition on his toeside edge.
* You should be looking for your landing under your leading arm. You know Brian is going to stomp this trick from shot 5, because he has spotted his landing already.
* Remember to keep low, with your weight centered, as you land back in.
* Try to land high on the wall to maintain speed.

STYLE MASTERS

An indy grab is great to combine with a frontside alley oop as it makes the air look big, solid and stylish. But you can throw in any old grab that suits your fancy. A boned front leg will also give your air that extra stamp of class.

Photo sequence—Tim Zimmerman.

5

6

7

8

9

10

BACKSIDE ALLEY OOP 180s
with Andrew Burton

LEVEL OF DIFFICULTY: 6.5 OUT OF 10

The backside alley oop, like the frontside alley oop, is a fun pipe trick that is relatively simple to learn. It is performed on the rider's frontside wall. For extra style points, make sure you throw in a grab. The alley oop is a 180 that will see the rider hit the wall forward and ride out forward.

GOLDEN RULES FOR BACKSIDE ALLEY OOPS
Step 1 – Approaching the Frontside Wall
- To make this trick easier to learn, approach the frontside wall on a toe edge quite straight on. But remember, the bigger you want to go, the less straight on you want to hit the wall (you will want to point it slightly more down the pipe).
- Keep your shoulders open a little as you pump up the transition.
- Stay very low and loose.

Step 2 – Leaving the Wall
- The take-off on this trick is from your toe edge. By leaving the lip on your toe edge, you will initiate the spin more easily.
- Try and look back into the pipe over your back shoulder.
- This is a very simple move to initiate, but many riders screw it up by leaving the wall way too early. Make sure you ride the wall all the way up and begin your air as you exit the pipe.

Step 3 – Re-entering the Pipe
- Re-entering this trick gets a little more difficult the bigger you go. However, it's a pretty easy move and you shouldn't have too much hassle landing back in the pipe.
- You should be landing back on your toe edge, pointing slightly down the pipe rather than directly across the pipe, as in the last two shots.
- Remember to keep low, with your weight forward, as you land back in.
- Try to land high up on the wall to maintain speed.

STYLE MASTER
You have to pull this move off with a funky grab to look like a pro and impress your friends. Andrew has gone the method grab, which is one of the most stylish-looking grabs and is quite simple to do. As you leave the lip, bring your knees up and grab the board on the heel edge, either in front of your front foot as Andrew has done, or between the legs. Any grab will look good if you are in control and go BIG.

9

10

11

FRONTSIDE 540s

with Jeff Christopherson

LEVEL OF DIFFICULTY: 7 OUT OF 10

Frontside spins in the pipe are a little different from spins off a kicker. A 360 off a kicker will have the rider take off forward, spin a complete rotation and then land forward. This is different in the pipe. When you spin 360, you actually land facing switch, and when you spin 540 in the pipe you land forwards. Spins in the pipe can be done backside and frontside, and on either your backside wall or your frontside wall.

Frontside 360s on the frontside wall are not the most stylish airs in the pipe and are only done by riders who want to hit the next wall switch. The frontside 540 in the pipe is kind of an equivalent to a 360 off a kicker, and is pretty much the basic for spinning in the pipe.

GOLDEN RULES FOR FRONTSIDE 540s

Step 1 – Approaching the Frontside Wall
- Keep low and loose and maintain a very sideways stance, with your hips and shoulders pointing towards your nose and tail.
- Make sure you approach the wall on a toe edge. Don't wash out and side slide on your approach or you will lose speed.
- As you approach the wall on your toe edge, start pumping the transition to maintain speed and to keep balanced.
- Hit the wall on a slight angle, pointing down the pipe. Don't head straight up the wall.
- Push up the wall with your hips whilst staying low.

Step 2 – Leaving the Wall
- As you approach the lip of the pipe, begin rotating your head and shoulders frontside. Notice in the third shot how Jeff has already begun opening up his shoulders for the spin.
- By the fourth shot, Jeff has fully rotated his upper body and has begun spinning his board off its toe edge as it leaves the lip. He is fully looking around the way he wants to spin.
- Once you have taken off from the lip, it's only a matter of maintaining your spin. Keep your head turned and your arms tight to your body, unless you want to grab, which takes a little practice. Jeff has gone the extra mile here and not only grabbed, but thrown in a nice bone for style.
- Just keep on looking around your front shoulder.

Step 3 – Re-entering the Pipe
- As you complete the spin and begin coming back into the pipe, you will spot your landing and will be facing forward.
- As you touch down, remember to stay low for balance and cushioning.

A Few Summary Points
- Always stay low on the approach and landing.
- Try not to take off from the lip too early or you will not get the spin or will land too far down the lip.
- Try to land high on the wall to maintain speed.
- Jeff's sequence proves that you don't need a great deal of height to pull off this move. Just maintain a nice tight spin and you'll be spinning like a pro in no time.
- Once you are a champ at doing 540s, hit the wall faster and try 720s and 900s.

5

6

7

8

9

10

11

BACKSIDE 540s
with Jeff Christopherson

LEVEL OF DIFFICULTY: 8 OUT OF 10

The backside 540 can be performed on either the frontside or backside walls of the pipe. Here Jeff is doing a backside 540 on the backside wall, which is a very stylish-looking trick. It is a more difficult move than a frontside 540 because it is pulled off on the more intimidating backside wall.

GOLDEN RULES FOR BACKSIDE 540s

Step 1 – Approaching the Frontside Wall
* Approach the backside wall on your heel edge, pointing a little down the pipe rather than straight up the wall.
* Keep low and open up your shoulders frontside in preparation for the backside spin as in shots 1 and 2 in the sequence.

Step 2 – Leaving the Wall
* This is the tricky part of the move because it is difficult to flatten out the base of your board whilst spinning at the same time. So concentrate on doing exactly that – as you hit the lip, begin spinning your head and shoulders backside. Flatten out your base as well or you will struggle to get the spin initiated.
* As you leave the wall, you should be spinning like a top. Try to suck your knees up and perhaps go for the grab if you think it won't stuff you up.

Step 3 – Re-entering the Pipe
* It's more than likely that you will have taken off from the lip a little early, which will force you back in the pipe with no problem. The key is to leave the lip late on the take-off so that you can land the move high on the wall.
* A little trick is to land the spin on your heel edge and slide the last portion of the spin on the snow as in shots 10 and 11. It isn't the perfect technique, but it's a good way to learn the trick and build up your confidence to do it bigger.

McTWISTS
with Rob Bak

LEVEL OF DIFFICULTY: 8.5 OUT OF 10

Not something on the McDonalds menu, the McTwist is a sick air that was developed by skaters in the 1980s and adapted to snowboarding. The McTwist is probably the easiest inverted air in the halfpipe, and is basically the combination of a frontflip and a little twist. There are different variations of the move, with the one that we have displayed being the less difficult but more stylish version.

Before you read how to do this move, perhaps check out the sequence showing a misty flip on page 226. The tricks are basically the same except that the McTwist is done in the pipe, whereas the misty flip is performed off a straight jump.

GOLDEN RULES FOR McTWISTS
Step 1 – Approaching the Backside Wall
- Approach the backside wall on your heel edge, pointing quite straight on up the wall.
- Keep low.
- Consider having your shoulders opened up a little to wind yourself up for the backside spin and flip.

Step 2 – Leaving the Wall
- As you hit the lip of the pipe, begin flipping your body towards the tail of your board.
- As you flip, bring your front arm across your body towards your tail as well, in order to initiate the spinning motion. Shots 2 and 3 highlight this perfectly as Rob leans right over and goes for the grab on his heel edge.
- It is very important to have begun turning your head in the backside direction.

- As you approach the backside wall, you will be on your heel edge, but as you begin the flip and spin, try flattening the base of your board on the lip.
- Go for the grab, as it will help you initiate the spin and flip as well as keep you balanced.

Step 3 – Re-entering the Pipe
- As you hit the wall of the pipe on the landing, keep your weight forward and stay low for better control.
- Try to land as high up on the lip as possible in order to maintain speed for the next hit.

1

2

3

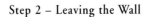

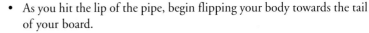

4

5

6

7

8

9

10

11

CRIPPLER
with Kendal Whelpton

LEVEL OF DIFFICULTY: 9.5 OUT OF 10

Also known as a Haakon flip (named after the legend of modern-day snowboarding Terje Haakonsen), the crippler is pretty much a frontside rodeo on the frontside wall of the halfpipe. The crippler tends to get a little more inverted than a rodeo and wins big points in a halfpipe comp. The complicating factor with this trick is that you land facing the opposite direction from the direction in which you took off. It also requires a bit of guts to try as you have to get inverted.

GOLDEN RULES FOR CRIPPLERS

Step 1 – Approaching the Frontside Wall
- Keep low and loose and maintain a very sideways stance, with your hips and shoulders pointing towards your nose and tail.
- Make sure you approach the wall on a toe edge. Don't wash out and side slide on your approach or you will lose speed.
- As you approach the wall on your toe edge, start pumping the transition to maintain speed.
- Hit the wall on a slight angle, pointing down the pipe. Don't head straight up the wall.
- Push up the wall with your hips whilst staying low.

Step 2 – Leaving the Wall
- As you hit the lip of the pipe, begin rotating your head and shoulders frontside. Notice in the first shot how Kendal has already begun opening up his shoulders for the spin.
- As you leave the lip, rotate your upper body frontside and flip over backwards. Think of yourself doing a backflip 360.
- Make sure you look over your front shoulder.
- Try to arch your back and stay crouched.
- Grab the board in any position. Kendal is grabbing lien here, probably the easiest grab.

Step 3 – Re-entering the Pipe
- As you complete the spin and flip, you will be re-entering the pipe switch, and should have no problem in spotting the landing.
- As you touch down, remember to stay low for balance and cushioning.

A Few Summary Points
- Always stay low on the approach and landing.
- Try not to take off from the lip too early or you won't get enough air and might hit your head on the lip.
- Try and land high on the wall to maintain speed.
- Make sure that as you flip backwards, you don't lift your legs out of the pipe, but rather, you get the air and flip your upper body back to initiate the backflip.

Photo sequence—Copper Mountain Resort.

1

2

3

4

5

6

7

THE HEAVE-HO
with Eric Shaw

LEVEL OF DIFFICULTY: 9.5 OUT OF 10

This trick has had so many names over the years that people don't know what they should be calling it. From the Michaelchuck to the backside rodeo, the name that seems to have stuck is the Heave-Ho. It's a pretty difficult air to perform – more from the point of view commitment than skill. Don't try it unless you are a pretty confident pipe rider and flipper.

The best way to visualize this trick is to imagine hitting the heel-side wall of the pipe and doing a Backside Rodeo as you would do off a straight jump. Some riders imagine they are doing a straight-up Backflip. If you are capable of pulling off Backside Rodeos off straight jumps, then this move is yours for the taking. Just make sure you stay committed the whole way through the move – otherwise you run the risk of hitting your head or snapping your neck on the lip.

1

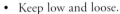

GOLDEN RULES FOR HEAVE-HOS IN THE PIPE

Step 1 – Approaching the Frontside Wall
- Keep low and loose.
- Keep your shoulders slightly open so that they point forward rather than sideways.
- Make sure you approach the wall on a heel edge and don't wash out. Keep your speed. You are far better going bigger than smaller when doing this move.
- Push up the wall with your hips whilst staying low to keep your speed up.

Step 2 – Leaving the Wall
- As you hit the top of the wall, make sure your whole board exits the pipe before flipping yourself.
- Initiatie the move by pulling off the lip on your heel edge (just like a Backside Rodeo).
- As you get in the air, turn your shoulders backside, along with your head.
- Begin a cartwheel over the tail of your board whilst turning your shoulders backside.
- Extend your head back so that you can spot your landing and keep the spin going backside.
- Make sure you grab your board (preferably method) so you can keep balanced and hold a tight flip and spin.

2

Step 3 – Re-entering the Pipe
- Possibly the most difficult part of this trick is landing back in the pipe.
- Because many riders who learn this move flick off their heels too early and too hard, they end up flicking themselves out of the pipe.
- The best way to make sure you land back in the pipe is to avoid spinning and flipping too early.
- As usual, keep low as you land and set yourself up for the next wall.

Photo sequence—Tim Zimmerman.

3

4

5

6

7

RAIL SLIDES MADE EASY

with Luke 'Mouse' Beuchat

LEVEL OF DIFFICULTY: 5 OUT OF 10

1

2

3

Sliding metal and wooden objects is fun. On a bad weather day there is nothing better than finding a disused rail or bench and sliding it to your heart's content.

If the rail is off the ground, there are two methods available to get on. The first and more difficult method involves ollieing on to the rail, as is described below. The second method involves building a snow ramp up to the rail and simply riding onto it. The second method is simple and requires no real explanation. However, the 'ollie-up' method is a tricky move and does warrant some description.

GOLDEN RULES OF RAIL SLIDING

Step 1 – Mounting the Rail
- Head towards the rail on a flat base and prepare to ollie onto the rail.
- As you approach the rail, head slightly left or right (depending on whether you are goofy or regular).
- Regulars should head towards the right of the rail (as has Mouse in the sequence), and goofies should head to the left of the rail.
- As you ollie on to the rail, turn your board 90 degrees in a frontside direction as Mouse does in the third shot.

Step 2 – The Rail
- The key is to land on the rail with a flat base. Do not land on your heel-side edge as this will almost certainly end in head injuries. In fact, even lean forward slightly to avoid sliding onto your back.
- To try to ensure that you land on a flat base, accentuate the bend in your knees. This will tend to flatten your base.
- Once you have locked onto the rail with a flat base, just keep sliding.

Step 3 – Leaving the Rail
- Just let the snowboard naturally slide off the end of the rail.
- Before you hit the snow again, rotate your snowboard 90 degrees and ride off forwards.

REMEMBER: Never lean back, and you don't need to go too fast!

4

5

6

7

8

50-50S MADE EASY

with Luke 'Mouse' Beuchat

LEVEL OF DIFFICULTY: 4 OUT OF 10

1

Doing a 50-50 is almost the same as doing a standard rail slide. However, instead of sliding the rail with your snowboard perpendicular to the rail, you point your nose directly down the rail.

GOLDEN RULES OF 50-50S

Step 1 – Mounting the Rail
- Head towards the rail on a flat base and prepare to ollie onto the rail.
- Unlike regular rail slides, head straight towards the rail.
- When you get close enough to the rail, ollie up onto it but keep your board pointing in the same direction down the hill. DO NOT turn the board.

Step 2 – The Rail
- The key is to land on the rail with a flat base. Do not land on an edge or else you will roll off the side of the rail.
- Keep your weight centered and keep your body loose. Do not tense up.
- Once you have locked onto the rail with a flat base, just keep sliding.

Step 3 – Leaving the Rail
- Just let the snowboard naturally slide off the end of the rail, land on the snow and keep riding. It's all too easy!

2

3

4

5

6

THE SNOWBOARDER TECHNICAL GUIDE

INTRODUCTION

To save time, money, life and limb, it is crucial for every snowboarder to have a good understanding of such things as board maintenance, buying a snowboard and avalanche awareness. The Snowboarder Technical Guide covers six key topics which will help you with the ability to ride better and safer.

BUYING A SNOWBOARD

If you are going to get seriously into snowboarding, it is much cheaper to buy a board than rent one. This Technical Guide provides you with some inside tips to help you purchase a board that best suits you and your riding style.

BOARD MAINTENANCE

To get the most out of snowboarding you need to ensure that your board is kept in tip-top condition. This is easy to do if you follow the steps in the Technical Guide.

BOARDERCROSS TECHNIQUES

Boardercross is a standard event at most snowboard competitions, yet very little has been written about boardercross racing techniques. The Technical Guide provides in-depth lessons on every stage of the boardercross race to help you become a boardercross pro.

BUILDING A SUPERKICKER

If you want to improve your freestyle snowboarding, the best way to do it is to build your own kicker. It is also super fun to build and session a kicker in the backcountry with your friends. The Technical Guide provides a step-by-step guide to building a super kicker.

HALFPIPE CONSTRUCTION AND MAINTENANCE

Most resorts around the world are adding halfpipes to their snowboard facilities. However, don't spend your money on a lift pass to ride a pipe unless you know how it is built and maintained – you may find yourself very disappointed. The Technical Guide takes you through the range of construction methods and maintenance procedures for halfpipes.

AVALANCHE AWARENESS

More and more riders are venturing out into the backcountry in search of powder and good locations to build kickers. If you are planning to go out back, you should have a good understanding of avalanches and what causes them. The Technical Guide provides you with an overview of avalanche awareness.

Left: *Rohan Smiles was smiling after hitting this perfect hip in the Tahoe backcountry. Photo— Gavin O'Toole.*

HINTS AND TIPS

Selecting a snowboard can be an exciting yet intimidating task. We all want the best board that we can afford and no one wants to fork out their hard-earned cash on a board that is either a lemon or not suited to their riding style and physique. In these few pages you will find some general guidelines that will help you select a board suited to your ability and riding style. Board selection is a logical decision-making process, so follow the guidelines.

WHAT TYPE OF RIDING?

Big air, halfpipe, backcountry, racing, all-mountain freeriding – what's it gonna be? Consider where you live. For example, if you live in Australia or on the USA East Coast, forget about buying a 164 cm+(64 in) powder, because you will seldom use it. The idea is, the more tricks you want to do, the shorter the board you should ride. If you want to cruise the whole mountain all day, getting the odd air here or there, then you won't want a short freestyle board; you will want an all-mountain 'freeriding' board. Alternatively, if you love the progressive, skate-influenced tricks on the Mack Dawg videos, then you will want something shorter – a 'freestyle' board.

Above: *Many snowboarders argue that freeriding is the soul of the sport. Here Jason Haynes glides through some New Zealand powder. Photo—Gavin O'Toole.*

SELECTING THE LENGTH OF YOUR SNOWBOARD

Now that you've selected the type of riding you're going to be doing – freestyle or freeride – it's time to select the length of your board. The length of the board will be determined by three factors – your weight, your height and the level of your riding (ie beginner, intermediate, advanced).

How much do you weigh?

As a general rule, the heavier you are, the longer your board needs to be. Thus, guys will generally ride a longer board than girls. Heavier guys should buy longer boards than lighter guys and small kids should ride shorter boards than bigger kids. You get the idea.

Here are some ideas on the recommended board size for certain weights. Remember, these suggestion are only guidelines and should not be used as hard and fast rules.

GUIDELINES FOR CHOOSING YOUR BOARD

Your Weight	40-50kg	50-60kg	60-75kg	75+kg
	(88-110lbs)	(110-132lbs)	(132-165lbs)	(165lbs)
Length of				
Freestyle Board	130-140cm	140-150cm	150-160cm	160cm+
	50-55in	55-59in	59-62in	62in+
Length of				
Freeride Board	135-145cm	145-155cm	155-165cm	165cm+
	52-57in	57-60in	60-64in	64in+

If you are a high intermediate or advanced rider, the best way to choose the right board length is to find a pro rider who has similar height and weight characteristics to you and then use his or her board length as a basis for selecting your board. Or work this logic backwards. If you want to ride like Terje Haakonsen in the pipe but you weigh 100 kg (220 lb), forget about getting a Burton Balance 156 – it will be too short for your weight. Stick to a board no shorter than about 160 cm (62 in). Of course, if you are a beginner, this method won't work, as what the pros ride is not really relevant to what a beginner should choose.

Above: *With new tricks being invented every year, freestyle riding represents the progressive element of snowboarding. Abe Tetar shows Terje Haakonsen that he can cut it with the big boys.*

How tall are you?

There is a similar principle to consider here. Generally, the taller you are, the longer your board should be. Of course, the two principles can work against each other. If you are tall but very light, the weight principle will say buy a shorter board but the height principle will say buy a longer board. Your best bet in these circumstances is to buy a medium-sized board.

What is your skill level: kook, getting good, or pro?

Be honest with yourself – if you aren't, only you will suffer. A general rule is that if your level of snowboarding is high, then you will be able to handle a longer board. Of course, it isn't necessary to buy a long board if you are an advanced rider. However, if you want to perform bigger airs and stick the landings, a longer board is the way to go. Also, be aware that as pipe airs get bigger, a general trend among pipe riders is to ride longer boards.

SELECTING THE STIFFNESS OF YOUR BOARD

OK, two steps down. You have selected the type of board (freestyle or freeride) and the length of board. Now things start to get more interesting. You need to select the flex pattern of your board. With the upsurge in pipe riding, flex has become a critical characteristic in board selection.

Stiff vs soft boards

A stiff board will hold a far better edge on hard-packed snow than a soft board. That's why race boards are super stiff. Similarly, as halfpipes are best ridden when the snow is firm, a good pipe board is stiff, as it needs to hold a good edge on the hard walls of the pipe. A good boardercross board will also be stiff, as it needs to negotiate gates on icy corners of the course. The downside of a stiff board is that it is much more difficult to control than a soft board.

A soft board is good if you are into popping big and small airs, pulling little tricks and, importantly, cruising powder. Soft boards are fun because they are less twitchy, easier to handle, easier to ollie and much easier to ride deep snow on. Of course when it comes to riding hard-pack and ice, the fun of riding a soft board disappears.

How do I tell if a board is stiff or soft?

1. Next time you are in a snowboard shop, grab a race board and grab a freestyle/freeride board.
2. Place the tail on the ground and hold the nose up so the board is on a 45-degree angle to the floor.
3. Place one hand behind the nose of the board. Make sure you place your hand below the nose, not right on the tip of the nose, otherwise the nose will bend, rather than the waist of the board.
4. Place your other hand in the middle (waist) of the board and push down hard so that the entire board bends (see photo, right).
5. Do this with both boards and you will find that the race board is much stiffer than the freestyle board.
6. Choose a few boards that you like and that you think wouldsuit your height, weight and ability. Perform the same tests as in steps (1) to (5), comparing the flex between the boards.

Making your decision on stiffness

When making the decision on stiffness, keep the following points in mind:

- Generally, as your weight increases, so should the stiffness of your board.
- If your level of snowboarding is not high, you should go for a softer board.
- If you like riding pipe, you should go for a stiffer board.

- If you prefer a board that is easier to control, you should go for a softer board.
- If you prefer just riding around the mountain and doing small tricks, you should go for a softer board.
- If you prefer riding super fast in all kinds of conditions, you should go for a stiffer board.

Don't underrate the importance of choosing the right flex. Ask the local shop legends for their advice and then ignore them (only joking). Just be aware that while many shop assistants can sound as if they know a lot about snowboarding, but often they don't have a clue. Keep an open mind and don't hesitate to question their comments if you are uncertain.

OTHER CONSIDERATIONS

By making these three decisions – the type of board, the length of the board and the flex of the board – you should pretty much be able to select your board. However, to really hone down your board selection, a few additional considerations will help.

How wide should the board be?

Board width is an important consideration in board selection. A board that is too narrow will cause your toes and heels to hang over the edge, which means that when you turn, they will dig into the snow and cause you to fall. If the board is too wide for your feet (a problem for many women and small kids), you will find it more difficult to initiate a turn and hold an edge. Make sure that you have 1–1.5 cm (0.4–0.6 in) of toe and heel overhang.

Keep in mind that a narrower board is quicker edge-to-edge and is more responsive. As a general rule, you should buy the narrowest board possible given your foot size and stance angles. Note that wider boards are good for freeriding as they float better on the powder and offer more surface area for good landings. Remember: super-fat boards have gone out with super-fat pants. Of course, if you have very large feet you really only have two solutions – either buy a very wide board or ride steeper angles on your bindings to reduce the toe and heel overhang.

Above: *Buying a snowboard is easy if you know how.*

Sidecut Radius

The sidecut of a snowboard refers to the curve of the board's edge, which can be clearly seen when the board is placed flat on the ground. To

determine the sidecut radius of the board, lay it flat on the ground. Now, using the curve of the sidecut as the starting point, draw a perfect circle next to it. The radius of this circle is the sidecut radius. Technically, the sidecut is a chord of a circle.

Most freestyle boards have a sidecut radius of between 7.5 and 8.5 m (25–28 ft). The smaller the sidecut radius, the deeper the sidecut – that is, the more pronounced the curve of the board's edge. Conversely, the larger the sidecut radius, the shallower the sidecut.

Together with the flex (stiff or soft), the sidecut of the board effectively determines the turning performance of the board. A deeper sidecut means shorter, more precise turns. Riding the pipe requires short, precise turns, hence pipe boards typically have deep sidecuts, usually between 7.6 and 7.9 m (25–26 ft). Take, for example, a Burton Balance 56 (the Terje Haakonsen pro model). This board has one of the deepest sidecuts of any freestyle board. Terje partly attributes his success to this feature. Subsequently, over recent years, there has been a trend among board makers to build boards with deeper sidecuts. However, the more sidecut a board has, the narrower it will generally be. Therefore, make sure your feet aren't too big for the board. Boards with deep sidecuts tend to be more difficult to control.

If you are not into pipe riding or racing, then a shallower sidecut will be sufficient. A board with a sidecut around 8 to 8.5 m (26–28 ft) will still have good turning performance and will be easier to control. Be aware that any board with a side radius over 8.8 m (29 ft) will have poor turning performance.

Directional or Twin Tip?

A directional board is one that has a longer nose than tail, often with a different shape, whereas a twin-tip board has a nose and tail of identical size and shape. In about 1993, the twin-tip revolution began. Everyone started doing skater-like tricks on boards. Spinning was the big thing so manufacturers of snowboards cut down the long noses on their boards so that the tip and tail were the same and riders could spin faster. Then, since 1996, riders started to go much larger and take their freestyle boards everywhere, such as in the powder, pipes and the backcountry. Riders realized that the benefits a twin tip were minimal, thus returned to directional boards. Of course, this is not to say you shouldn't buy a twin tip.

When you're choosing a board, heed the following guidelines in relation to twin-tip and directional boards. If you want to be a freerider, then definitely go for the directional because you probably won't be riding switch too often. If you want to do small flatland tricks and lip tricks in the pipe, a twin tip may be a good option. However, if you want to do large freestyle moves, a directional board is the way to go.

THE FINAL DECISION – GRAPHICS

Naturally, the graphics on a board will determine how well you ride and how cool you will look when you are hanging out at the pipe in spring (this is a joke, in case you didn't realize it!). So make sure your board looks cool – otherwise nobody will like you or think you rip!

HOW TO CHOOSE A BOARD

Ask the following questions before you buy a board.

1. What type of riding will I be doing–freestyle or freeride?
2. How much do I weigh?
3. How tall am I?
4. What is my level of skill–beginner or advanced?
5. How stiff do I want my board to be?
6. How big are my feet?
7. Do I want a deep sidecut board?
8. Do I want a directional or a twin tip?
9. What sort of graphics am I into?

BOARD MAINTENANCE

TRICKS OF THE TRADE

Ever wondered why your friend's board goes faster than yours? Why your friend does bigger jumps? Well your friend probably looks after his/her base better than you do ,spending hours every night preparing his/her base so he/she can extract that extra inch of speed out of it.

Since it is only your base and your edges that touch the snow when you are riding, if you ensure that these are kept in peak condition (well waxed and well tuned), you will be pretty much guaranteed of having a fast board. You can do most of the tuning that your base requires yourself, thereby saving valuable dollars, which can then be spent on your next snowboard adventure. However, when major work is required, a snowboard shop may be the only port of call.

SELF-MAINTENANCE TUNE-UPS
EDGE TUNING
Requirements
1. Edge tool or file
2. Wire brush
3. De-burring stone

Procedure
The first thing to do is take all the burrs out of the edges. Grab your de-burring stone and run it along both edges. Next, it's time for sharpening. Unless you are a World Cup snowboard technician, it is not recommended that you sharpen your own edges using files. Although files do the best job, you need to know what you are doing and have your board secured properly in the correct position.

The easiest and most foolproof way to sharpen your edges is to purchase a special edge-sharpening tool. These things are easy to use – it's just a matter of running the tool along your edges. Don't be afraid to use a bit of force. If the edge tool becomes clogged with edge filings, take your wire brush and clean them off. Remember, there is no need to sharpen your edges as often as you wax your board. In fact, it's not recommended that you do this, since it may cause a concave base and also lead to your edges wearing out super quickly.

Once you have finished sharpening your edges, it's time to de-tune the edges around the nose and tail. De-tuning enables the snowboard to initiate turns more easily and stops the edge catching when traveling in a straight line. Begin your de-tuning at the point where the nose and tail begin to turn up. Round off the edges on the nose and tail using a file. The amount of de-tuning required will depend on your personal preference.

BASE CLEANING
Requirements
1. 1 x base cleaner
2. 1 x old rag

Procedure
Before you begin any work on the base of your board, you should clean the base. You can buy a base cleaner from most

Right: *Buying an edge-sharpening tool from your local snowboarding shop makes tuning easy.*

Right: *This is how the experts do it. A World Cup file and a precise technique.*

Right: *To really get your edges razor sharp, go to your local shop. Shops typically use a Montana Edge Sharpener.*

Right: *Use a file or ruler to determine where your nose and tail start to turn up. This will provide you with the reference point to start de-tuning.*

Right: *To complete the de-tuning, round off the edges on the nose and tail using a file.*

reputable snowboard shops. The purpose of a base cleaner is to clean all the dirt out of the pores of the base, hence ensuring that your wax job is effective. Spray the base cleaner onto the base, then wipe it off using an old rag. Remember that you are trying to remove dirt from the pores of the board.

REPAIRING BASE GOUGES
Requirements
1. 1 x P-Tex stick/candle (appropriate colour for your base)
2. 1 x metal scraper
3. 1 x cigarette lighter or burner

Procedure
Set your board up so it is horizontal, base facing up. Light your P-Tex stick using the cigarette lighter. Hold the

Above: *Use a cigarette lighter to light the P-Tex candle, holding the P-Tex candle in the blue part of the flame until it starts to burn by itself.*

P-Tex stick in your writing hand and the lighter in the other hand. Keep the P-Tex stick in the flame of the lighter until it is burning by itself. Once the P-Tex Stick is burning, put the lighter down and pick up the metal scraper. The idea now is to fill the gouges in the base of your board by dripping the P-Tex into them. The problem is that if the P-Text burns at the wrong temperature, it carbonizes (turns black), meaning your repair job looks terrible and will most likely fall out after a few days on snow. The idea is to control the temperature of the P-Tex by rolling it against the metal scraper. Any carbonizing that occurs on the P-Tex stick can be rolled off on the metal scraper. By working the P-Tex stick with the metal scraper, you should be able to perform a satisfactory repair. But remember, practice makes perfect. Don't expect to get it right the first time.

Above: *Once the P-Tex candle starts to burn, drip it into the gouge.*

Once the P-Tex has dried in the gouge (this should only take a few minutes), scrape the excess P-Tex off with the metal scraper so that the base is flat again. Don't be afraid to use a lot of force to remove the excess P-Tex.

Above: *When the iron is hot, hold the wax against the iron and drip it over the base of the board.*

Above: *Once you have dripped the wax all over your board, use the iron to push the wax into the pores of the board.*

WAXING YOUR BASE
Requirements
1. 1 x block of wax
2. 1 x iron with no holes in the base

Procedure
By now your base should be nice and clean. Set your board up so it is horizontal, base facing up. Plug your iron in. Test the heat of the iron by touching the wax against it. If the wax starts to smoke, the iron is too hot. Reduce the temperature of the iron until the smoke from melting the wax is kept to a minimum.

Hold the iron upside down with the pointy end facing your board. Now melt the wax by touching it against the iron. Dribble the wax down the edges of the base first, then down the middle. Remember that the base area closest to your edges gets the most work, so you most likely want to use a slightly harder wax here (ie a wax for colder temperatures).

A universal wax is probably sufficient for the centre of your base. Once you have dribbled the wax all over the base, use the iron to evenly distribute the wax over your whole base. Use strong, powerful strokes – imagine you are trying to force the wax into the pores of the base. When the top sheet of your board starts to get hot, you know the wax is getting in. When you finish waxing, go read a mag and let it dry. Note: Make sure you don't leave the iron in one spot for too long, otherwise your base will start growing bubbles.

BUFFING YOUR BASE
This is the most critical step if you want to maximize your speed.

Requirements
1. 1 x plastic scraper
2. 1 x Scotch Brite® pad (scourer)
3. 1 x structure brush

Procedure

Now it's time to scrape off the excess wax. Remember the only useful wax is in the pores of the base. Any other wax will slow you down. Thus the idea is to scrape off all excess wax. Take your plastic scraper and use long strokes from tip to tail to remove ALL excess wax. If you want to be super technical, place your board in a cold place (eg refrigerator) for half an hour or so. Excess wax comes out of the base when the board is chilled. Scrape this wax off. Finally, you need to polish your base to get it up to tip-top speed. Use a Scotch Brite® pad (or scourer) to remove any excess wax and give the base a nice smooth finish. Next you need to structure the base using a structure brush or carbide sandpaper block. If the snow is cold, then the structure should follow the direction

Above: *After allowing the wax to dry, take a plastic scraper and remove all excess wax.*

Above: *To finish, take a Scotch Brite® pad (scourer) and buff the base to perfection, working from nose to tail.*

of the base, ie tip to tail. If, however, the snow is warm and slushy, then you should structure the base at a 30-degree angle. Structuring your base allows the melted snow to leave your base more quickly. You are now ready to rip it up and go super fast.

BINDING MAINTENANCE

Requirements

1. 1 x Phillips head screwdriver – sizes 2 and 3
2. 1 x shifter
3. Allen key (depending on your bindings)

Procedure

The final step in DIY board maintenance is to inspect your bindings. Your bindings enable you to control your board. If your bindings are falling apart, it's like trying to drive a car without a steering wheel. Binding maintenance simply involves checking to see that all screws, both mounting screws and strap screws, are tight. There is nothing worse than losing a screw on the mountain, especially on a powder day.

It's also helpful to spray some lubricant (WD-40 is always good) into the moving parts of your bindings, ie ratchets and clips. This keeps them running smoothly and prevents rusting.

SHOP MAINTENANCE
BASE WELDING

Requirements

1. You will need some cash.

Procedure

Go to a snowboard shop. If you have any major gouges in the base of your board, it is probably best to get a shop to repair the P-Tex. A major gouge means a gouge that goes to the core of the board. Most snowboard shops have P-Tex guns, which enable the technician to burn the P-Tex at the right temperature. This means the P-Tex does not carbonize (turn black), so

Above: *Shops typically use a P-Tex gun to repair base gouges. P-Tex guns prevent the P-Tex from carbonizing.*

when it dries on your board it will be super strong. DIY jobs are prone to falling out.

BASE GRINDING

Requirements

1. Some more cash would be helpful.

Procedure

Find a snowboard shop. When your base is no longer flat or there are numerous long shallow gouges in the P-Tex, then it is best to take your board into a snowboard shop to get the base ground by a grinding machine specifically designed for snowboards. Be wary of taking your board to a ski shop, since a ski base grinder is not really designed for snowboards.

To determine whether your base is still flat, perform the following steps:

- Find a ruler.
- Drag the ruler along your snowboard.

If the whole ruler always touches the whole of your base, then your base is flat. If, however, you can see a space between the ruler and the base, for example in the middle of the base or on the edges, then your base is not flat. If your base is not flat, take it in for a base grind. A base that is not flat makes a board slower and more difficult to control.

Go out and kick your friend's butt in the speed stakes!

Above: *To get your base flat again, take it to a reputable snowboard shop for a base grind.*

BOARDERCROSS TECHNIQUES

HOW TO WIN RACES

Since 1994, boardercross racing has taken off in a big way. It now has its own dedicated world tour – the Swatch Boardercross, presented by O'Neill. There is also talk that boardercross will soon be introduced to the Winter Olympics. Snowboarding companies such as Palmer are setting up specialized boardercross racing teams and making snowboards specifically for racing boardercross. Most importantly, there are thousands of boardercross competitions, happening every year at local mountains across North America, Japan, Europe, Australia and New Zealand. To be successful in any of these competitions the rider needs to have a firm grasp of track techniques and crucial race tactics. What is provided here is a run-down of the key techniques and tactics that can be utilized when racing boardercross. Using these won't guarantee that you will win, but it will certainly enable you to raise your boardercross racing to the next level.

Above: *This is boardercross racing. Photo—Peter Murphy.*

Boardercross racing is similar to motocross racing except it is carried out on the snow. Between four and six snowboarders race simultaneously down a course filled with man-made obstacles. The first two riders (three riders where there are six in each heat) to cross the line at the bottom of the course proceed to the next round. This knockout format continues until there are only four riders (six where there are six in a heat) remaining, who then compete in the final.

Boardercross courses vary considerably in steepness, length and difficulty, but they typically consist of three main man-made obstacles.

1. **Whoopdy Doos:** These are 0.9-1.2 m (3-4 ft) humps that are shaped out of snow and placed across the course. Usually, two or three whoopdy doos are placed together, with about 2-3 m (6-10 ft) between each.

Where two whoopdy doos are placed together, it is called a double jump; where three are placed together, it is called a triple jump.

2. **Banks or Berms:** Banks or berms are placed on corners of the course. They look like the sloped corners on a velodrome track. Berms enable riders to take the corners of the boardercross course with more speed. They also enable riders to generate speed out of the corners.

3. **Tabletops:** Tabletops are jumps placed on the course. They are added to most courses to make the racing more spectacular. Typically, tabletops are placed near the start of the course or near the base of the course, as these areas are where most spectators' attention is focused.

76

GOLDEN RULES FOR BOARDERCROSS RACING

Five key things to remember when racing boardercross.

1. Win the start. If you get out in front early on in the race, then you will more than likely win the race or finish in the top two. Being out in front ensures that you are not caught up in the carnage that ensues when two or three riders enter a bank together.
2. Base is faster than edge. This is actually a giant slalom racing technique but applies equally to boardercross racing. Wherever possible, you should try to keep your board on a flat base because the P-Tex base is much faster than the metal edges.
3. Snow is faster than air. This rule says that it is generally quicker to stay on the snow rather than launch off a jump. In some cases, especially where you need to clear several small bumps, it may be quicker to travel through the air but generally you will be able to complete the boardercross course more quickly if you stay on the snow.
4. Do not miss the practice session. Boardercross racing is all about knowing what is around the next corner so that you and your board are totally prepared for it. The practice session is the perfect time to dial yourself into every nook and cranny of the course.
5. Wear a helmet unless you want to end up like Biff in *Back to the Future*.

TRACK TECHNIQUES

The Start

As with most races, the start is crucial to boardercross racing. Each competitor has his or her own starting gate. The gate is typically a metal frame, which the rider uses to pull himself or herself onto the course.

Placed in front of the gates is a wooden boom gate, which is controlled by the start marshal. To start the race, the start marshal shouts 'Racers ready!', then he or she can drop the boom gate at any time in the next 5 seconds. As the start marshal drops the boom gate, he or she shouts 'Go!'

The following two start techniques will help you improve your boardercross starts.

1. Watch the start marshal's hand and not the boom gate. The start marshal controls the boom gate with his or her hand. As soon as the start marshal's hand starts to move to drop the gate, you should be pulling out of your gate with every ounce of strength in your body.
2. Adjust your pulling technique to the steepness of the start. The pulling technique refers to how you pull out of the gates. There are two primary pulling techniques – the full pull and the half pull. The full pull requires you to have your arms fully extended before you pull yourself onto the course. The half pull requires you to have your arms less than fully extended – that is, they are bent at the elbows. Where the start of the boardercross course is flat it is best to use the full-pull technique, since you will require as much momentum as possible when you leave the gates. But when the start track is steep, the idea is to get onto the course as soon as possible and use the steepness of the course to generate speed. So where the start is steep, use the half-pull technique. The exact extent of your half pull will depend on the steepness of the start. The steeper it is, the less pull you need. The best idea is to fine-tune your start during the practice session.

Above: *In the gates ready for some action. Photo—Peter Murphy.*

Pre-ollieing

Pre-ollieing is the backbone of successful boardercross racing. It enables you to maintain your speed through bumps and jumps of varying sizes. If you want to be a boardercross racer, you need to be able to pre-ollie to perfection.

The idea of a pre-ollie is that you want to go over a whoopdy doo or a tabletop and maintain as much speed as possible. To maximize your speed through whoopdy doos and tabletops, you need to have three things in mind:

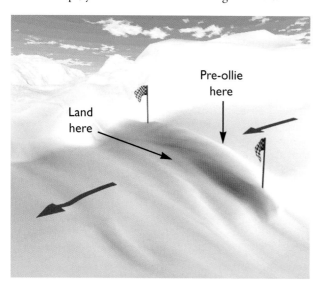

1. Minimize the amount of time you are in the air, as this will slow you down.
2. Minimise the amount of the whoopdy doo or tabletop you absorb with your legs, as this will only wash your speed off.
3. Land as high up as possible on the downside of the whoopdy doo or tabletop. This will allow you to gather more speed as you depart the obstacle.

A pre-ollie is simply an ollie (see page 204) performed before the lip of the whoopdy doo or tabletop. The idea is to perform the ollie at the correct point on the upside of the whoopdy doo or tabletop so that you float nice and low over the jump and land near the top of the downside of the jump. The correct point to start your pre-ollie will depend on the size of the whoopdy doo or tabletop. This is something you will need to perfect during the practice session.

Whoopdy Doos

There are essentially two ways to negotiate whoopdy doos – the pre-ollie and the 'jump the lot' method. Which method you use will depend on the number of whoopdy doos and the space between them.

The pre-ollie method is particularly appropriate where there is a single whoopdy doo. However, where there is more than one whoopdy doo, you will need to decide whether to pre-ollie each whoopdy doo or jump all of them.

Where there are two whoopdy doos located close together, it is generally quicker to air both of them (known as doubling). This is one of the rare cases where air is faster than snow. If it's impossible to clear the whoopdy doos together, you will have to pre-ollie them.

When jumping more than one whoopdy doo, there are some key points to bear in mind to ensure that you maximize your speed.

1. Minimize the time you are in the air. This means the path you take through the air from the lip of the first whoopdy doo to the downside of the last whoopdy doo should be as straight as possible. Unlike your trajectory off a normal jump, which has the shape of a deep arc, your trajectory

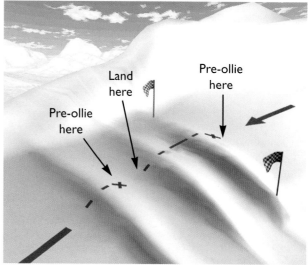

from first whoopdy doo to last whoopdy doo should be a very shallow arc. The idea is to use your speed so that you can skim over all the whoopdy doos.

2. Land on the downside of the final whoopdy doo. This allows you to have a smooth landing and to minimize any loss in speed.
3. Make sure you can clear the whoopdy doos. Perfect your strategy during the practice session, otherwise you will be exiting the competition pretty quickly. Where there are three whoopdy doos in a row, the best strategy may be to double the first two and pre-ollie the last one.

Banks

Banks are placed on courses to be used. Too often, competitors ignore the banks and edge hard around corners. This is where the rule 'base is faster than edge' comes into its own. Banks allow you to leave your board on its base through most

Above: *Using the banks to genererate power. Photo—Peter Murphy.*

78

of the corner, so it will be much quicker to use the bank than edging hard around a corner. Further, as banks are sloped, you will be able to pump some extra speed as you depart.

The best way to negotiate a bank is to take a path through the centre of the bank then pump down through the bank as you exit. You will be pleasantly surprised by how much extra speed you can generate when you use banks properly.

Tabletops

There is one simple rule about tabletops – pre-ollie. Pre-ollieing a tabletop is the quickest way over it. If you want to go to Hollywood and do some fancy air, be prepared to be knocked out. Of course, if you have a large lead, doing a nice air is fine, and great entertainment for the spectators.

RACE TACTICS

Boardercross racing is not just about negotiating the man-made obstacles on the course, it's also about negotiating the moving obstacles – your competitors. In fact, your competitors are probably your biggest obstacles, because their actions are totally unpredictable. Here are some race tactics that may help in different situations.

1. Get in front. This is the number one race tactic. If you are in front, you are less likely to be knocked over by another competitor.

2. If you are in a heat and coming second, be content. If you are coming second and the other competitors are well behind, it's not worth the risk to try to overtake the leader. There is a possibility that you could both crash and end up coming last. Save your fancy passing moves for the final.

3. If you are going into a bank together with two or three other riders, it may be better to pull back. The majority of falls in boardercross occur when riders enter a bank simultaneously. Whether a fall occurs will depend on what your competitors are like. If they are not high-quality riders, a fall will most likely occur and everyone will go down. This is one situation where you should pull back and ride around the ensuing crash. If your competitors are very aggressive and like to push and shove, this may also be an appropriate time to pull back, especially if you are not a six-foot giant.

GO RACING

With all this in mind, it is time to go racing, so go down to your local hill and enter a boardercross competition. Most of all, remember that boardercross racing is supposed to be enjoyable, so have some fun out there!

Above: *Going to Hollywood over the final kicker. Photo—Peter Murphy.*

BUILDING A SUPERKICKER

THE BEST METHODS

Kicker riding has become one of the most popular and progressive parts of snowboarding. The beauty of kicker riding is that you often don't need to spend your hard-earned cash for a lift ticket and it's super fun. All it takes is a group of friends, some imagination and a bit of hard work.

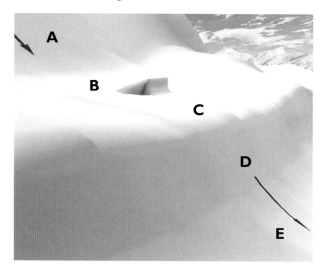

WHAT MAKES A GOOD KICKER?

A. A steep run-in is usually good, as it enables you to get a lot of speed without having to hike too far. Also, a steep run-in enables to speed check, giving you more control on your way to the kicker.

B. A flat section in the run-in is also a good idea, as it enables you to steady yourself as you prepare to hit the kicker. If you are going too fast, the flat section before the kicker can be used to speed check. This flat section also makes the transition from the steep run-in to the kicker a lot smoother and helps you maintain balance.

C. A good kicker usually has a gap or flat section to clear. The size of this depends on how big and fast you want to go. Obviously, the bigger the gap, the faster you need to hit the jump and the bigger you will go.

D. A steep landing is crucial – we talk about this further on.

E. A run-out with no rocks, trees, bumps or sudden deviations is best.

STEPS TO BUILDING A SUPER KICKER

Location

1. Find a good landing area (Section E in the diagram). A good landing will be steep and at least 9 m (30 ft) long. There should be plenty of snow and no rocks, trees or bumps. If you are unable to find a steep enough landing, consider building a landing ramp.

2. Make sure there is a good run-out (Section F in the diagram).

3. Make sure there is a good run-in which is steep enough for you to gather speed (Sections A and B in the diagram). To determine whether the run-in is good enough, hike up to where you think you will need to start your run-in to the kicker. Imagine where the

kicker will be, plug in and straight line it all the way to where you think you will place the kicker. This should tell you whether or not you will have adequate speed for the run-in. Remember, if you are on soft, deep snow, you may have to perform this step two or three times in order to pack down the run-in and get a better idea of whether the run-in is long enough and steep enough.

4. Once you have worked out the landing and the run-in, work out where you will place the kicker. Make sure you consider how much gap or flat you want to clear (refer to Section D in the diagram).

Building the Jump

1. It is important that you have the right tools to build the jump. The best tool that you can get is a collapsible snow shovel. These babies are tough, lightweight and can make building a jump as easy as putting a few Lego blocks together. One thing to remember: don't buy a plastic shovel! Plastic shovels are weak, can't dig through hard snow and will break. Metal shovels are more expensive, but consider the money saved on lift tickets. If you don't have any shovels and the snow is soft, consider digging with the nose/tails of your boards. However, this is inefficient and not highly recommended.

2. Grab a bunch of snowboards and create a frame for the kicker against which you can pile snow. The frame will have a back wall and two side walls.

3. Start piling the snow up against the boards, creating a mound of snow. Remember, make the pile of snow at least twice the width you think you want the kicker to be, because the actual kicker area always ends up a lot narrower than its base.

4. As you pile the snow up, pack in the sides to give the kicker strength.

5. Make sure the kicker is long enough, not too sharp or too 'kicky'.

Finishing Off

1. Pack all the snow in around the sides so that the jump isn't going to collapse when you go off it. Try and pack it with the boards rather than shovels, because boards have a greater surface area and pack the snow down better.

3. If possible, take a bag of salt with you so that you can spray it on the kicker when you have finished it. The salt will make the kicker nice and hard so that it won't collapse.

2. Take your board and smooth the top off so that you have a nice, smooth take-off.

4. Race up to the top so that you can be the first off the jump.

REMEMBER

1. Make sure that you pick a landing with a good gradient or you will end up with your knees in your mouth every time you land.
2. Look out for rocks and stones in the landing before you build the kicker.

HALFPIPE CONSTRUCTION AND MAINTENANCE

THE MAJOR TECHNIQUES

Picture this: you rock up to your favorite snowboard resort, all psyched to have the day of your life in their halfpipe which, you've been informed, has been freshly cut, only to find that it looks like little more than your grandmother's baking tray! And what's worse, you paid $50 of your hard-earned cash for it! Well, don't be ripped off any more – we will take you through the ins and outs of halfpipe maintenance. By learning the different techniques involved in halfpipe maintenance, you can plan your next trip so that you don't waste time and money at a place which promises more than it is able to deliver.

The International Snowboard Federation (ISF) is the governing body for the sport of snowboarding. It sets the standards for judging halfpipe events, and construction of world-class halfpipes. According to the ISF construction manual:

> In freestyle snowboarding, snow gives the sport a new expression: higher jumps, more time to execute the manoeuvres, smoother and easier landings. Creative and extravagant, the halfpipe is a very specific discipline of snowboarding!

Good halfpipe construction provides the platform for a high standard of riding. Organizers of serious snowboarding venues and events aid the standard of halfpipe riding by constructing halfpipes to exacting standards.

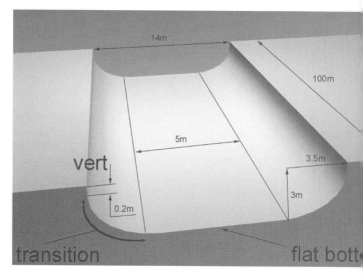

Above: *Thanks to a Pipe Dragon, Andrew Burton is able to boost big in the Copper Mountain halfpipe.*

HAND SHAPING

The oldest method known to man, hand shaping is the way resorts can produce and maintain a halfpipe if they have insufficient funds to invest in some proper halfpipe equipment. A very tedious and time-consuming method, hand shaping takes a lot of teamwork and a dedicated group of people to continually keep the pipe up to scratch. Shaping a pipe by hand will give a fantastic finish if the shapers are experienced, but resorts which maintain their pipe this way never have a consistently better-shaped halfpipe than the resorts which use a machine. A proper shaping machine can be run through a rutted pipe at the end of a day and have the walls in perfect shape within half an hour. A team of shapers who are using shovels will take hours/days to do the same job.

ISF HALFPIPE CONSTRUCTION STANDARDS

All measurements in meters.	Min.	Rec.	Max.
1. Inclination (degrees)	15	17	20
2. Length of each wall	80	100	120
3. Width from wall to wall (inner)	11	14	18
4. Inner height of walls	2.5	3	4
5. Transition radius	2.5	3.5	5.5
6. Bottom flat	3	5	6.5
7. Vertical (90%) at the top of the radius	0.1	0.2	0.4
8. Platform width	2	4	
9. Protected area (platform from coping to fence)	2		
10. Start area (above pipe/height)	2	3	5

Source: ISF Construction Manual.

Advantages of Hand Shaping
- No set-up costs, only ongoing payment of staff to shape the pipe.
- Provides a well-shaped pipe.

Above: *Shaping blades are one of the cheapest ways to shape a halfpipe. The problem is that they do not provide a good finish. Photo —Peter Murphy.*

Above: *Hand shaping is a technique as old as halfpipes themselves. It is one of the worst techniques used to regularly maintain a halfpipe.*

Disadvantages of Hand Shaping:
- It is such a labor-intensive method that it is never used as frequently as necessary. Try convincing a bunch of underpaid/unpaid riders to get the shovel out and shape the pipe every couple of days. The reality is, the pipe will need shaping every few days if not more frequently.
- A resort has the ongoing expense of paying staff to shape the pipe.

Overall effectiveness: 3 out of 10 – there is no comparison between halfpipes at resorts with and without a pipe-shaping machine.

SHAPING BLADE
There are various shaping blades on the market, which are usually made by the resorts that operate them. They are basically a hunk of metal in a half-moon shape that attaches to a snow groomer. They are designed to push up each wall, thereby cutting a perfect transition. The reality is that if you put a shaping blade up against an icy halfpipe wall, the icy wall will come off better and the blade will break or just simply not work.

Advantages of the Shaping Blade
- Cheap to make.
- Good to dig the initial transition in the wall before manicuring with a shovel.

Disadvantages of the Shaping Blade
- Biggest drawback is it pushes the snow, which is very difficult, when the snow is icy/hard.
- Usually leaves small holes in the walls where the snowpack hasn't bound properly.
- Often doesn't get rid of kinks and highways.
- Often creates over-vert.
- Takes too much time to get a good wall and then still requires hand shaping with a shovel.

Overall effectiveness: 6 out of 10 – waste of money.

BACKHOE
Your ordinary earth-digging backhoe can become an excellent transition shaper when used correctly. If operated by a skilled driver, the backhoe can have its arm set to a certain radius and slowly move along the walls, cutting a near-perfect transition. It can be used instead of a pipe-shaping machine such as a Pipe Dragon or other shaping tool. It digs an excellent pipe but it is slow and inefficient to use on a daily basis. Japanese resorts are big users of backhoes, but they still finish off their pipes with a Dragon.

Advantages of the Backhoe
- If operated by a skilled driver, it will dig a near-perfect halfpipe.
- Inexpensive capital outlay relative to a Pipe Dragon/Master as many resorts already own or have cheap access to a backhoe.

Disadvantages of the Backhoe
- Backhoes are too slow to use on a daily or regular basis – they are best used for getting the initial shape of the pipe.
- Backhoes require very skilled operators.

Overall effectiveness: 7 out of 10 – not as easy to use as a Pipe Dragon/Pipe Master.

Above: *Backhoes are great for digging the initial shape of the walls.*

PIPE DRAGON

A Pipe Dragon is a hydraulically powered grooming machine that is attached to a snow groomer and used to form the half-pipe's smoothly curved transitions and vertical walls. The Pipe Dragon works by digging the wall as it passes along it, thereby removing unwanted ruts and creating a perfect transition. It also fills the ruts in as it passes along the walls and leaves a beautiful corduroy finish to the wall. Each time the Pipe Dragon is run down a wall, it takes away about 8-13 cm (3-5 in) from the wall. Therefore, each time the pipe is shaped, it gets about 15-25 cm (6-10 in) wider; after numerous shaping sessions, the pipe must be filled in and re-built from scratch. The Pipe Dragon is the most widely used shaping machine in the world. In fact, it is the standard pipe groomer for competition halfpipes.

Above: *Pipe Dragons are the most popular and arguably the best halfpipe-shaping tool. Photo courtesy of Weisse Arena Corp.*

Advantages of the Pipe Dragon
• Quick and easy to use. Park the Dragon near the pipe, connect it to the groomer when needed and run it up each wall once. It takes around 20-30 minutes per wall, minimizing expensive groomer time and allowing a resort to shape the pipe regularly at little cost.
• Gives perfect 2.4-3 m (8-10 ft) transitions without over-vert.
• Leaves a beautiful corduroy finish without chunks and holes in the walls, unlike the shaping blade.
• Removes ruts and highways with exceptional precision.

Disadvantages of the Pipe Dragon
• The pipe must be rebuilt every now and again as it gets too wide from being cut too many times.
• Resorts need to be prepared to fork out a bit of cash for one of these – about USD$45,000 (includes shipping).
• Requires a very skilled operator.

Overall effectiveness: 9.5 out of 10 – won the Squaw Valley 'Groom-off' in 1998 against the Pipe Master and Scorpion.

PIPE MASTER AND SNOW TURBO GRINDER

The Pipe Master by Kassbohrer and Snow Turbo Grinder by HiTe Metal are similar machines in terms of the techniques they use to shape the pipe. Both machines attempt to pull the snow that is inside the pipe and relocate it elsewhere to maintain perfectly smooth transitions. They fill in holes and highways and takes out bumps. Despite these similarities, the Snow Turbo actually weighs about half as much as the Pipe Master, and is the most widely sold pipe-shaping tool.

Unlike the Pipe Dragon, the Pipe Master and the Snow Turbo Grinder do not spit snow out of the pipe. The advantage of this is that both perform extremely well in poor snow conditions. They are able to maintain perfect halfpipes when there is less than a 15 cm (6 in) base. This is because they utilize snow in the pipe most efficiently. The Pipe Master is becoming popular with resorts which operate groomers supplied by Kassbohrer, due to its lower repair and maintenance costs. The Snow Turbo Grinder can in fact be fitted to four different types of groomers – Bombardier, Kassbohrer, Prinoth and Leitner.

Advantages of the Pipe Master and the Snow Turbo
• Can be used in bad snow conditions more effectively than a Pipe Dragon.
• Gives perfect 2.4-3 m (8-10 ft) smooth transitions.
• Minimizes expensive groomer time, thus enabling a resort to shape the pipe very regularly at little cost.

Disadvantages of the Pipe Master and the Snow Turbo
• Not as robust and capable of digging through ice as the Pipe Dragon.
• Not as cheap to buy as a shaping blade.
• Potentially difficult to use in a pipe that is full of fresh snow, as it doesn't blow the snow out.

Overall effectiveness: 9 out of 10 – if your resort has one of these, you'll be riding one of the best pipes in the world.

Opposite: *Mouse Beuchat requests a fly-by from the Snowbird control tower. Damn you, Maverick!*

AVALANCHE AWARENESS

BEING SAFE IN THE BACKCOUNTRY

More and more, snowboarders are returning to the roots of snowboarding – the backcountry. They are doing this to find new terrain, untracked powder and good locations to build backcountry kickers. Unlike in in-bounds terrain, no avalanche control is carried out in the backcountry. Thus it is essential that snowboarders who venture into the backcountry have a solid understanding of the dangers associated with avalanches. Those who use the backcountry as their natural playground owe it to themselves and to their fellow users to ensure that their activities in the backcountry are safe and responsible. This means understanding avalanches.

The formation of an avalanche is a natural and complex process that occurs as the snowpack adjusts to the changing weather conditions and the pull of gravity. It is not possible, even for experts, to predict an avalanche with absolute certainty. However, there are factors that indicate if a slope will be especially prone to an avalanche. There are steps you can take to avoid being caught in an avalanche. And if you or one of your friends are caught in an avalanche, there are guidelines that should be followed. The information here will not enable you to predict avalanches, but it will help you gain a better understanding of the dangers in the backcountry and how to take some necessary precautions.

WHAT CAUSES AVALANCHES

The danger of an avalanche is caused by three factors known as the 'Avalanche Triangle' – the snowpack, the terrain and the weather.

A. The Snowpack

The snowpack consists of several layers of snow and results from various dumps that occur throughout the season. The critical factor for avalanches is the strength of the bonding between the layers. The strength of the bonding between the layers is affected by:

1. Snow crystal type: It is a common misconception that snow crystals have a six-sided, symmetrical shape. Snow can take on other interesting shapes too, such as hexagonal plates, columns, and needles. The exact shape of the snow crystal will depend on the air temperature and saturation at the end of its creation. In turn, the shape of the snow crystals will determine the strength of the bonding between the layers in the snow-pack. However, what makes things more difficult is that the shape of the snow crystals is constantly changing as the weather patterns change and new snow falls.

2. Internal snowpack changes (metamorphism): Changes in the weather continually influence the snowpack, making the bonding between the layers either weaker or stronger. Further, the difference in temperature between the surface and the base of the snowpack has a strong metamorphic effect. The best way to determine the strength of the bonding between the layers is to dig a cross-sectional pit. This will give you a good idea of the different layers that exist in the snowpack on a particular slope. When digging

a pit, always look for the presence of loose, sugary snow. This type of snow is known as depth hoar and causes a very unstable snowpack. But remember, the information gathered from a cross-sectional pit dug on one slope will not necessarily apply to another nearby slope.

B. The Terrain

The location and gradient of a slope will be two important factors that affect how prone the slope is to an avalanche. If the slope is on the leeward (protected) side of the mountain, then it will most likely receive a lot of wind-deposited snow and may be extremely unstable. Windward slopes are generally the safer areas, but they are not totally immune to slides either.

Avalanches occur most commonly on slopes with gradients of between 30 and 45 degrees. Any slope between these gradients represents the most danger and should be treated with extreme caution. Large avalanches have also been recorded on slopes with inclines ranging from 25 degrees to 60 degrees. The most dangerous are those with 30 to 45-degree gradients.

In the Northern Hemisphere, north-facing slopes tend to be more dangerous during the mid-winter period. These slopes tend to remain in the shade, so the bonding between the layers is not strong. South-facing slopes tend to be most dangerous during the spring, especially on sunny days. During spring it is usually recommended that any activities to be carried out in the backcountry should be done before midday or after 6 pm. Note that in the Southern Hemisphere these rules are reversed – north-facing slopes are more dangerous during spring and south-facing slopes are more dangerous during mid-winter.

Ground cover is the other terrain variable that affects how prone a slope is to an avalanche. Large boulders, trees and bushes all help anchor the snow to the mountain. No ground cover or a large clearing on a slope indicate that a slide is more likely to occur in that area.

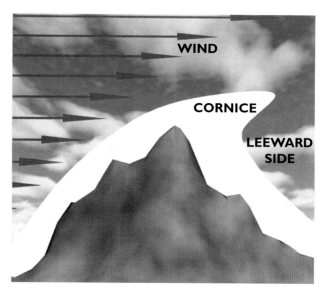

WIND

CORNICE

LEEWARD SIDE

Above: *Avalanches can occur anywhere – in-bounds, even directly under lift lines.*

C. The Weather

Changing weather is a very important determinant of avalanche danger. Extreme care should be taken after unusual changes in precipitation, temperature and wind. The effect of weather conditions will also vary greatly between mountains in the interior and mountains on the coast.

The coastal climate is characterized by huge, dense, frequent snowfalls and mild temperatures. The depth of snow, warm air and relative lack of air space within the snowpack results in a tendency towards strengthening over time. Avalanche cycles generally run during and immediately after storms. The Coast Mountain Range of British Columbia in Canada and the Cascades in Washington State, USA are good examples of areas affected by coastal climate.

The interior climate is characterized by shallow snow cover, light fluffy snow, cold temperatures and long dry spells between storms. These conditions result in a snowpack whose layers tend to weaken over time. In this climate, the avalanche cycles are not tied to the storm cycles; they can occur at any time. The Rockies of Colorado are a prime example.

When thinking about the effect of weather on the slopes, the following points should be borne in mind.

- Storms present the most dangerous conditions, as most avalanches occur during or shortly after storms.
- Winds with of 25 km/h (15 mph) or higher will cause an extreme increase in avalanche hazards. As the wind accelerates on the windward side of a slope, it picks up snow and deposits it on the leeward slope, thus greatly increasing the danger on leeward slopes.
- New snow falling at a rate of 2.5 cm (1 in) per hour or more indicates an increasing avalanche danger. When more than 30 cm (12 in) falls in less than a 24-hour period, the avalanche danger will be extreme.
- Higher temperatures cause snow to lose its cohesive strength as the snow crystals change shape. Low temperatures cause dry snow to remain loose and unstable. On average, new snow will settle and stabilize when the temperature is near freezing.

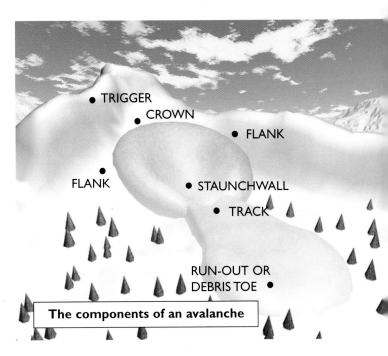

The components of an avalanche

TYPES OF AVALANCHES

There are two main types of avalanches – the loose-snow avalanche and the slab avalanche. The loose-snow avalanche or sluff generally occurs on the surface in new snow or wet spring snow. This type of avalanche often begins at a point and spreads out as it goes, gradually gaining momentum. Although they can be huge and destructive, loose-snow avalanches of such magnitude do not often occur. It is very rare that a loose-snow avalanche will bury a person.

In contrast, slab avalanches are very dangerous. They occur over large areas when a cohesive body of snow separates as a moving slab from more stable snow, leaving a well-defined fracture line. There are two families of slab avalanches – the soft-slab avalanche and the hard-slab avalanche.

The soft-slab avalanche is caused by a rapid build-up of fresh snow. Due to the quantity of new snow, the pull of gravity is much stronger than the bonding effect between the layers. Thus the new layer of fresh snow releases before it has a chance to properly bond to the old surface layer. In contrast, a hard-slab avalanche can take with it any number of layers. A major cause of hard-slab avalanches is the formation of depth hoar in the lower layers of the snowpack. This makes hard-slab avalanches extremely difficult to predict.

AVALANCHE SAFETY EQUIPMENT

The majority of avalanche victims die within the first 25-30 minutes of being buried. Carrying the right safety equipment and knowing the correct rescue procedures can help avoid such deaths.

Transceivers

Transceivers are small, low-powered, electromagnetic devices that transmit a constant signal when turned on. The transceiver is worn against the body. It should not be put in your backpack as this can be torn off by avalanches. If one of your friends is buried in an avalanche, you will need to turn your transceiver to 'receive' so you can locate him or her. Using a transceiver efficiently and quickly takes practice, so put some time aside, bury a transceiver in the snow and practice finding it.

Above: *This is a typical avalanche transceiver. If you are going into the backcountry, it is essential.*

Some things to remember when using avalanche transceivers:

- Never use rechargeable batteries. There is a tendency for the power to drop off abruptly.
- Change your batteries regularly. Do not run them until they are fully discharged. Five dollars spent today may save your life.
- Wear your transceiver against your body, under your outer layers – don't carry it in your pack or pocket.
- Even if you ride alone, carry a transceiver – this could save searchers hours of looking for you.

Snow Shovels

There is no point having an avalanche transceiver if you can't dig your friend out. These days there are plenty of light-weight collapsible shovels on the market. You need to ensure that the shovel blade is of a decent size so you can shift snow rapidly.

Avalanche Probes

An avalanche probe looks and works like a lightweight tent pole. Probes are used to systematically poke around the avalanche debris looking for buried victims. Probes are an excellent means by which you can pinpoint an avalanche victim once you have located him/her with a transceiver.

First-aid Supplies

Any backcountry enthusiast should have a first-aid kit in his or her pack. One of the most important items in the kit is medical tape, so make sure you have some.

Mobile Phones

If you are stuck in the backcountry or one of your friends has been caught in an avalanche, a mobile phone is the quickest way to call in the Search and Rescue team.

Avalanche Awareness

If you are heading into avalanche-prone territory, familiarize yourself with the appropriate procedures to follow should you or one of your friends be caught in an avalanche. Although you never really want to be put in a situation where you have to dig your friend out of an avalanche, knowing how to may save his or her life.

GOLDEN RULES OF AVALANCHE AWARENESS

There are three golden rules for avoiding avalanches:

1. Always, always, always cross an avalanche path one at a time. Never cross together.
2. Never enter a slope above your friend. Allow your friend to clear the slope before you make your descent.
3. Always have an escape route planned. If you trigger an avalanche, you will have a brief moment to use your momentum to carry you to a safety zone, provided you have identified one in advance. Ridges, big trees and lower-angle slopes are all good safety zones.

INTERNATIONAL SCALE OF AVALANCHE HAZARD

Most resorts publish an avalanche bulletin daily. The level of avalanche danger is rated according to an international scale. The ratings mean the same whether you are in Verbier, Switzerland or Snowbird, Utah. The avalanche bulletins are compiled by avalanche experts, so believe what they say.

Low

Natural avalanches are very unlikely, human-triggered avalanches are unlikely. Travel is generally safe in all terrain for travelers of all skill levels.

Moderate
Natural avalanches are unlikely, human-triggered avalanches are possible. Use caution in steeper terrain, especially on aspects identified in the avalanche advisory.

Considerable
Natural avalanches are possible, human-triggered avalanches are probable. Be increasingly cautious in steeper terrain.

High
Natural and human-triggered avalanches are likely. Travel in avalanche terrain is not recommended.

Extreme
Widespread natural or human-triggered avalanches are certain. This is not a good time to go into the backcountry.

TAKE AN AVALANCHE COURSE
If you spend a lot of time in the backcountry or seriously want to get into backcountry snowboarding and mountaineering, you will benefit from an avalanche course. Most countries run intensive courses during the winter. Just be aware that what is provided here is only a guide and can never replace a comprehensive avalanche course. At the risk of sounding like a 'No Fear' slogan, it needs to be said that you should take care out there, as nature does not forgive.

SELECTING A ROUTE

Before you go out and ride down any slope in the backcountry, you need to think about whether the route you are taking is safe. You should bear the following points in mind:

- Obtain information about local snowpack conditions, weather and avalanche hazards.
- Look out for evidence of old slide paths, such as bent or broken trees. Old slide paths indicate the possibility of more action.
- Avoid hollow-sounding areas and slopes that go 'whomp' when you travel on them. This indicates the collapse of the weak layers of snow and that the slope is precariously close to sliding.
- Leeward slopes are breeding grounds for avalanches.
- Cornices often break off well back from their edge on tops of ridges and hills. Detour around all overhaning snow and do not climb beneath corniced areas.
- Be wary of convex slopes, as these are extremely avalanche-prone.
- If a slope looks dangerous, stay well away. When hiking, keep to ridge tops or close to wooded areas. Do not hike directly up an open face.

SEARCHING FOR A VICTIM

If one of your friends is buried in a slide, the following steps will help you locate him or her.

1. Before beginning to search, look for further slide danger and select a safe escape route should another slide occur. Designate a look-out person to warn of new slides.
2. Mark the last spot where the victim was seen.
3. Perform a quick search for any clues. Probe briefly with an avalanche probe in suspected areas.
4. If you have transceivers, immediately turn them to 'receive' and commence searching systematically.
5. If the victim is not located, decide whether or not to go for help. Consider the time needed to reach help and have help return. Remember that half of all avalanche victims die in 1 hour; many are dead in 5 minutes.
6. If your party is large, send two people for help immediately after a quick search has been conducted (if it has failed).
7. If you do not have transceivers, begin a probe search for the victim. Mark all areas that are probed and mark any clues that are dug up.
8. Primary probing areas are places where slide debris has accumulated. Check the toe of the avalanche, side of the slide path and all around any exposed obstacles such as trees or rocks. Persons are often hung up in these spots by the current of the avalanche snow flow.
9. Probing should be carried out in an organized manner. The correct method of probing is to insert the probe in a straight line, with each probe separated by 75 cm (29 in). Designate someone to dig up everything hit with probes.

WHAT TO DO WHEN CAUGHT OR BURIED IN AN AVALANCHE

If you are caught in an avalanche, you should remember the following things:

- Discard all cumbersome equipment, especially your pack.
- Make swimming motions (breaststroke) with your arms and attempt to stay on the surface of the slide.
- Do not waste vital energy fighting the flow, but rather try to ferry your way to the other side of the avalanche path.
- Grab trees, bushes or rocks to stabilize your position.
- As you feel the slide slowing down, make a last fight to gain the surface.

If you are buried by an avalanche, take the following steps:

- Attempt to get a hand above the surface.
- Keep one hand in front of your face to prevent icing up and suffocation.
- Take a slow deep breath and calmly hold it until the snow has settled around you.
- You will be extremely disoriented. Do not waste energy trying to extricate yourself, unless you can see light through the snow.
- Do not panic! Remain calm and wait for assistance.

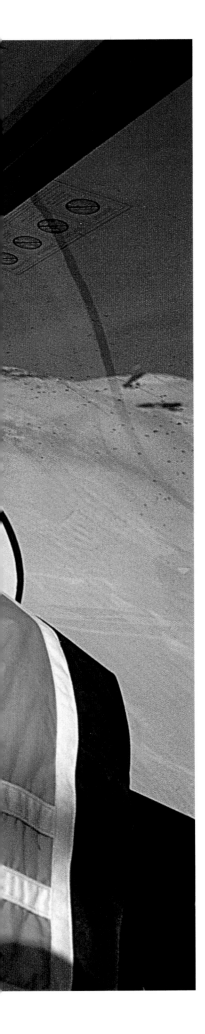

THE SNOWBOARDER RESORT GUIDE

INTRODUCTION

As you flick through snowboarding magazines and watch the latest snowboarding videos, you are constantly teased with images of your favorite riders cruising some of the most awesome mountains on the planet. It's the desire of almost every snowboarder to travel and sample new terrain in different parts of the world. Whether it be in the next state or the next country, snowboarding somewhere different is the ultimate dream. It's exciting to travel to new resorts and explore different terrain. Nothing can replace the feeling of anticipation as you board the first chairlift in the morning, scoping out new lines or examining a perfectly manicured pipe.

Whether you have traveled 20 minutes or 20 hours to get to your snowboarding destination, there is nothing worse than finding out that the resort is far from what you expected. The terrain is uninteresting, the freestyle facilities are downright terrible, and the resort's marketing document, which promised untracked tree runs and the best halfpipe in the country, was simply not true.

In the Snowboarder Resort Guide, we aim to help you maximize your snowboarding experience when you visit new resorts. We do this by providing objective reviews on 50 snowboarding destinations in eight countries across the globe. The Snowboarder Resort Guide is the ultimate snowboarding terrain guide. Whilst we don't tell you where to stay and eat in our reviews, we give you the most objective, reliable and detailed rundown on the terrain and snowboarding facilities available at each of the 50 resorts covered. All of the reports have been prepared by the same group of riders, who have personally visited each of the 50 resorts covered. The team has over 50 years of combined snowboarding experience. For these reasons the information provided is consistent and credible.

The 50 resorts we have chosen are not necessarily the best 50 resorts in the world. Rather, they represent some of the best snowboarding destinations in the USA, Canada, Australia, New Zealand, Japan, Austria, Switzerland and France. There is a good cross-section of resorts, from gigantic super resorts such as Whistler/Blackcomb to lesser-known resorts such as Gerlos. This mix has been provided to enable you to compare and contrast different snowboard destinations so you can select a place that best suits your needs.

To acquire the most from the Snowboarder Resort Guide, you will need to absorb every facet of the reports. Study the statistical tables. They will provide you with information on the number of lifts, the vertical drop and how to find out about the latest snow conditions. The resort overview will provide you with a feeling for the resort. What level of development exists? Is it snowboarder-friendly? Finally, and most importantly, the terrain section will enable you to decide whether the mountain has good freeriding terrain or whether it is better for park and pipe riding. Also, it will let you know such things as where to find powder turns or where to be in bad weather. Most of all, the Snowboarder Resort Guide will help to ensure that your next snowboarding trip is as epic as the ones you read about in the snowboard magazines.

We hope that the Snowboarder Resort Guide not only comes in handy for planning your next trip, but also makes for entertaining reading.

Left: *The crew on a fantastic winter's day, cruisin' to the summit. Days like this are few and far between, so make the most of the conditions and go ballistic.*

UNITED STATES OF AMERICA

The USA is a massive country, with over 270 million people living in fifty states across some nine million square kilometers. It is the place where anything can happen and everything does happen. Arguably the home of snowboarding, the USA is one of the most enjoyable travel destinations in the world. Its landscape is vast and extremely varied. Similarly, its ethnic cultures vary across states and suburbs. The USA cannot be compared to any other place in the world and is a country that every snowboarder must visit at least once in a lifetime.

THE MOUNTAINS AND CLIMATE OF THE USA

America is littered with hundreds of snow resorts, ranging from small backhills to huge corporate money-spinners. The best places to snowboard in the USA are in three distinct regions across the country: (a) The West Coast; (b) The Rocky Mountain States; and (c) The East Coast. Needless to say, each region is characterized by its own unique landscape. In the west there are the sharp alpine peaks of the North Cascades in Washington, and the Rockies in Utah. The tree-laden mounds of the Appalachians characterize the landscape in the East Coast.

Weather varies immensely between the two seaboards of the USA. It is dictated largely by the huge masses of mountains that spread across a significant portion of the country. Given its geographical location, each mountain region has its own unique weather patterns and snow conditions. It's difficult to compare the light dry powder of Utah in the Central Rockies to the wet Pacific snow of Mt Baker Washington on the West Coast.

Pacific North West: Stretching from Alaska in the Arctic Circle to the southern parts of the Sierra Nevadas in California, the West Coast of the USA is bombarded constantly throughout winter by strong Pacific storms which dump huge amounts of wet heavy snow across the coastal ranges. The West Coast mountains consistently record some of the highest average snowfalls in the USA. Sunshine varies considerably during winter. Resorts in northern California record about 75% sunny days each season. Go a little further north towards Seattle, though, and sunny days can be as rare as hen's teeth during Thanksgiving.

Opposite: *Arguably the home of snowboarding, the USA is the mecca for most snowboard travelers who want to push themselves to the limit. Here Bear Agushi frontflips his way into the Utah backcountry.*

The Rockies: The Rockies are a vast range of mountains spreading from the deserts of New Mexico to the prairie-lands of Alberta in Canada. Covering some seven US states, they span regions that have enormous climatic variation. Due to the distance of the Rockies from the surrounding oceans, the climate of the Rocky states in winter is much cooler than that of the west. Hence the snow is much drier. The Rockies receive numerous sunny days throughout the winter. Storms that travel from the Pacific have the moisture sucked out as they travel via jet streams across the western deserts and dump light dry powder.

The East Coast: Whilst snowboarding in the western states of the USA often means powder, sun and more powder, conditions on the East Coast are different. East Coast snowboarders usually have to put up with Arctic temperatures, ice, rain and slush for most of the season. When cold sub-Arctic air crashes with warm humid air from the Gulf of New Mexico, the snow can fall in large quantities across the northeastern states. However, these days are few and far between, and as a result, snow resorts have become expert at making and storing snow to ensure that riders are able to enjoy many fine hardpack days on the East Coast.

SNOWBOARDING IN THE USA

The USA was the birthplace of snowboarding over three decades ago and since then has never looked back. Resorts across the nation have embraced snowboarding so fully that they lead the world in providing facilities to keep snowboarders coming back to their slopes. The incredible popularity of snowboarding has made it a mainstream sport across the country. Every teenager who wants to be cool snowboards – or claims to. Resorts are littered with riders, and at certain places, snowboarders can outnumber skiers. Terrain, conditions, facilities and attitudes can vary across the nation, but you are guaranteed of some awesome riding in the USA.

Below: *A lone rider scopes out the endless lines in the US backcountry. Photo—Gavin O'Toole.*
Opposite: *Scott Nelson enjoying the steeps at Brighton. Photo—Gavin O'Toole.*

CALIFORNIA
USA

OVERVIEW

California is world-famous for a lot of things, such as Hollywood, Disneyland, motorways and, of course, snowboarding. The riding terrain and conditions can vary vastly across this massive state. In the south are the dry San Bernadino Mountains surrounding LA and in the north are the powder-covered peaks of the Sierra Nevada range.

Northern California: Lake Tahoe is one of the best US snowboard destinations in the world. The mountains receive good snowfalls and good weather.

Southern California: Southern California is home to sun, surf and Hollywood. Here you can be guaranteed sunny days, great pipes and parks, and warm weather. However, don't go to Southern California if you want powder and big terrain. For that, you will have to head up north to Tahoe.

Snowboarding in California: California is known as America's home of skateboarding and surfing, so it's no surprise that the resorts and the riders in this state are particularly freestyle-orientated. As a result, there are very few resorts in California that do not have a good halfpipe and snowboard park. However, the huge Pacific storms play havoc with the maintenance of the pipes and the parks. Fortunately, competition amongst the resorts guarantees good-quality halfpipes and snowboard parks. As far as freeriding goes, Tahoe is the place if you are after good steeps and powder. The mountains around Lake Tahoe offer plenty of high alpine riding. The peaks in this area are characterized by bowls, cliffs, chutes, cornices and glades. The terrain in northern California is, without a doubt, close to the best in the USA.

This guide will concentrate on the resorts in northern California, including one of the giant resorts of the USA, Squaw Valley.

Opposite: *Boosting big off a California super kicker, a local spins his way to stardom.*
Below: *Rohan Smiles churning some powder above Lake Tahoe. Photo—Gavin O'Toole.*

LAKE TAHOE
USA

OVERVIEW

Lake Tahoe is one of the world's most picturesque alpine lakes. It borders two states, California and Nevada. It takes about 1.5 to 2 hours to drive around the lake and over 13 resorts are located on its shores. Further, some of the most extreme backcountry is located close to Lake Tahoe in an area known as Donner Pass.

Lake Tahoe is arguably the premier snowboard destination since the freestyle facilities at each resort are excellent and the backcountry is some of the best in the world. The freestyle facilities are superb because the resorts compete fiercely to attract snowboarders. Consequently, snowboarders are provided with perfectly manicured halfpipes and parks. Tahoe is also the home to Standard Films, Mack Dawg films and countless other snowboard media. As a result, the resorts in the area are home to numerous pro snowboarders. For these reasons, the resorts invest plenty of money in snowboarding so that they can gain the maximum media exposure.

ACCOMMODATION IN TAHOE

Lake Tahoe is dotted with small towns and holiday condos. There is rarely a shortage of accommodation in the area and it is very affordable, especially if you are in a group of 4 or more. The Lake can be divided into two main regions: (1) North Shore; and (2) South Shore. Choosing a place to stay

Below: *Luke Fitcher launching a method around Lake Tahoe. Photo—Gavin O'Toole.*

will depend on which resort you want to ride. If you are going to ride the resorts on the north shores of the lake, then don't stay on the south shore, as it is at least a 45-minute drive away and public transport is not good. Check out the local vacation rental agencies as they offer great deals on short to medium-term stays. You can also find accommodation by picking up the local newspapers at any supermarket and other retail outlets. These advertize all types of accommodation. In addition to staying in houses or condos, you may wish to save money and stay in a motel, which when shared can be very cheap. However, what you save on staying in a motel you spend on food, as you don't have cooking facilities.

NORTH SHORE

Truckee: The gateway to most of the North Shore resorts is a town called Truckee. It is the most developed town on the North Shore and has all your typical fast food stores (McDonalds, Burger King, Subway, Little Caesar's) as well as Italian and Chinese restaurants. There are two big supermarkets and a few banks. It is a thriving tourist town in winter and employment opportunities are good. Truckee lies only about 10 minutes from Boreal, 15-20 minutes from Squaw Valley, Alpine Meadows and Sugar Bowl, about 40 minutes from Mt Rose and about an hour from the South Shore.

Kings Beach: Kings Beach is a small town located right on the lake and it is heavily developed with vacation homes. The town has far less in the way of restaurants than Truckee. It has one supermarket (Safeway), a movie theatre, a giant outdoor hot-tub, an indoor gym and a few small snowboard stores. It is a quaint town and only about 20-30 minutes' drive from Squaw Valley, Alpine Meadows and Mt Rose, about 40 minutes from Sugar Bowl and the rest of Donner Summit, and about 45 minutes from South Shore.

Tahoe City: Tahoe City is another small town located on the lake. It is probably a little more resort-like than nearby Kings Beach and Incline Village. There is some good nightlife in Tahoe City, with a few cool bars. There is a Safeway in Tahoe City for all your grocery needs and the town is only about 10-15 minutes' drive from Squaw Valley and Alpine Meadows, 25-30 minutes from Boreal and Sugar Bowl, about 40 minutes from Mt Rose and about an hour from South Shore.

Incline Village: Incline Village is located in Nevada. It's small in terms of its business district, but is packed with vacation condos and houses. About the same size as Kings Beach, Incline Village doesn't have a lot in the way of places to dine or get fast food. Opposite Christmas Tree Village Shops there is a supermarket and a pretty good snowboard store called Porters. Incline Village is the closest town to Mt Rose, about a 20-minute drive. It is about a 35 to 45-minute drive from Squaw Valley and Alpine Meadows, about a one-hour drive from Boreal and Donner Summit, and about 30 minutes from South Shore.

Crystal Bay: Crystal Bay is a very small town on the Nevada/California border. The only real accommodation here is in casinos, which are its major attraction. Crystal Bay

Above: *Dave Lee, demonstrating a smooth and clean rodeo above Lake Tahoe.*

is about a 25-minute drive from Mt Rose, and a 35 to 45-minute drive from Squaw Valley, Alpine Meadows, Boreal and Donner Summit, and about 30 minutes from South Lake.

SOUTH SHORE

South Lake Tahoe: South Lake Tahoe is the biggest town in the Tahoe region and is on the Nevada side of the border. This means that it is home to many casinos and wedding chapels as well as some of Tahoe's best powder. If you are interested in short-term accommodation and don't require cooking facilities, check out the casinos, as they are cheap and pretty cosy. For entertainment, there is a lot more happening in South Lake than up on the North Shore, primarily due to the casinos. There is a Planet Hollywood for the tourists, and McDonalds, Subway, and Pizza Hut outlets for the junk food addicts. The major problem with the South Shore is that it is about a one-hour drive to Lake Tahoe's two best resorts, Squaw Valley and Alpine Meadows.

SQUAW VALLEY
CALIFORNIA, USA

STATISTICS

Average Annual Snowfall

	1100 cm	440 in

Elevations	(m)	(ft)
Top:	2760	9055
Base:	1891	6204
Vertical Drop:	869	2851

Lifts

Surface Lifts:	4
Double Chairs:	10
Triple Chairs:	9
Quad Chairs – Fixed Grip:	1
Quad Chairs – Express:	4
Six Chairs – Express:	0
Gondolas:	1
Cable Cars:	1
Funiculars:	0
Total:	30

Contact Details

Phone:	+1 530 583 6985
Fax:	+1 530 581 7106
Email Address:	squaw@sierra.com
Internet Site:	www.squaw.com

RESORT REVIEW

Squaw Valley has to be one of the most incredible resorts in the world for snowboarding. Riding at Squaw Valley is comparable to riding at some of the big European resorts. The size of the terrain, the snow, the weather and the facilities all combine to offer an amazing destination.

Squaw boasts one of the USA's biggest and most advanced lift systems. With 30 lifts including a brand new Funitel and luxury cable car, over 49,000 people can be lifted up to the six alpine peaks per hour. Squaw is also one of the resorts most committed to snowboarding; this is evident when you ride its park and pipe.

Left: *Bear Agushi over some rocks in the Granite Chief bowls.*
Above: *Mouse Beuchat styling a stalefish in the Squaw Park.*

TERRAIN

FREERIDING

Squaw Valley comprises six adjoining mountains – Snow King (2,300 m/7,550 ft), Broken Arrow (2,444 m/8,020 ft), KT-22 (2,499 m/8,200 ft), Emigrant Peak (2,652 m/8,700 ft), Squaw Peak (2,719 m/8,900 ft) and Granite Chief (2,758 m/9,050 ft). Extreme skiers and snowboarders flock to Squaw thanks to the resort's unbeatable steeps and freeriding terrain. The area is vast, with more open alpine terrain than nearly any other resort in North America.

Powder Turns: The bowls, chutes and glades off the KT-22 lift are some of the best and steepest in the USA. Head up the lift, pan right and you will see some of the sickest lines. These lines are constantly ridden by Squaw locals. Once a storm has passed, KT-22 gets stocked with deep powder and is usually the first to open thanks to its more sheltered position. Whilst the terrain off Siberia lift is not as challenging as KT-22, it is consistently pitched and long for some good untracked turns. You will notice that the terrain in these areas gets tracked very early in the day. When this happens, it's time to head over to the Granite Chief Lift, which accesses some medium-length steeps, and heaps of little rock drops, not to mention the cornice along the top of the ridge. This cornice can reach over 6 m (20 ft) in height. A short hike up to the Granite Chief Peak will place you above some sick chutes and cliffs which end up in a nice powder-filled bowl.

Trees: Traverse to the skiers' right, across Granite Chief towards Snow King Peak, and drop the glades in this area or head to the trees below the Red Dog Lift, which usually holds the powder the longest after a dump. The runs at Red Dog may not be as exciting as some of the other parts of the mountain, but the area usually provides safe haven in bad weather. The trees offer shade for the powder, keeping it drier, even days after the last dump.

Cliffs/Chutes: For the cliff-jumping types, the cliff band at the top of Squaw Peak, known as the Palisades, offers some insane drops and chutes. In addition, the terrain directly under the KT-22 lift is some of the most extreme in the USA.

Bad Weather: When the weather closes in, head to the tree runs under the Red Dog Lift, which provide good definition in fog and protection from the wind. The Snow King Peak at the top of the Red Dog Lift is lower in altitude and usually attracts less fog then the rest of Squaw Valley. This illustrates the beauty of Squaw – the vast number of lifts and varied terrain means there is always an escape from bad weather and windy conditions.

Avoiding Crowds: It is difficult to avoid crowds at Squaw as it is the pinnacle resort in the USA. However, usually when the mountain is crowded, the best spot to ride is Granite Chief, as it is tucked away at the very back of the resort.

FREESTYLE

Central Park, located at High Camp midway up the mountain, is Squaw Valley's main area for freestyle riding. The park usually comprises several tabletops and two world-famous halfpipes, and is open from 9 am to 9 pm, 7 days a week. If you want to ride the park and pipe at night, purchasing a night pass for only USD$15 will give you access to the Tram, Riveria Chair and Central Park from 4 pm to 9 pm. The flat light around dusk can be a problem; sometimes it's best to wait until the sun has completely gone down. Once night falls, the park is lit up with huge spotlights and is an awesome place to session. It's also fun to do laps of the tram.

Above: *James Smart flipping off Granite Chief in Squaw Valley.*

Halfpipes: Squaw boasts two halfpipes shaped regularly by a Pipe Dragon. Both are located at Central Park. They are 100 m (333 ft) long and have perfectly shaped 3.5 m (12 ft) walls. The night pipe is cut most days with a Pipe Dragon at around 3 pm and is the best-shaped pipe in Tahoe.

Snowboard Parks: The park consists of two wide tabletops which vary in length and height. The smaller tabletop is great for intermediates, whilst the larger tabletop is great for those who want to try some big, progressive moves. The Squaw park is often sessioned by some of the world's best snowboarders. The tables can be hit individually or in succession, with a short lift at the bottom of the second kicker bringing you back to the top of the park.

ALPINE MEADOWS
CALIFORNIA, USA

STATISTICS

Average Annual Snowfall

	1005 cm	402 in

Elevations

	(m)	(ft)
Top:	2617	8637
Base:	2071	6835
Vertical Drop:	546	1802

Lifts

Surface Lifts:	1
Double Chairs:	5
Triple Chairs:	4
Quad Chairs - Fixed Grip:	0
Quad Chairs - Express:	1
Six Chairs - Express:	1
Gondolas:	0
Cable Cars:	0
Funiculars:	0
Total:	12

Contact Details

Phone:	+1 530 583 4232
Fax:	+1 530 581 4499
Internet Site:	www.skialpine.com
Email:	info@skialpine.com

RESORT REVIEW

Alpine Meadows is the best-kept secret of all the Tahoe resorts. It is the equivalent of Squaw Valley but without the glitz. Situated right next door to Squaw, Alpine (as the locals call it) has much the same terrain but a lot more room to move. It has everything: groomers, steeps, tight trees, wide-open trees and bowls, natural and engineered hits, cliff bands, cornices and super technical chutes. No wonder top pros like Tom Burt and Nate Cole call Alpine home.

Alpine boasts 809 rideable hectares (2,000 acres), 549 verical meters (1,800 feet) and over 100 designated runs in-bounds, and, thanks to a generous open boundary policy, many more just a short hike out-of-bounds. Alpine is serviced by 12 lifts, including one high-speed detachable 6-seater chair, possibly the fastest chair in the world and worth the ride just by itself. And with an average snowfall of 402 inches, the 75 hectares (185 acres) of snowmaking, accessed by 10 of the 12 lifts, is not often needed. Open from November all the way through to the end of May, Alpine's halfpipe is regularly maintained by a Scorpion shaping machine.

Right: *Darius Heristchian boosting high into the Alpine Meadows air space. Photo—Gavin O'Toole.*

TERRAIN

Above: *Peter Coppleson kicking back in the trees.*
Photo—Gavin O'Toole.

FREERIDING

Alpine Meadows consists of two peaks, Ward Peak (2,633 m/ 8637 ft) and Scott Peak (2,526 m/8289 ft), both of which contain some of the most amazing steeps and freeriding/freestyle terrain in North America.

Powder Turns: Where does one begin? The best place to start on a powder day is the Summit Six Chair. But be early, otherwise you'll miss out. As you get on the chair, don't forget to check the whiteboard to see which areas are open and which are not. Avalanche danger is real at Alpine, and ducking ropes can make you very dead. In fact, a few years ago the entire base lodge was destroyed by an avalanche.

To the right, as you head up the chair, you can see numerous steep lines down the Wolverine Bowl, which empties out into Waterfall and The Face, and deposits you back at the base of Summit Six. For something a little more cruising, make a left off the chair and head down Sun Spot into Alpine Bowl. From here you can access a lot more of the area. Keep

to the skiers' left and you will come to the Roundhouse Chair, which accesses much of the intermediate terrain on the front side of the area. Ride to the skiers' right, catch the Alpine Bowl Chair and look to the left. There are numerous steeps, both advanced and expert, accessed only by a short traverse. With names such as the Palisades and Keyhole, you know you're going to find a sick line.

Head past the bottom of Alpine Bowl and down to the base of Scott Chair. This is the steepest chair at Alpine and offers the most consistent pitch on the entire mountain – experts only and of course, right under the lift. If show-boating is not for you, go a bit more to the skiers' left and you will come to some steep lines through a tight rock garden and some open trees. Got game? Ride the 'Chute That Seldom Slides' – maybe it will, maybe it won't. Heading off the left off the chair, follow the traverse, ride the tight trees and you will come to the Promised Land, but don't forget to cut left at the bottom, unless, of course, you want to hike back up the road.

Trees: Head to the Promised Land, to the skiers' right off Scott Chair, or to Hidden Knolls off Sherwood Chair, or to the skiers' left of the Chute that Seldom Slides. There are just too many options!

Cliffs/Chutes: If you're into rock jumping, then Alpine is for you. Head down under Scott Chair, keeping to the skiers' left for one drop right after another. Take the High Traverse and drop into any one of the chutes in Alpine Bowl. Make sure you've been watching your weight – these chutes are tight.

Bad Weather: Keep to the front side and stay on Roundhouse or Weasel Chairs in and around the trees or head inside to the bar. Try and find Hot Wheels – to the skiers' left of Weasel – for a sick gully/natural halfpipe.

Avoiding Crowds: The easiest way to avoid the crowds is to stay away during the holiday periods, especially Christmas and Presidents' Week. Otherwise, just try to stay off the beaten track. There is plenty of room in the trees or bowls, but it is hard to avoid crowds in the lift lines, especially on Summit Six and Roundhouse.

FREESTYLE

Halfpipes: Alpine has invested in the services of a Pipe Scorpion to groom its halfpipe. The 'Gravity Cavity' halfpipe is right under the Roundhouse Chair at the base of Sympathy Face. It is shaped every couple of days and a day or two after a big storm. It is generally suited to intermediate and advanced riders.

Snowboard Parks: The snowboard park contains a permanent boardercross course called 'Roo's Ride'. It is situated to the skiers' left of the Kangaroo Chair. The park also consists of a few tabletops, ranging from a beginner 6 to 10-foot (1.8–3 m)kicker to a pro standard 50 to 60-foot (15.2–18.3 m) monster. The Kangaroo Chair basically runs the length of the park so it is very easy to run laps all day.

SUGAR BOWL
CALIFORNIA, USA

STATISTICS

Average Annual Snowfall

	1270 cm	508 in

Elevations	(m)	(ft)
Top:	2555	8382
Base:	2097	6880
Vertical Drop:	458	1502

Lifts

Surface Lifts:	2
Double Chairs:	0
Triple Chairs:	0
Quad Chairs – Fixed Grip:	7
Quad Chairs – Express:	2
Six Chairs – Express:	0
Gondolas:	1
Cable Cars:	0
Funiculars:	0
Total:	12

Contact Details

Phone:	+1 916 426 9000
Fax:	+1 916 426 3723
Email Address:	info@sugarbowl.com
Internet Site:	www.sugarbowl.com

RESORT REVIEW

Sugar Bowl has proven over the years to be one of the USA's premier snowboard areas. Many of America's top pros call it their local resort and it has featured very heavily in all the good videos over the years. Located at the top of Donner Pass, Sugar Bowl gets the most snow in the Tahoe region (over 500 inches per year) and keeps it the longest, well into spring and summer. The resort has begun upgrading its lift system, with the installation of a few high-speed quads, and the recent purchase of a Scorpion pipe-shaping machine. The area has a brand-new day lodge and a second cafeteria located slightly up the mountain. The vibe at the resort is very snowboarder-friendly, and on many days, snowboarders outnumber skiers.

Sugar Bowl has some excellent backcountry in an area known as ASI. This area has both steep chutes and cliffs as well as natural rolling terrain which is perfect for building kickers. ASI regularly features in the snowboard videos produced by Standard Films. Once the powder has been tracked at Sugar Bowl, ASI is the perfect place to head.

Left: *Sugar Bowl groom their pipe with a Scorpion, which keeps it in perfect condition. A local rider gets inverted in the freshly cut Sugar Bowl Pipe. Courtesy Sugar Bowl Resort.*

TERRAIN

FREERIDING

Although Sugar Bowl doesn't offer the vertical of some of the other nearby resorts, the in-bounds freeriding terrain is sensational. Comprising 4 alpine peaks at around 2,438 m (8,000 ft), the terrain at Sugar Bowl is characterised by large open alpine bowls and ridge-lines with just enough trees to offer shelter and seclusion. The resort has it all, from beginner and intermediate groomers to steeps, cliffs, cornices and chutes.

Powder Turns: For steep powder turns, head up the Silver Belt Chair to the top of Mt Lincoln (2,555 m/8,383 ft). This gives access to plenty of the more challenging and longer runs on the mountain. Mt Disney Peak (2,424 m/7,953 ft) offers some nice ridge-line riding and can collect some nice powder stashes on windy days. Another great powder run is to take the Crows Nest Chair and hike up to Crows Nest Peak. The run down is unsurpassed.

Cliffs/Chutes: Chutes and cliffs are a very good reason to come to Sugar Bowl, with the pick of them being located to skiers' left of the Silver Belt Quad. Within this area are the Sugar Bowl Palisades, a collection of absolutely sick cliffs and chutes which are strictly for experts only. No rider will find

Above: *Richard Hegarty, frontside rodeo in the Palisades. Photo—Gavin O'Toole.*

the terrain here easy and there is plenty to keep you amused long after the lifts close.

FREESTYLE

Like most of the resorts in the Tahoe area, Sugar Bowl has invested heavily in snowboarding to try and cement a place in this rapidly growing market. They have allocated a whole run for a snowboard park and employed the design services of Noah Salasnek. Further, they have recently invested in a Scorpion to shape their pipe.

Halfpipes: The pipe at Sugar Bowl varies greatly, depending on how regularly it is cut. It is generally in good condition as it is shaped by a Scorpion pipe-shaping machine. However, the area receives a lot of sun, so the snow quickly becomes extremely slushy and the pipe loses shape.

Snowboard Parks: Designed by snowboarding legend Noah Salasnek, 'Noah's Park' is one of Lake Tahoe's better park set-ups. Located off the Mt Judah Express Lift, the park offers some great kickers, ranging from beginner to advanced, and is super long.

UTAH
USA

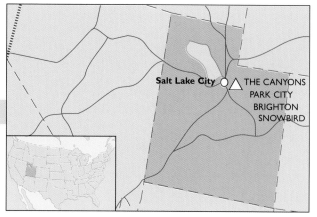

OVERVIEW

Utah, located in the USA Rocky Mountains, prides itself on having the 'greatest snow on Earth' and boasts the most resorts within easy reach of an international airport. Most of the snowboarding resorts in this state are located around Salt Lake City, home to about one million people. Within a 30 to 60-minute drive from the Salt Lake City International Airport there are nine snowboarding resorts and some of the best backcountry terrain in the USA.

Although Utah is the breeding ground for the USA's best riders, many Utah resorts have only opened their doors to snowboarding in the last few years. The Alta and Deer Valley Ski Resorts still don't allow snowboarders.

The Salt Lake City resorts are located in two big canyons that run east–west, beside the city. The closest canyon to downtown Salt Lake City is Big Cottonwood Canyon. In this canyon you will find the resorts of Brighton and Solitude. Next to Big Cottonwood Canyon is Little Cottonwood Canyon, where you will find Snowbird (known as 'the Bird' to the locals) and Alta. Also in this canyon you will find an area known as Grizzly Gulch. This area is more commonly known as the Utah backcountry. The Gulch has natural rolling terrain and is the perfect place to build kickers. Grizzly Gulch frequents the pages of *Transworld Snowboarding*. Other resorts, located slightly further from Salt Lake City, include Park City, The Canyons, Snowbasin and Powder Mountain.

As Salt Lake City is hosting the Winter Olympics in 2002, resorts in Utah are upgrading their lift systems. In particular, Snowbasin, Park City and The Canyons are investing heavily in resort infrastructure. This is great for snowboarders traveling to Utah in the lead-up to the Olympics.

Below: *Extreme lines in the Utah backcountry. Photo—Gavin O'Toole.*

Above: *The Unita Mountains in northern Utah offer some of the best hiking in the USA outside Alaska. Photo—Gavin O'Toole.*

Given that over half the population of Utah is Mormon, the state has very strict laws and ethics. However, you would struggle to find a more hospitable community in the USA and a better environment for snowboarders to visit. Mormons are extremely friendly and courteous. Contrary to what you may think, the Mormon religion is not some strange and secret religious sect. The Mormons are very open and helpful. You will be blown away by the hospitality you will receive in Salt Lake City.

ACCOMMODATION

Accommodation, in the form of motels, is available mostly around downtown Salt Lake City, which is about a 40-minute drive from most resorts. Motels, condos and houses are also available in the suburbs, such as Sandy, which are closer to Little and Big Cottonwood Canyons. Check the local papers and bulletin boards at supermarkets for the best deals.

If you are in the Salt Lake City area for a short time and think you might want to ride all the Salt Lake resorts, definitely stay in Salt Lake City rather than on mountain or in Park City because it is a far more central location and much cheaper. Also, Salt Lake City is a great place to hang out, as it has a large snowboarder population and plenty of things to do off the snow.

HINTS AND TIPS

- Salt Lake City is a big city, unlike most American ski towns, therefore there is an abundance of accommodtion, jobs and off-snow activities.
- A car is very handy as not much budget accommodation exists near the slopes. Although snow buses run up and down Big and Little Cottonwood Canyons, if you are staying far from the pick-up locations, getting to the hills may be a little tricky. So if you're in town for a short stay with a few friends, look into hiring a car and staying somewhere further from the resort. What you spend on a car you will save on accommodation.
- Having a car to get around means that you can easily access the nine resorts in the Salt Lake area. Don't limit yourself to one resort if you can help it, because all resorts in the Salt Lake area are well worth visiting.
- Utah gets some of the lightest and deepest powder on earth, so bring a long board and a snorkel!

BRIGHTON
UTAH, USA

STATISTICS

Average Annual Snowfall

1270 cm	508 in

Elevations	(m)	(ft)
Top:	3203	10509
Base:	2670	8760
Vertical Drop:	533	1748

Lifts

Surface Lifts:	0
Double Chairs:	3
Triple Chairs:	2
Quad Chairs – Fixed Grip:	1
Quad Chairs – Express:	1
Six Chairs – Express:	0
Gondolas:	0
Cable Cars:	0
Funiculars:	0
Total:	7

Contact Details

Phone:	+1 801 532 4731
Fax:	+1 435 649 1787
Email Address:	info@skibrighton.com
Internet Site:	www.skibrighton.com

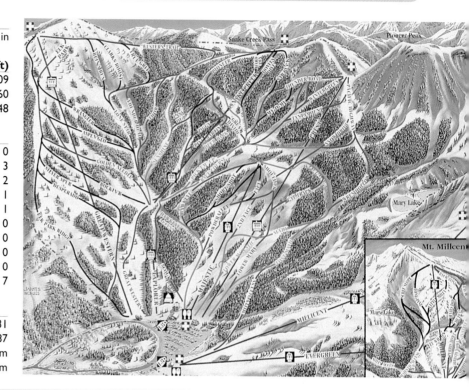

RESORT REVIEW

During the eighties and most of the nineties, many of Utah's resorts didn't allow snowboarders on their slopes. One exception was a little-known resort called Brighton. Brighton welcomed snowboarders from the beginning. It has since developed a good reputation in the international snowboard community for offering a very friendly atmosphere, not to mention some awesome riding.

Brighton is undoubtedly the home of snowboarding in Utah and is the stomping ground for many of the USA's best riders. In some parts of the resort, all you will find are snowboarders, as the terrain is perfectly suited for snowboarding. Brighton is famous for receiving an average of 500 inches (13 m) per season of the lightest and driest powder in the world. However, be wary that 30 cm (1 ft) of Utah powder on top of ice is simply not enough as you just sink straight through it unless you have pulled out your long board.

The lifts at Brighton run from mid November to April. They are open from 9 am until 9 pm, 7 days a week, except on Sundays, when they close at 4 pm. The resort has been modestly developed, with two high-speed lifts and plans for lift upgrades. A large day lodge is located at the base of the resort, offering a range of food at typical resort prices. Visitors to the resort are able to drive directly to the base of

the hill and park in a large parking lot no more than 100 m (330 ft) from the lifts. Access to the mountain is easy up Big Cottonwood Canyon, but check conditions because the road is occasionally closed to 2WD vehicles.

Right: *Brighton offers some of the best in-bounds cliffs in the world. Mikey Basich playing in his backyard. Photo—Gavin O'Toole.*

TERRAIN

FREERIDING

The terrain at Brighton ranges from steeps to flats. There are rollers, wind-lips, rocks and cliffs which can provide hours of entertainment to adventurous riders. What Brighton lacks in vertical, it makes up for in natural hits and drops, not to mention amazing Utah powder.

Brighton's greatest downfall is the brevity of its runs. For beginner and intermediate riders, the groomed terrain offers good length. However, for powder junkies who are after long ,open powder fields, Brighton is not the place to ride. Further, most of the steep terrain becomes flat midway down a run. However, the variability of the terrain means that after you have ridden the steeps at the top, you can ride the groomed runs and the countless hits off the sides of the runs.

Cliffs: The Millicent Lift is an old double chair and would have to be one of the slowest in the USA. However, the terrain it accesses provides Brighton with its reputation. Once off the chair, a two-minute traverse to the skiers' right leads to clusters of the world's best in-bounds rock bands. Here the cliffs range from small to large, with steep landings that are almost always full of deep powder. Even days after a dump, powder can still be found in the rock bands.

Powder Turns: When the powder comes, go straight to the Millicent Lift and hit the rock drops or the powder bowls at the top of Mt Millicent. Even when the powder around the mountain has been chewed up, this area has the best powder stashes. Also, the Great Western High-speed Quad offers some more advanced terrain, which is awesome after a dump. For some out-of-bounds riding in this area, get off the Great Western Chair and traverse to the skiers' right until you pass out-of-bounds. From here, head down the powder fields until you hit the road, then walk back a few hundred metres to the Great Western. Alternatively, cut to the skiers' left about three quarters of the way down and traverse through the trees until you make it back to the Great Western Chair.

Early Morning: Check out the Millicent Lift for powder stashes. If the sun's out and it is icy, ride the Great Western Chair – this terrain tends to soften up the quickest as it faces the sun.

Bad Weather: Ninety percent of Brighton's terrain is below the tree line, so when the weather is foggy, the trees are a great haven and provide visibility and definition. In bad conditions, ride the Great Western Chair – it is the fastest and offers plenty of tree riding.

Avoiding Crowds: The terrain around the Millicent Lift is never crowded, probably because it is one of the slowest lifts in the world. On busy days, head straight to this area because there is never a queue and there is a lot of good terrain.

Hiking: For the hikers, a 10 to 20-minute hike up Pioneer Peak will lead to some of Brighton's best powder riding through trees. For the brave-hearts, the 20-minute hike to the top of Mt Millicent will bring you to some of the largest do-able cliffs in the country.

Above: *Spot the rider? Bear Agushi puts a perfect Brighton kicker to the test.*

Beginners: Cruise the runs accessed by the Crest High-speed Quad.

FREESTYLE

Halfpipes: For pipe enthusiasts, Brighton maintains a half-pipe at the top of the Majestic Lift. The pipe is shaped a few times per week with a Pipe Master shaping machine. However, more often than not, the condition of this pipe is far from perfect. Pipe riders really need to go elsewhere in Utah, such as Park City or Snowbird, where the resorts put more effort into maintaining their halfpipes.

Snowboard Parks: The terrain under and around the Millicent Lift is always littered with natural kickers and hits which make the area one big snowboard park. If this area isn't working, head up the Majestic Double Chair and check out the snowboard park, which generally comprises kickers, tabletops, a spine and a quarterpipe and is suited to all abilities. The only problem is that the park stays very icy until late in spring, so pack your helmet.

SNOWBIRD
UTAH, USA

STATISTICS

Average Annual Snowfall

	1270 cm	508 in

Elevations

	(m)	(ft)
Top:	3353	11001
Base:	2365	7759
Vertical Drop:	988	3241

Lifts

Surface Lifts:	0
Double Chairs:	0
Triple Chairs:	0
Quad Chairs – Fixed Grip:	7
Quad Chairs – Express:	1
Six Chairs – Express:	0
Gondolas:	0
Cable Cars:	1
Funiculars:	0
Total:	9

Contact Details

Phone:	+1 801 742 2222
Fax:	+1 801 933 2298
Email Address:	lccbird@aol.com
Internet Site:	www.snowbird.com

RESORT REVIEW

Snowbird is Utah's answer to Europe and is one of the state's biggest resorts, with about 1,000 m (3,300 ft) of vertical and some of the longest and steepest terrain in the region. The terrain and the huge amounts of powder received by Snowbird have shaped many of Utah's best big mountain snowboarders. Unlike the terrain at Brighton, Snowbird's terrain is consistently steep. There are very few flat spots. This makes the powder riding an out-of-this-world experience.

The lift system at Snowbird is considerably underdeveloped considering the abundance of incredible terrain on offer. Nonetheless, the resort management has laid down plans for renovation of the lift system, which has begun with the installation of a brand new high-speed quad which takes riders up to the Little Cloud Bowl – the Gadzoom Lift.

Left: *12 feet off the lip and 24 feet above the bottom of the pipe, Mouse Beuchat puts on a show.*

TERRAIN

FREERIDING

The freeriding terrain at Snowbird is by far the best in Utah. The mountain offers long groomed runs for beginners and steep powder runs for advanced riders. The terrain at Snowbird is more like the European Alps than any other North American resort (except perhaps Jackson Hole). Unlike nearby Brighton, The Canyons and Park City, the steeps at Snowbird are steep and long, without flat spots. Therefore, a rider can take full advantage of powder days without having to regularly unbuckle and hike or traverse. The terrain at Snowbird is characterized by cliffs and rocks of varying size, all with great landings.

Powder Turns: Powder is the reason riders come to Snowbird. With over 500 inches per season, it is certainly one of the powder capitals of the world. Due to its proximity to Salt Lake City, Snowbird gets very crowded any day of the week, and powder can be tracked out within hours after a dump. When it has dumped, head straight up the Tram and follow the ridge line under the Tram for about 183 m (200 yards). From here you can either go straight or drop into the steeps to the left. Follow this line all the way to the bottom of the valley and do it again.

Also, if you are prepared to wait in line, check out the 'Little Cloud Bowl' and 'Road to Provo' runs – they collect tons of powder but are often closed due to avalanche danger. Overall, on a powder day, all of Snowbird goes off. On a hard pack day, go to the pipe.

Bad Weather: Much of the resort's terrain is below the tree line, offering good protection from fog and wind. In bad conditions, ride the Gad No. 2 Lift, which offers long runs sheltered by trees. This area collects heaps of snow and is steep and fun.

Avoiding Crowds: Avoiding crowds at Snowbird is hard to do because of its popularity. It is very close to Salt Lake City and attracts most of the city's 'ski dog/powder junkie' population. It seems Snowbird is about the only resort in the world where the skiers hit the powder and not the groomed. This aside, when it is busy, check out the Gad No. 2 Lift or the Gadzoom High-speed Quad. On powder days, expect to queue for at least 20 minutes on the Tram and the Little Cloud Chair because these are the lifts to the best powder.

FREESTYLE

Halfpipes: Thanks to extremely high lift pass prices (relative to nearby Brighton) and the lack of a park and pipe, Snowbird hasn't generated a strong freestyle scene. However, things are set to change since Snowbird added a Pipe Dragon to its inventory at the start of the 1998/99 season. Snowbird's winter pipe is located in a superb position at the lower end of the mountain, and is set on an excellent gradient. The pipe is shaped a few times per week and is most often in good condition. If you are after some good pipe action, consider 'the Bird' before Brighton. When summer comes, the pipe moves its way to the top of the resort and operates through until June. Just be aware that during the season the pipe is extremely hard, so wearing a helmet is good protection from brain damage.

Below: *Sasha Ryzy leaves a trail of glory at Snowbird, Utah. Photo—Gavin O'Toole.*

THE CANYONS
UTAH, USA

STATISTICS

Average Annual Snowfall

762 cm	305 in

Elevations	(m)	(ft)
Top:	2859	9380
Base:	2073	6801
Vertical Drop:	786	2578

Lifts

Surface Lifts:	0
Double Chairs:	0
Triple Chairs:	0
Quad Chairs – Fixed Grip:	5
Quad Chairs – Express:	3
Six Chairs – Express:	0
Gondolas:	1
Cable Cars:	0
Funiculars:	0
Total:	9

Contact Details

Phone:	+1 801 649 5400
Fax:	+1 435 649 7374
Email Address:	info@thecanyons.com
Internet Site:	www.thecanyons.com

RESORT REVIEW

Formerly known as Park West, then Wolf Mountain, The Canyons is now owned by the ski resort giant American Skiing Company, and is set to become one of the largest resorts in North America. The American Skiing Company has bold plans for development of the resort before the 2002 Winter Olympics in Salt Lake City. Development has already begun, with massive upgrading of the once old and slow lift system. The aim is to have 22 lifts accessing some 2,833 hectares (7,000 acres) of rideable terrain, making it the largest ski area in Utah (and possibly the largest in North America).

The resort is located in the Park City area, about 30-40 minutes' drive from Salt Lake City Airport. Its location on the backside of Big Cottonwood Canyon means that The Canyons does not receive the quantity of snow enjoyed by nearby Brighton and Snowbird (about 300 inches/ 760 cm per year) as there is much less snowfall on this side of the valley.

The Canyons is one of Utah's most rider-friendly resorts, offering a Pipe Dragon-shaped halfpipe and a small snowboard park. However, it is yet to develop the 'hard-core' snowboard scene that exists at Brighton and Snowbird. A large proportion of the clientele at The Canyons are destination skiers and snowboarders staying in Park City – the resort is currently tailored to beginner intermediate skiers who enjoy groomed trails.

Above: *Jason Haynes puts on the brakes at the Canyons. Photo— Gavin O'Toole.*

TERRAIN

Above: *Mr Hollywood powders his nose in the Utah backcountry. Photo—Gavin O'Toole.*

FREERIDING

Nearly all of the terrain at The Canyons is groomed runs cut through the trees. Overall, it is an enjoyable place to ride, especially on a fresh layer of powder. There are plenty of well-pitched runs that are reasonably long. The problem is that the runs get moguled very quickly due to the large number of skiers who frequent The Canyons. The terrain is more suited to riders who don't mind cruising trails with small hits along the way, rather than powder junkies.

As far as extreme riding goes, the in-bounds terrain doesn't match up to Brighton and Snowbird. The in-bounds terrain lacks the cliffs and real steeps that make for an ultimate freeriding experience. The biggest advantage of the freeriding terrain at The Canyons is that most skiers who visit do not venture off the groomed, thus there is plenty of great freeriding in the trees. The trees at The Canyons hold good powder for several days. This is unlike Snowbird, where every inch of powder on the mountain gets tracked out in hours.

Powder Turns: The pick of the in-bounds steeps are found at Ninety-Nine 90 Peak. The North Face here presents some of the steepest terrain on the mountain.

Chutes: The closest thing that The Canyons offers to chutes is a bunch of runs called 'The Chutes', located on skiers' right, off the Super Condor Express Lift. Whilst short, they are challenging and well worth the effort.

Bad Weather: About 95% of the terrain at The Canyons is cut out through the trees so when the visibility is bad, most of the terrain is good to ride because the trees provide good definition and protection from the wind.

Avoiding Crowds: The new lift system at The Canyons and its distance from Salt Lake City (compared to that of Snowbird and Brighton) means that it doesn't get too crowded. However, this is set to change as the resort gains a higher profile and becomes a destination resort rather than a day trip resort.

FREESTYLE

Halfpipes: The Canyons is showing great commitment to freestyle snowboarding and maintains a well-shaped pipe located above the gondola. The halfpipe is shaped a few times a week with a Pipe Dragon and therefore has good transitions and big walls.

Snowboard Parks: The Canyons offers a park which is generally more suited to beginners and intermediate riders. It offers a series of tables that are generally small in size. The Canyons does not have a reputation for building good parks for advanced riders.

Natural Hits: The trails at The Canyons offer heaps of fun riding with cat-tracks, hips and little jumps scattered along the runs. In addition, a natural gully snakes its way down the mountain, making an awesome natural boardercross course. The terrain isn't too undulating, so there isn't much in the way of natural rollers and tabletops. Nevertheless, the consistent gradient and length of trails makes the riding at The Canyons fun. Also, the new high speed-quads mean that you spend more time on the snow.

PARK CITY MOUNTAIN RESORT
UTAH, USA

STATISTICS

Average Annual Snowfall

	880 cm	352 in

Elevations	(m)	(ft)
Top:	3075	10089
Base:	2123	6965
Vertical Drop:	952	3123

Lifts

Surface Lifts:	0
Double Chairs:	4
Triple Chairs:	5
Quad Chairs – Fixed Grip:	1
Quad Chairs – Express:	0
Six Chairs – Express:	4
Gondolas:	0
Cable Cars:	0
Funiculars:	0
Total:	14

Contact Details

Phone:	+1 435 649 8111
Fax:	+1 435 647 5374
Email Address:	info@pcski.com
Internet Site:	www.pcski.com

RESORT REVIEW

Above: *Park City keeping the rich entertained. Photo courtesy of Park City Mountain Resort (Scott Sine).*

Park City is an old mining town which once flourished in the silver mining era of the 1800s. It was the epitome of the 'Wild West', with drunken miners running amok in the bars by night, then mining silver by day. Nowadays, things are slightly different, with Park City being the winter destination of the USA's high society. Unlike nearby Snowbird and Brighton, most visitors to Park City come from around the USA rather than from Salt Lake City.

The centre of attention in Park City, and a major site of the 2002 Winter Olympic Games, is the Park City Mountain Resort. This ski area is also known as Park City, which can be rather confusing at times. Park City is the site of the Olympic snowboarding halfpipe and downhill events. This is quite ironic, since Park City Mountain Resort did not allow snowboarding until 1996, and has done little to support snowboarding since it opened its lifts to snowboarders.

Park City is the home of the US Ski and Snowboard Team, and they actually have a whole run to themselves. No one else on the mountain is able to access this run. Snowboarders are a definite minority at the resort and those who do ride there are a pretty mellow and friendly crowd. However, despite the small number of snowboarders, Park City is putting a lot of work into maintaining its halfpipe as it prepares for the Olympics.

TERRAIN

FREERIDING

The Park City region averages about 350 inches of snow per season and the low altitude of the resort provides for plenty of gladed runs and trails cut through trees, very similar to its close neighbor, The Canyons. Park City's terrain is largely intermediate, with very little in the way of challenging steeps, cliffs and rock bands compared to nearby Snowbird. The back bowls at Park City, especially Jupiter Bowl, are an excellent feature of riding at the resort. There are a handful of steeps and cliffs to drop, but if that's primarily what you're looking for, Snowbird or Brighton would be a better option. Park City Mountain Resort provides a little of everything, with a well-developed lift system including four six-person high-speed lifts. This is the most of any resort in the world. Overall, the runs at Park City are long, with consistent gradient. However, they tend to be moguled out very quickly due to the high number of skiers that frequent the mountain.

Powder Turns: Jupiter Bowl is the pick of the steeps when the powder has fallen. It's an expansive area accessed by the Jupiter Lift. Because of its location at the back of the resort, many people stay away from this area and keep it untracked some time after a snowfall. It is best to traverse hard to skiers' right once getting off the Jupiter Lift. The further to the right you traverse, the less tracked is the powder.

Hiking: Jupiter Peak (not to be confused with Jupiter Bowl) is the pick of the in-bounds hiking, with plenty of steeps and great powder long after the last dump. Drop into Puma Bowl and ride through to the bottom of McConkey's High-speed Six-person Chair. Pinecone Ridge also offers some awesome tree riding if you are happy to hike for it.

Above: *Park City offers one of the best pipes in Utah.*

FREESTYLE

Halfpipes: The site of the 2002 Winter Olympic Halfpipe competition, the Park City Resort halfpipe is located near the bottom of the mountain on 'Pay Day', next to the Pay Day High-speed Six-person Lift. Shaped relatively regularly by a Snow Turbo Grinder, the pipe has a good fall line and is lit up at night. Pipe riders looking for a place to ride in the Salt Lake area should put Park City at the top of their list, as the resort offers one of the best-shaped pipes in Utah.

Snowboard Parks: Unfortunately, Park City's resort management is still not interested in enticing the snowboarder dollar and has neglected to maintain a good snowboard park. If you want a park, you are better off going to Brighton. Better still, grab your shovels and head up to Grizzly Gulch.

Below: *Luke Fitcher enjoying deep Utah powder.*
Photo—Gavin O'Toole.

COLORADO
USA

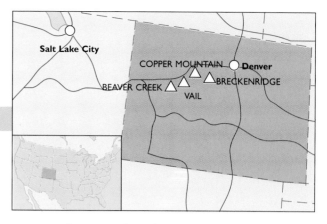

OVERVIEW

The Rocky Mountains characterize much of the Colorado landscape, with big rolling hills towering 4,267 m (14,000 ft) above the plains. There are a number of distinct regions within Colorado which make for excellent riding.

Colorado terrain is generally flat when compared to many other places in the USA and the lift-accessed terrain is largely boring relative to other US and overseas destinations. To make up for this, Colorado resorts are way ahead of other US resorts in providing the very best facilities for riders of all abilities.

SUMMIT COUNTY

Summit County is definitely the pick of the destinations for a touring snowboarder. Whether your journey is for a week or a season, the opportunities for riding in this area are huge. Much like Lake Tahoe in California, Summit County comprises a number of resorts which are located close to each other. The Interstate 70 highway passes near most of the resorts in the area, making this area a perfect place to visit if you wish to experience more than one resort during your stay. Whether it be Arapahoe Basin (or A-Basin), Beaver Creek, Breckenridge, Copper Mountain, Keystone, Loveland or Vail, you will definitely experience some awesome riding. But make sure you pick your destination wisely, as conditions, facilities and terrain can vary significantly.

Below: *The high alpine peaks of Colorado rise above the dense forests of Copper Mountain's front face. Photo courtesy of Copper Mountain Resort.*

WEATHER AND SNOW CONDITIONS

Being located so far from the coast and in the middle of the desert, Colorado resorts receive incredibly dry snow, reliable seasons and good weather. Unlike the Pacific North West and East Coast, where rain, fog and ice can plague resorts for days/weeks on end, the weather in Colorado is generally consistent, with storms bringing the powder in between sunny breaks. Most resorts boast between 250 and 350 inches a year in snow.

The weather and snow conditions in Summit County are unique. Generally, most snow falls in March. However, on the continental divide , at places such as at A-Basin, the bigger dumps can occur in April. Snow conditions will vary per resort according to the elevation and the location of the mountain. A-Basin gets the most snow in the area and holds it longer due to its elevation and the fact that 62% of its slopes are north-facing. Breckenridge's east-facing slopes mean that spring snowboarding comes a little earlier each year than at Keystone and Copper Mountain. Copper's slopes are mostly north-facing so, like A-Basin, the snow can stay longer and firmer during the season. Although Keystone receives the least snow in the region, it has extensive snow-making capabilities.

ACCOMMODATION

You have various accommodation options when staying in Colorado. Firstly, you can stay in the resort villages. This is more affordable if you secure a package deal which may offer lift passes and lodging all together. Secondly, you can stay in a nearby town in a motel if it is short term, or a condo if you have a few more bucks or a big group to split the cost. If you want to spend your time in Summit County, then the towns of Frisco or Dillon (both located on the I-70) are the most likely to provide decent accommodation. If you are after a good deal on motel accommodation in Frisco, there are a number of places you can try.

TRANSPORT

Buses run from the major towns to each resort every day, so even if you don't have a car it is still pretty easy to get around. Obviously having a car is the easiest, most convenient way to get around because the resorts in Colorado are so spread out.

HINTS AND TIPS

- Summit County is very spread out. A car is a big help if you want to access several resorts on your trip.
- Staying at the resorts will generally be more expensive than staying in the towns of Frisco or Dillon. However, staying in these towns means a drive up to the resorts of between 20 minutes and an hour each day.
- Altitude sickness is a definite reality in Colorado, with the average base elevation being around 2,743 m (9,000 ft) and lifts soaring up to 3,962 m (13,000 ft).
- Drink plenty of water and bring headache tablets.
- If you are feeling a little altitude sickness, stay away from high-protein foods and eat plenty of carbohydrates.

Above: *Andrew Burton shows his fellow riders how its' done in the Copper Mountain Pipe.*

COPPER MOUNTAIN
COLORADO, USA

STATISTICS

Average Annual Snowfall

711 cm	284 in

Elevations	(m)	(ft)
Top:	3753	12313
Base:	2960	9711
Vertical Drop:	793	2601

Lifts	
Surface Lifts:	4
Double Chairs:	6
Triple Chairs:	5
Quad Chairs – Fixed Grip:	0
Quad Chairs – Express:	4
Six Chairs – Express:	1
Gondolas:	0
Cable Cars:	0
Funiculars:	0
Total:	20

Contact Details

Phone:	+1 800 458 8386
Fax:	+1 970 968 2711
Email Address:	wc@ski-copper.com
Internet Site:	www.ride-copper.com

RESORT REVIEW

As you drive west along the I-70 from Denver, you will pass the town of Frisco and be greeted by the 'in your face' slopes of Copper Mountain. The resort, a stone's throw from the motorway in Summit County, is one of the best snowboard destinations in Colorado. Compared to the nearby resorts of Vail, Breckenridge and Beaver Creek, Copper is a modestly developed resort with much less accommodation and retail infrastructure. However, with investment of over USD$66 million into Copper Mountain in the 1998/99 season and a further USD$500 million to be spent between now and 2002/03, Copper Mountain will be transformed into another the USA mega-resort. The early signs of redevelopment include Colorado's first high-speed six-person chair and multiple high-speed quads which whisk riders up the slopes.

With some 20 lifts (of which five are high-speed) accessing 985 hectares (2,433 acres), you are guaranteed maximum time on snow. Extensive snow-making and good average annual snowfalls ensure long seasons beginning in November and extending through to May.

Right: *After cruisin' up the I-70 Freeway in his Porsche 911, champion halfpipe rider Todd Richards puts in a hard day at the office. Photo—Gavin O'Toole.*

TERRAIN

FREERIDING

The terrain at Copper Mountain is pretty similar to that of most other Colorado resorts. Nearly all the riding is on runs cut through the dense pine forests. There is very little in the way of open bowl riding compared to Europe or some other US resorts. This is despite the fact that the highest lifted point at Copper Mountain is on Union Peak at 3,753 m (12,313 ft). The terrain is broken up into three distinct areas, stretching from the beginner terrain in the west, through the intermediate terrain in the centre to the advanced slopes on the east side of the mountain. Most of the lifts take you from the base in the valley floor to close to the top. Here, shorter lifts access the peaks and ridge tops.

Powder Turns: Start with the Spawlding Bowl, as the powder here is most often dry and deep. Next, visit Copper Bowl, which is south-facing but can collect heaps of snow after a dump. If they are tracked or not working, try Union Bowl. The Upper Enchanted Forest offers some double black steeps and isn't a bad spot to try if you don't mind a few chair rides. Also, double black in Colorado isn't necessarily double black at places such as Jackson Hole, Wyoming or Chamonix in France!

Trees: The Glades in Copper Bowl are definitely the pick of the tree riding, but also try the Enchanted Forest. Generally, Copper offers some good tree riding high up on the mountain, but as you descend, the forests become very dense.

FREESTYLE

Halfpipes: Copper Mountain really only began offering half-pipes in 1997/98, but since then has become the leader in Colorado, with arguably the most consistently shaped pipes in the state. The resort offers three pipes for all abilities and it makes an excellent effort at maintaining all of them. The location and quality of the beginner and intermediate pipes will vary season by season but the main pipe is located on the Carefree Run not far from the village base. The location of the main pipe is perfect because it receives direct sun on its left wall in the morning and on the right wall in the afternoon. This ensures that neither wall deteriorates quickly. However, there is a slight problem when it's icy, as it doesn't get the chance to soften up on cool days. The gradient of the pipe is perfect, just under 20 degrees. The pipe is cut a few times per week with a Pipe Dragon, ensuring that the walls are in tip-top shape for boosting big or learning the basics. The only thing lacking is a rope tow or magic carpet (as at Breckenridge) because hiking the pipe at 3,000 m (9,800 ft) is an absolute nightmare. Also, remember to take along a big bottle of water as the high altitude causes dehydration and the closet food outlet is in the Copper village.

Snowboard Park: The snowboard park at Copper Mountain is almost as good as the pipe. The park runs parallel to the American Eagle High-speed Quad Chair and contains between 10 and 20 hits on a 427 vertical meter (1,400 ft) run. The park suits riders of all abilities from beginners to pros and has tabletops, spines, rollers and kickers. The landings are long and steep and are groomed on a regular basis, which ensures that they are smooth. However, be wary that not many of the landings receive strong sunlight for most of the season and they are almost always very firm, to say the least. The best time to hit the park is after lunch, when the sun has had a chance to soften things up. Also, depending on the time of the season, there is a boardercross track that runs from the bottom of the park down to the village and is great for racing your buddies on.

BEAVER CREEK
COLORADO, USA

STATISTICS

Average Annual Snowfall:

	838 cm	335 in

Elevations	(m)	(ft)
Top:	3488	11444
Base:	2255	7398
Vertical Drop:	1233	4045

Lifts	
Surface Lifts:	1
Double Chairs:	4
Triple Chairs:	3
Quad Chairs – Fixed Grip:	0
Quad Chairs – Express:	6
Six Chairs – Express:	0
Gondolas:	0
Cable Cars:	0
Funiculars:	0
Total:	14

Contact Details

Phone:	+1 970 460 5601
Fax:	+1 970 845 5722
Email Address:	eagle@vailresorts.com
Internet Site:	www.snow.com/beavercreek

RESORT REVIEW

Beaver Creek is not the most highly renowned resort amongst snowboarders. This is good, since it is one of Colorado's best-kept secrets, until now. Situated 16 km (10 miles) west of Vail on the I-70, Beaver Creek is yet another ritzy Colorado resort, similar to sister resort Vail. Beaver Creek, Vail, Keystone and Breckenridge are all owned by Vail Resorts Inc, and a pass at one resort gives access to all the others. This is handy if you rock up to Vail and find that the lift queues are huge. A 10-minute drive down the Interstate 70 will see you in the much-less-crowded Beaver Creek.

Just like Vail, Beaver Creek boasts the latest in lift innovation, with 6 of the 14 lifts being high-speed quads. And what's important for snowboarders is that Beaver Creek is highly committed to providing the very best in man-made facilities such as snowboard parks and halfpipes.

Left: *Bear Agushi tries to impress his co-author Mouse Beuchat with this monster-sized method in the pipe.*

TERRAIN

FREERIDING

Beaver Creek Resort comprises Beaver Creek Mountain, Grouse Mountain and Arrowhead Mountain. The terrain off Arrowhead is short and flat. In contrast, Grouse Mountain presents the best terrain for riders who are after steeps. A steeper resort than Vail, Beaver offers 1,230 m (4,040 ft) of vertical across 658 hectares (1,625 acres). Whilst the runs are long, the layout of the resort across the three mountains makes it impossible to access all the vertical in one hit. It is necessary to catch several lifts to really appreciate all the vertical and the terrain at Beaver.

Powder: Unfortunately, unlike Vail, Breckenridge and Copper, there are no large powder bowls at Beaver Creek, meaning that most of the good steeps are in narrow corridors cut through the trees which unfortunately get moguled out very quickly. However, get in early after a dump and you will be pleased. Try the modest double blacks off the Westfall Lift or head up the Birds of Prey High-speed Quad and burn down the Golden Eagle Run.

Trees: Get up the Strawberry Park Express Lift and cut your way down to the Grouse Mountain Express. Head to the peak of Grouse Mountain and cut your way through the Royal Oak Glades.

FREESTYLE

Snowboard Parks and Halfpipes: Beaver Creek has an excellent halfpipe and snowboard park located on Moonshine about halfway up the Centennial Express Lift, which caters for riders of all abilities. The halfpipe is shaped a few times per week by a Pipe Dragon. The park comprises an array of tabletops, spines, kickers, rails and logs for your jibbing pleasure. JP Walker would be a very happy lad in this park.

Below: *The BTW kicker crew scan the Beaver Creek super park.*

BRECKENRIDGE
COLORADO, USA

STATISTICS

Average Annual Snowfall

	760 cm	304 in

Elevations	(m)	(ft)
Top:	3962	12999
Base:	2926	9600
Vertical Drop:	1036	3399

Lifts	
Surface Lifts:	8
Double Chairs:	7
Triple Chairs:	1
Quad Chairs – Fixed Grip:	0
Quad Chairs – Express:	6
Six Chairs – Express:	0
Gondolas:	0
Cable Cars:	0
Funiculars:	0
Total:	22

Contact Details

Phone:	+1 970 453 5000
Fax:	+1 970 453 3210
Email Address:	breckenridge@vailresorts.com
Internet Site:	www.snow.com/breckenridge

RESORT REVIEW

Back in 1985 when the rest of Colorado snubbed snowboarding and snowboarders, Breckenridge (or Breck) decided to host the first ever World Snowboard Championships. Since then, Breckenridge has developed one of the greatest reputations in the USA for providing the very best in snowboarding facilities. Consequently, champion riders such as Todd Richards and Morgan LaFonte call Breck home.

The resort is spread across four mountain peaks, simply named Peak 7, Peak 8, Peak 9 and Peak 10. The village of Breck is huge and has a great snowboard scene thanks to the greater availability of budget accommodation when compared to other Summit County resorts.

With 22 lifts accessing some 139 runs across 827 hectares (2,043 acres), Breck is big. In typical Colorado fashion, 6 of the 23 lifts are high-speed quads, which ensure maximum time on snow. The major downfall of Breck is its close proximity to Denver (137 km/85 miles). This means big crowds, especially on weekends, hence the massive parking lots for day-trippers. One consolation is the free shuttle access from the parking lot up to the lifts.

Thanks to a great snow-making system, Breck ensures up to 6 months of riding each season and is one of the first resorts in Colorado to open each season.

Right: *A view of Breckenridge across the Peak 8 Halfpipe.*

TERRAIN

FREERIDING

The four peaks that make up Breck are essentially flat on the front and steep on the sides. The area is very spread out and although the lift system is well laid out, getting from one area to another can be a massive pain in the butt, with long uncomfortable traverses. Each of the peaks towers high above the tree line. The problem is that the lifts don't extend far beyond the dense evergreens. This means the full vertical of the mountain is not utilized. Peak 7 and Peak 8 offer the best advanced riding. If you don't mind a hike, you'll be pleased with what's available at Breck. But don't expect anything extreme. Like much of Colorado, the terrain is pretty flat and most of the runs are long, groomed trails.

Powder Turns: Horseshoe, Cucumber and Contest Bowls off the t-bar at Peak 8 are probably the pick of the powder runs and are classed as 'Expert', being double black diamonds. Although short, the terrain is relatively steep and you can make the run long by following it down through the trees to the bottom.

Trees: Head over to Peak 10 and ride the trees in an area called 'The Burn'. Just make sure you stay to the right at the bottom as the trees get a little tight. If you don't mind a hike, head out to the Peak 7 Glades, which are a little fun but a bit of a hassle to get to.

Hiking: If you fancy a bit of high-altitude hiking, then give the 30 to 40-minute hike to the top of Peak 8 a go. There is some great riding on the way down through Imperial Bowl. Even better, traverse the ridge to Lake Chutes, which provides some of the sickest in-bounds chutes in the region. Just be aware that Imperial Bowl is south-facing and can crust up quickly in spring. Also consider the hike out to Peak 7.

FREESTYLE

Halfpipes: Breck has got one of the best halfpipe set-ups in Colorado. With a park and pipe in two locations, one at Peak 8 and another at Peak 9, Breckenridge is at the forefront of snowboarding in Colorado. The halfpipe set-up at Peak 8 is one of very few in the world that offers its own lift to save riders the hassle of a high-altitude hike. A magic carpet whisks you back up to the top of the pipe in only a few minutes. Once at the top of the pipe, take advantage of the riders' hut. It has a vending machine for refreshments and snacks or you can heat up your own lunch in the microwave. A large sound system pumps out tunes until the sun goes down. The pipe is shaped by a Pipe Dragon on a regular basis and can vary from OK to excellent. Be wary that in spring, the left wall of the pipe gets baked by the sun and crumbles away quickly.

Snowboard Parks: With two of the largest parks in the USA, Breckenridge doesn't hold back when it comes to pleasing riders. If you want to spend time practicing your latest moves, head to Breck, as their park has a complete range of kickers and tabletops to suit all abilities.

Above: *Launching into the valley, Breckenridge offers one of the best snowboard parks in Colorado. Photo—Gavin O'Toole.*

Above: *Peak 7 glades hold some incredible powder stashes. Peter Coppleson finds the secret spots. Photo—Gavin O'Toole.*

VAIL
COLORADO, USA

STATISTICS

Average Annual Snowfall

867 cm	347 in

Elevations	(m)	(ft)
Top:	3491	11453
Base:	2475	8120
Vertical Drop:	1016	3333

Lifts	
Surface Lifts:	11
Double Chairs:	5
Triple Chairs:	3
Quad Chairs – Fixed Grip:	1
Quad Chairs – Express:	10
Six Chairs – Express:	0
Gondolas:	1
Cable Cars:	0
Funiculars:	0
Total:	31

Contact Details
Phone:	+1 970 476 9090
Fax:	+1 970 845 2609
Email Address:	eagle@vailresorts.com
Internet Site:	www.snow.com/vail

RESORT REVIEW

Situated 160 km (100 miles) west of Denver on the Interstate 70, Vail is the largest single snowboard mountain in North America, with 1,879 rideable hectares (4,644 acres). Vail gives new meaning to the term 'express lifts', with 10 high-speed chairs ensuring that you can clock many vertical miles in a day. The resort is spread across a ridge that runs east to west, providing steeper terrain on the eastern side and easier slopes across to the west. Most of the terrain on the front side of the valley is north-facing, ensuring long seasons and better-quality snow. However, the famous Vail Back Bowls located on the back side of the ridge offers open bowl and gladed terrain in often bottomless powder.

Although Breckenridge was the first major resort to embrace snowboarding in Summit County, Vail has now taken the lead when it comes to providing freestyle facilities. The resort offers an excellent park and pipe set-up and a huge snowboard school. Catering mostly for the destination traveler, Vail Village is huge and epitomizes Colorado ritziness. There is a heap of accommodation, which is just as well, as the resort caters for 1.5 million visitors each season.

Left: *Bear Agushi pokes indy out of a perfect Vail halfpipe.*

TERRAIN

Above: *Local Vail boy Brody getting upside down off an icy Vail tabletop.*
Left: *The world-famous back bowls of Vail. Photo—Gavin O'Toole.*

Powder Turns: It goes without saying that the best powder riding at Vail is in the 1106 hectares (2,734 acres) of the legendary Back Bowls. These five scoops of almost treeless heaven face south and collect dry Colorado powder after each dump. Over 5 miles (8 km) wide, the terrain is huge and offers steeps, chutes, cliffs, rock drops and glades – terrain that is not common in Colorado.

Trees: Head over to Ouzo Glade, then to the trees on Seldom and Never.

FREESTYLE

Halfpipes: Vail has traditionally been the market leader in Colorado when it comes to halfpipes. Shaped by either their own Snow Turbo Grinder or Beaver Creek's Pipe Dragon two or three times per week, Vail's pipes are consistently well shaped, long and fun. Just watch out in spring when the sun melts one wall into slush and leaves the other rock-hard.

Snowboard Parks: As with their halfpipe set-up, Vail boasts a massive park each season which is maintained by experts who understand what it takes to construct a good kicker. With tabletops, spines, kickers and rails, Vail's park is a great place to practice your tricks and break your butt. Vail rates highly when it comes to snowboard parks.

FREERIDING

With the exception of the Vail Back Bowls, snowboarding at Vail is through snowy corridors cut through dense pine and aspen forests. Much of the terrain is groomed and gets moguled out very quickly by the thousands of ski dogs that frequent the hill. Expect to come to Vail and get it deep with the resort boasting over 335 in (8.67 m) of snow per season. To make up for the predominantly flat and unchallenging freeriding terrain, Vail offers 1,016 m (3,335 ft) of lift-accessed vertical, ensuring that your thighs burn on each run.

WYOMING
USA

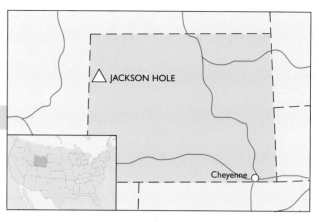

OVERVIEW

Wyoming is like the last frontier of the USA. It is the epitome of classic American cowboy country. It seems everyone wears cowboy hats and cowboy boots and drives a pick-up (when not riding a horse). Lying on the eastern edge of the Rocky Mountains, Wyoming offers some of the USA's best extreme snowboarding. The Grand Teton mountain range that passes through the state peaks at over 4,260 m (14,000 ft). Yellowstone National Park, which is located on the state's western border, offers one of the most beautiful and truly awesome landscapes in the world.

The mountains in Wyoming collect massive dumps of snow throughout the season, resulting in over 11 m (400 in) per year, and the snow is almost as dry as that found in Utah. Two sensational snowboard resorts lie within the Teton range near the small town of Jackson – Jackson Hole and Grand Targhee. In this guide we will concentrate on Jackson Hole.

WEATHER AND SNOW IN WYOMING
December storms, which travel via jet streams from the Pacific, continually pound the Grand Teton Mountains with snow. Jackson Hole is blessed with good consistent snowfalls throughout the whole season. Throughout January and February the powder days are frequent. The weather is usually at its coldest in January and begins to warm up in the following months. Snow will fall regularly through to April, which means powder days can extend well into spring. Cowboy country certainly has more to it than simply rustling cattle.

Opposite: *Something about the alpine air gets riders like Rohan Smiles high. Photo—Gavin O'Toole.*
Below: *Luke Fitcher in cowboy country. Photo—Gavin O'Toole.*

JACKSON HOLE
WYOMING, USA

STATISTICS

Average Annual Snowfall

975cm	390 in

Elevations

	(m)	(ft)
Top:	3185	10449
Base:	1924	6312
Vertical Drop:	1216	4137

Lifts

Surface Lifts:	2
Double Chairs:	2
Triple Chairs:	1
Quad Chairs - Fixed Grip:	2
Quad Chairs - Express:	1
Six Chairs - Express:	0
Gondolas:	1
Cable Cars:	1
Funiculars:	0
Total:	10

Contact Details

Phone:	+1 307 733 2292
Fax:	+1 307 733 5585
Internet Site:	www.jacksonhole.com

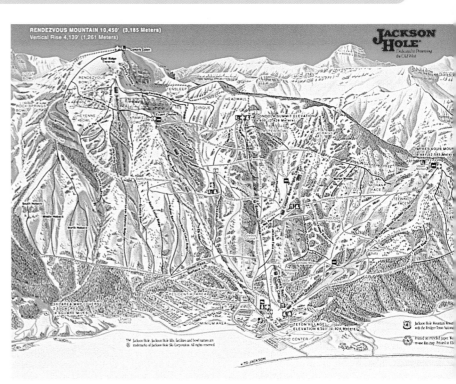

RESORT REVIEW

Jackson Hole is the extreme snowboarding capital of the USA. The in-bounds terrain at Jackson Hole is rivalled only by some of the European resorts. The resort has the largest lift-accessed vertical rise in the USA at 1,262 m (4,139 ft), and the second largest in North America, behind Whistler/Blackcomb. It is an incredible place, and it attracts the biggest egos in the USA, all convinced that they will tame its endless chutes, cliffs, rocks, bowls, faces and ridges.

In typical Wyoming fashion, Jackson Hole seems to be lost in time. The cowboy theme runs strong, and it's common to run into characters such as Lloyd Christmas (Jim Carrey from *Dumb and Dumber* and urban cowboys who try to feel a little rugged by dressing up in their million-dollar cowboy outfits.

However, new ownership of the resort has seen a lot of changes, including a new name – 'Jackson Mountain Resort'. With the installation of 9 new lifts, 3 new mountain restaurants and more snow-making, Jackson Hole is on its way to becoming an American super-resort.

Right: *Jackson Hole is a big mountain with plenty of vertical. It is little wonder the mountain breeds some of the best freeriders on the planet. Photo courtesy of Layshock and Jackson Mountain Resort.*

TERRAIN

FREERIDING

Jackson Hole is the home of freeriding in the USA and is one of the only places in North America that is similar to Chamonix in France. The terrain is big and steep with cliffs, chutes, gullies, peaks and trees characterizing the landscape. There are probably more in-bounds cliffs and chutes at Jackson Hole than at any other resort in North America and it's a place which can really put your riding skills to the test.

The infamous Corbet's Couloir is a Jackson Hole landmark, and is accessed directly by the Tram, which also accesses most of the expert terrain at Jackson. Overall, Jackson Hole definitely offers the best freeriding in North America. A season at Jackson Hole will increase your freeriding ability tenfold, because the runs are longer, steeper and gnarlier than anywhere else in the USA. The terrain is consistently pitched with very few flat spots, unlike many other big North American resorts.

The Tram accesses the best terrain on the mountain but is the biggest pain in the butt to ride. On most days you will have to wait in line for anywhere between 20 and 60 minutes to access the summit. Once up the top, you can either stay high on the mountain and ride the upper lifts or head back to the bottom and wait in line again.

Powder Turns: It's no secret, the pick of the powder riding is a run that begins at the summit and takes you through Rendezvous Bowl to Rendezvous Trail to the Hobacks. Although the Hobacks don't open until about 9:30 am, the 1,262 vertical meters (4,139 ft) you get out of this course will give you Mr Universe thighs. If you want to avoid the Tram, head up the Bridger Gondola and ride the Study Plots and Sundance Bowl under Amphitheatre Traverse. This spot is sheltered, so when high winds force the Tram to close, this is the spot to be.

Trees: The best tree riding is in Moran Woods off the Casper Chair. Alternatively, head to the Mushroom Chutes past Tower Three under Thunder. Also, give the terrain out towards Saratoga Bowl a go.

Early Morning: When the conditions are good, ride the south-facing and lower elevations in the morning as they end up very moguled by late afternoon. When it's firm, stick to the groomers on the southern faces.

Bad Weather: When the wind is blowing and/or the fog is thick, stay right away from the Tram. The last thing you want to do is drop into Corbet's Couloir without realizing it. Try any of the runs among the trees from mid-mountain level down.

Avoiding Crowds: Jackson Hole is an isolated resort and generally doesn't get all that crowded. When the crowds get too heavy, give the terrain out beyond the 'Apres Vous' Double Chair a go. Make the traverse to the area boundary towards Saratoga Bowl and enjoy some well-spaced trees in some secluded powder stashes.

FREESTYLE

Halfpipes: If the natural terrain isn't working, Jackson Hole offers a halfpipe which is shaped by a Snow Turbo Grinder and can range from awesome to terrible. Most riders don't head to Jackson for its pipe, but rather for the incredible natural terrain. However, when the snow is bad, it's good to have the option to ride a good pipe.

Snowboard Parks: Don't bother coming here for snowboard parks. Jackson Hole doesn't have them.

Natural Hits: The natural landscape of Jackson Hole makes for a freestyler's paradise, with tons of little hips, gullies, rocks and cat-tracks to boost some air off. The pick of the runs for the best in freestyle terrain is a long top-to-bottom gully known as the 'Gros Ventre'. This gully winds its way down the mountain and offers stacks of quarters, hips and drops to have some fun on.

Above: *When it dumps, there is no better place in the US for freeriding than Jackson Hole. Photo courtesy of Bob Wooda/Wade McKoy and Jackson Mountain Resort.*

MONTANA
USA

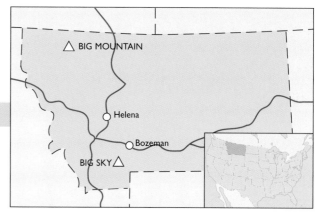

OVERVIEW

Montana is a massive state that stretches some 650 miles (1,040 km) from the flat prairie-lands in the east to the towering Rockies in the west. The resorts in Montana are relatively uncrowded and you rarely wait in lift lines. The smaller resorts of Montana tend to get mostly local town traffic whereas the big resorts get the majority of interstate destination travelers.

Considered to be in the middle of nowhere for so long, wealthy city slickers are setting up second homes in the state to try and escape the urban grind.

The resorts scattered around Bozeman, such as Big Sky and Bridger Bowl, enjoy good snowfalls during winter, with seasons being long and powder being plentiful. Just remember to bring your long johns when you ride in Montana, because the mercury often sits below -7°C (20°F) in the winter months. This ensures that the powder is dry and stays fresh many days after a dump.

WEATHER AND SNOW IN MONTANA

Montana is such a huge state, with terrain that is incredibly large and diverse, that its weather varies significantly. The biggest snowfalls occur in the east, where the Rocky Mountains meet the sky. Most storms travel east from the Pacific or southwest over eastern Oregon and Idaho. Be wary, the conditions in Montana can be exceptionally cold, thanks to its distance from the Pacific.

Opposite: *Riding into a cushion of clouds, Peter Coppleson descends from heaven. Photo—Gavin O'Toole.*
Below: *Jared Winkler mid-rodeo, lost in the forests of Montana.*

BIG SKY
MONTANA, USA

STATISTICS

Average Annual Snowfall

	1016 cm	406 in

Elevations	(m)	(ft)
Top:	3399	11152
Base:	2125	6972
Vertical Drop:	1274	4179

Lifts

Surface Lifts:	3
Double Chairs:	3
Triple Chairs:	3
Quad Chairs – Fixed Grip:	1
Quad Chairs – Express:	0
Six Chairs – Express:	0
Gondolas:	1
Cable Cars:	1
Funiculars:	0
Total:	12

Contact Details

Phone:	+1 406 995 5000
Fax:	+1 406 995 5900
Internet Site:	www.bigskyresort.com

RESORT REVIEW

Situated 72 km (45 miles) south of Bozeman, Montana, Big Sky offers 1,416 hectares (3,500 acres) of diverse terrain spread across the two peaks of Lone Mountain and Andesite Mountain. As you turn off Highway 191 toward Big Sky, the 3,403 meter (11,166 ft) volcano-shaped peak of Lone Mountain immediately catches your eye. Big Sky, formerly known for its predominantly intermediate terrain, has changed its focus, with 43% of its terrain suiting expert riders in search of the best in steeps, chutes, bowls and powder.

Big Sky is the jewel in the crown of Montana ski resorts, with the Boyne Ski Company investing millions of dollars in the resort. They have created a fantastic year-round vacation retreat. High-speed quads, gondolas and cable cars, as well as condos and luxury hotels, are all part of the Big Sky theme. Unlike its neighbor, Bridger Bowl, Big Sky is a destination resort. But most of the Bozeman locals go and ride at Bridger Bowl, mainly because the tickets are cheaper.

Left: *Sasha Ryzy up to her neck in it. Photo—Gavin O'Toole.*

TERRAIN

FREERIDING

Much of the riding at Big Sky is below the tree line in moderate trails cut from the dense pines. However, Lone Peak is the total opposite, and is the spot for all your free-riding needs, with the very best in steep chutes, narrow couloirs and wide-open powder fields.

Big Sky really has the two extremes – nice cruising runs and super-steep extreme runs. It doesn't really have anything in between. It seems to lack natural gullies and nice droppable rocks and cornices. The mountain also lacks the undulating and unpredictable terrain that makes riding so much fun. However, it is worth going to Big Sky just to ride the Tram and the extreme terrain on Lone Mountain. Just be aware that the Tram gets very packed and you can wait for up to 45 minutes on a typical powder day.

Powder Turns: The answer is simple – take the Tram to the top of Lone Peak and check out Marx and Lenin Chutes for some better than average riding. If you want to get away from the Tram, hit the Challenger Lift, which provides access to Moonlight, Midnight and Big Rock Tongue Runs.

Cliffs and Chutes: If you are up for some sick drops, then check out the Little and Big Couloirs. Little Couloir is the steepest run on the hill and is definitely worth a visit.

FREESTYLE

Snowboard Parks and Halfpipes: Don't bother coming to Big Sky if this is what you are after.

Above: *The Lone Peak cable car cruising above some of the steepest chutes in the lower 48. Photo courtesy of Big Sky Ski and Summer Resort.*
Below: *One of the most breathtaking views in Montana, Lone Mountain dwarfs the Big Sky landscape. Photo courtesy of Big Sky Ski and Summer Resort.*

VERMONT
USA

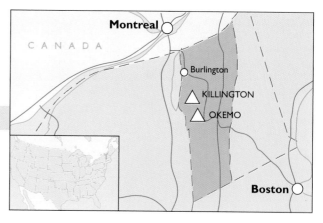

OVERVIEW

Vermont is located on the East Coast of the USA. It is one of the New England states, bordered on the north by the Canadian province of Québec, on the east by New Hampshire, on the south by Massachusetts, and on the west by New York. It is interesting to note that the name of the state is derived from the French words *vert* (green) and *mont* (mountain). Not surprisingly, Vermont is known as the Green Mountain State. It is one of the smallest states in the USA.

The main mountains in Vermont are the White Mountains in the northeast and the Green Mountains that stretch north–south through the centre of the state. The Green Mountains are home to Vermont's highest peak, Mt Mansfield at 1,339 m (4,393 ft).

The majority of ski resorts in Vermont lie off Route 100, which winds its way through the Green Mountains. Over 15 resorts lie within 32 km (20 miles) of Route 100, including some of the East Coast's best-known resorts. Resorts such as Killington and Stratton grace the sides of Route 100. In fact, this area may have the greatest congregation of resorts

Opposite: *If you hit Vermont at the right time you can find some good powder. Jef Billo's timing was spot on.*
Photo—Tim Zimmerman.
Below: *No matter how icy the snow, the Vermont locals go big. Here Shawn Shouldis launches a huge indy. Photo—TimZimmerman.*

on a single highway anywhere in the world. It should be noted that the resorts of Vermont have much lower elevations than those in Utah and Colorado.

WEATHER AND SNOW CONDITIONS

Winters in Vermont are long and cold – damn cold. Temperatures generally hover around –6°C (21.5°F) to –8°C (about 17.5°F).

Relative to Tahoe and Utah, the snowfall in Vermont is not huge. Average annual snowfall across the Green Mountains is around 6 m (20 ft). However, due to a geographical peculiarity, a resort known as Jay Peak, located in the north of the state, receives a whopping 7.9 m (26 ft) of snow. This is more than some of the famous resorts of Colorado, such as Keystone and Steamboat.

The low temperatures, combined with the dry weather, mean that the resorts often have icy conditions. These icy conditions are a breeding ground for top riders, since a fall usually means severe injury. Little wonder the riders in Vermont live by the creed, 'stick it or pay'.

KILLINGTON
VERMONT, USA

STATISTICS

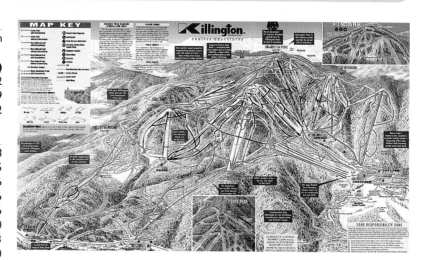

Average Annual Snowfall

	635 cm	254 in

Elevations

	(m)	(ft)
Top:	1293	4242
Base:	323	1059
Vertical Drop:	970	3182

Lifts

Surface Lifts:	8
Double Chairs:	5
Triple Chairs:	6
Quad Chairs – Fixed Grip:	6
Quad Chairs – Express:	6
Six Chairs – Express:	0
Gondolas:	3
Cable Cars:	0
Funiculars:	0
Total:	34

Contact Details

Phone:	+1 802 422 3333
Email Address:	info@killington.com
Internet Site:	www.killington.com

RESORT REVIEW

With 33 lifts accessing some seven different summits across 486 hectares (1,200 acres) of terrain, Killington is the mega-resort of the East Coast. But the amazing statistics don't end here. Killington is traditionally the first East Coast resort to open and last to close each season, thanks to good natural snowfalls (on an East Coast scale) and a massive snow-making system which seems to blow snow practically 24 hours a day. In fact the Superstar trail boasts a 25-foot base by April, allowing the resort to stay open until summer each year. Thanks to these amazing snow credentials and its proximity to many major US cities, Killington receives crowds like no other resort in the world.

Because Killington comprises seven separate areas, there are plenty of flat crossovers and traversing is a way of life for snowboarders who like to get around the mountain. Be sure to carry a trail map at all times if you are new to the resort because you will be bound to get lost or end up at the wrong base area and have to somehow hitch a ride back with some crazy Jerseyite.

Right: *Killington has a good reputation for building quality halfpipes. Jef Billo wouldn't disagree.*
Photo—Tim Zimmerman.

TERRAIN

FREERIDING

Killington is divided into seven mountain areas plus an area called 'Pico'. Generally a flat resort compared to the best of the west, Skye Peak, Killington Peak and Bear Mountain have the pick of the more challenging terrain. Skye Peak's Vertigo and Needle's Eye are the better steeps, whilst Outer Limits and Devil's Fiddle on Bear Mountain are the best choices in this area, but on a powder day only. While Killington does offer some good steeps, don't head to any of them if it hasn't snowed in the preceding days, or you'll be riding icy bumps the whole way down. Bear Peak is the most enjoyable area to ride in spring and is a little warmer and softer in winter than Skye and Killington Peaks.

Whilst Snowshed is a beginner area, it offers the best day lodge in the resort. Ram's Head is another beginner area and the home of the magic carpet. It is the first place to open for the season and is fun before winter and in spring. Snowdon has predominantly easy terrain but does offer a few steeps and some decent tree riding into the Low Rider Zone. Just be wary of Snowdon's super-slow lift system.

Killington Peak is the highest of all the peaks. Here you can hike to 1,293 m (4,241 ft). Give the Big Dipper Glades a go or head skiers' right of the Canyon Quad Chair for some better steeps.

Powder Turns: On the few days when natural snow falls at Killington, the powder usually gets tracked out by mid-morning, although if you know where to go there are usually untouched trails. If you are feeling bad-ass, cutting ropes will ensure freshies, but if not, you can try the South Ridge Chair, which is a long run on a side of the mountain nobody goes to. Your best bet is to befriend a local, who will show you powder turns all day.

Early Morning: The sun doesn't hit the pipe until 10 am, so early in the morning it is best to take runs up the gondola and make turns on the fresh corduroy. Never go to Bear Peak in the morning as it receives afternoon sun and is usually glare ice and freezing cold early in the morning.

Bad Weather: Bad weather plagues the East Coast often, and the only thing to do is to take gondola runs. Riding down isn't so bad, and the cabins provide shelter from the wind, rain, sleet, ice or snow.

FREESTYLE

Halfpipes: Killington's halfpipe is as close to ISF regulations as you can get. It is almost 130 m (400 ft) long, with the walls usually at 3 m (10 ft) and is meticulously maintained with a Snow Turbo Grinder about three times per week. It is also serviced by a tow rope and is lit for night riding.

Snowboard Parks: Killington hires full-time staff each season who are completely devoted to making sure the parks are in tip-top shape. Snowdon hosts the alpine park, which allows skiers and snowboarders alike and is generally geared to a beginner crowd, with flat landings and little kids standing all over the place. Stay away if you are averse to landing on someone's head, but don't write it off entirely, as some days it's better than the real snowboard park. The official snowboard park is on Bear Mountain, and has all the ingredients of a park in a Mack Dawg video. There are hips, rails, jumps, and the token tree jib as well. The best freestyle area at Killington is the permanent boardercross course on Bear Peak, which usually contains the best jumps, as well as spines and rollers. There is a trail running alongside that keeps most of the novices off the actual course.

Above: *When the sun goes down, the lights come on and the riding continues at the Killington pipe. Photo courtesy of Killington Resort.*

OKEMO
VERMONT, USA

STATISTICS

Average Annual Snowfall

	388 cm	155 in

Elevations

	(m)	(ft)
Top:	1050	3445
Base:	334	1095
Vertical Drop:	716	2349

Lifts

Surface Lifts:	3
Double Chairs:	0
Triple Chairs:	3
Quad Chairs – Fixed Grip:	3
Quad Chairs – Express:	4
Six Chairs – Express:	0
Gondolas:	0
Cable Cars:	0
Funiculars:	0
Total:	13

Contact Details

Phone:	+1 802 228 4041
Email Address:	okemo@lidl.tds.net
Internet Site:	www.okemo.com

RESORT REVIEW

While not as big as nearby Killington, Okemo boasts one of the best freestyle set-ups in New England, and a commitment to snowboarding like no other resort in the USA. Like most other resorts in the region, Okemo pumps out snow constantly and, thanks to 95% snow-making coverage, manages to keep its doors open well into spring each year. Many of the East Coast's top halfpipe and jump riders come from Okemo, thanks to their amazing park and pipe set-up, which has been upgraded recently to provide the very best in freestyle facilities.

Left: As the stalactites hold on for dear life, Shawn Durst shows off his method style. Photo (left and above)—Tim Zimmerman.

TERRAIN

laps of the pipe and park throughout the day. Thanks to park design specialists 'Stimilon', Okemo's newly designed park puts the resort ahead of its competitors and makes the cost of a day pass all the more worthwhile. Once you are ready for a break or shelter from harsh East Coast weather, head into 'The Yurt' hut and enjoy a beverage or snack while listening to the tunes pumping out of the sound system outside.

Left: *Indy poke performed by Eerik Ilves after a fresh dump. Photo—Tim Zimmerman.*
Below: *No tree could stop Eerik Ilves grabbing his tail. Photo—Tim Zimmerman.*

FREERIDING

Okemo's terrain is predominantly flat and it gets very crowded with families and other punters from the New England area, especially Connecticut. The upper mountain is the place to ride if you are into steeps, but be wary of the mogul fields, which usually exist in the steeper areas. The best way to ride Okemo is to enjoy the groomed runs. Plenty of jumps, rollers, whales and assorted obstacles exist on the runs. Just remember to stay as far away as you can from Sel's Choice, or else you'll be up to your neck in moguls the size of VWs. One good thing about Okemo is that you will never get lost, as all trails eventually lead to the bottom.

FREESTYLE

The Halfpipe: Both of Okemo's pipes are exceptionally well maintained by Pipe Dragons. They are amongst the best in the USA and accordingly, many of America's top pipe riders call Okemo home. Thanks to 'The Pull' Lift, you are able to out-lap any pipe hiker and maintain your energy for endless pipe runs.

Snowboard Parks: Okemo offers snowboarders the luxury of two snowboard parks. The park located on the Exhibition Run is targeted more towards the beginner and intermediate riders whilst 'The Zone' park, located at Lower Sel's Choice, is geared towards the rippers who want to boost big. The Zone is serviced by 'The Pull' Lift, which is great for doing

CANADA

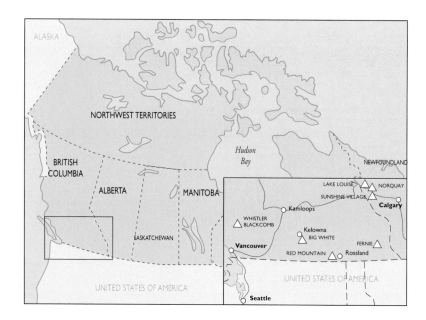

Canada is the world's second largest country by land mass, stretching the whole width of the North American continent from the Pacific Ocean in the west to the Atlantic Ocean in the east. It reaches from the USA border in the south all the way up to the North Pole. If you flew a plane across Canada you would cover some 5,309 km (3,300 miles) and cross six time zones. It is made up of 12 provinces – British Columbia, Alberta, Saskatchewan, Ontario, Manitoba, Quebec, New Brunswick, Newfoundland, Nova Scotia, Prince Edward Island, North-West Territories and the Yukon. Each province has its own culture and Quebec even has a different language – French, as opposed to English. Despite its large land size, the population of Canada is modest – only 28 million people.

THE MOUNTAINS OF CANADA

Canada is not only huge in surface area but it is also home to some very large mountains. Most of the snowboarding in Canada is on two major mountain ranges. The first is known as the Coast Mountains of British Columbia (BC) and is located along the west coast of BC. The second is the Canadian Rockies, which stretch along the western border of the province of Alberta. Alberta is the neighboring province to BC. Contrary to what you may think, the highest point in the Coast Mountains, Mt Waddington (4,016 m/13,252 ft), is higher than the highest point in the Canadian Rockies, Mt Robson (3,954 m/13,048 ft). Yet the Rocky Mountains are a much larger mountain range, extending from northern Canada deep into the USA.

Unlike most of the resorts in the Canadian Rockies, which lie inside national parks, most of the resorts in the Coast Mountains, particularly Whistler/Blackcomb, lie outside national parks. This allowed these resorts to be developed more quickly. It is well known that it took Sunshine Village, a resort high up in the Canadian Rockies, almost 20 years to win approval to install a new lift.

SNOW CONDITIONS IN CANADA

Canada is renowned for its intense winters. The Coast Mountains are bombarded throughout the season by huge storms that roll in off the Pacific and dump, on average, over 9 m (30 ft) of snow. The Canadian Rockies receive storms that push in from the Pacific and push down from the freezing

Right: *It's a rare occasion when you find such a good staircase run. Franz Waddler thanks his lucky stars. Photo— Alex Guzman.*

Above: *Vancouver is one of the most beautiful cities in the world. It is a place where the Coast Mountains of British Columbia meet the freezing Pacific Ocean.*
Below: *Riders stand in awe of the mighty Canadian Rockies. Little wonder Canada breeds so many good big-mountain riders. Photo— Gavin O'Toole.*

Alaskan hinterland. These storms also dump well over 9 m (30 ft) of snow on the Canadian Rockies each year. Due to their proximity to the BC coastline, the snow that falls in the Coast Mountains tends to be wetter than the snow that drifts onto the jagged peaks of the Canadian Rockies.

SNOWBOARDING IN CANADA

Canada has fast become one of the hottest spots in the world for snowboarding, due to a number of factors. Firstly, the awesome natural terrain has allowed extensive resort development, with lift-accessed terrain that is both long and steep. Second, the weather patterns across the country (particularly in the west) lead to regular snowfalls of light, dry powder. Finally, most resorts across the country have opened their doors to snowboarding in a big way and provide the very best in man-made snowboarding facilities.

The majority of resorts are located in British Columbia and Alberta. There are also some decent-sized resorts in Quebec, on the east side of the country. Mont Ste-Anne and Tremblant are both located in Quebec. However, in this guide we will concentrate on resorts in BC and Alberta. In particular, we're going to take you riding in Whistler/Blackcomb, Big White, Red Mountain, Fernie, Lake Louise, Sunshine and Norquay. These resorts dish up some of the best that Canada has to offer.

GETTING TO THE MOUNTAINS IN CANADA

If you are going riding in any of the resorts in BC, your best bet is to fly into Vancouver and organize a connecting bus or plane to the resort. If you are going riding in the Canadian Rockies, it's best to fly into Calgary, then jump on a bus to Banff, which is the major resort town below all the moutains. If you can, find a travel agent with expertise with Canada.

ACCOMMODATION

Motels and hotels are everywhere you go in Canada so there is no issue finding somewhere to stay; it's just a question of how much you want to spend. Sometimes you'll pay CAN$20, but at other times you'll need to fork out CAN$80 per person for a night's accommodation. It's simply a case of searching smart and choosing the right style of accommodation to suit the duration of your visit and your budget. Some of the resorts offer accommodation in the mountain resort village. Visitors to other resorts may have to go to a nearby town to get the best deal. Hostels are also very popular throughout Canada and most resort towns have at least one hostel. One night at a hostel costs CAN$20 if you have International Youth Hostel membership.

HINTS AND TIPS

- Canadians dislike being confused with Americans.
- Canada has a good transport system, excellent roads and, most importantly, credit cards are accepted in almost every location.
- Be aware that there is a Goods and Services Tax (GST) as well as provincial taxes in Canada. Currently, the GST is 7%, and the British Columbia Tax is 7%; there is no provincial tax in Alberta.
- As in the USA, tipping is a way of life in most Canadian service industries and is typically 15–20% of the final price.

Below: *Peter Coppleson enjoys some Canadian powder. Photo—Gavin O'Toole.*

WHISTLER/BLACKCOMB
CANADA

STATISTICS

Average Annual Snowfall

	914 cm	366 in

Elevations	(m)	(ft)
Top:	2284	7493
Base:	675	2214
Vertical Drop:	1609	5279

Lifts	
Surface Lifts:	7
Double Chairs:	0
Triple Chairs:	3
Quad Chairs – Fixed Grip:	0
Quad Chairs – Express:	12
Six Chairs – Express:	0
Gondolas:	3
Cable Cars:	0
Funiculars:	0
Total:	25

Contact Details

Phone:	+1 604 938 7703
Fax:	+1 604 938 7527
Email Address:	blackcomb@whistler.net
Internet Site:	www.blackcomb.com

RESORT REVIEW

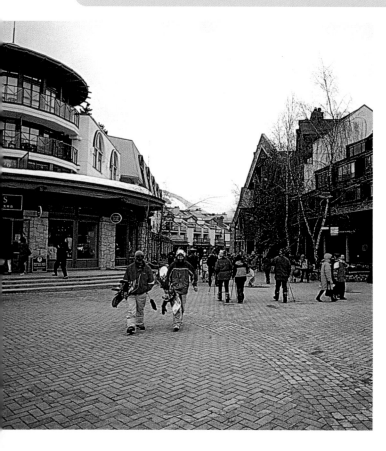

Whistler/Blackcomb has been rated the number one snowboard destination in North America by leading American magazines for the last two years. In 1996 it received top honours from all three major North American ski magazines. This is not surprising given the size of its terrain – over 2,800 hectares (6,920 acres) of skiable terrain and 1,600 m (5,280 ft) plus of thigh-burning vertical. Add to this an hourly lift capacity of over 26,000, three halfpipes and two parks, and it soon becomes clear why magazines keep throwing superlatives at Whistler/Blackcomb.

The Whistler/Blackcomb legend began in 1960 when a group of businessmen, led by Franz Wilhelmsen, formed the Garibaldi Lift Company, with the aim of developing an alpine ski area for the 1964 Olympics. The Olympics were never held at Whistler, but the dream continued and the resort grew. Today, it's the largest ski resort in North America.

Whistler is renowned for its freeriding terrain and Blackcomb is renowned for its freestyle facilities. Whistler is a freerider's paradise. It is a mountain with seven different bowls, plus cliffs, tree runs and endless supplies of powder. Blackcomb offers a great park and one of the best halfpipes in the business, both sponsored by Nintendo 64 (N64).

Left: *Mouse and Shane stroll through the stylish Whistler village.*

Whistler/Blackcomb receives an extraordinary amount of snow. This means an abundance of powder days throughout the season. On the flip side, so much snow means plenty of bad weather. Whistler is not famous for its sunny days. If you love powder and can handle bad weather, then the twin mountains of Whistler/Blackcomb will suit you.

Whistler/Blackcomb has the latest in lift technology, with 17 lifts on Blackcomb and 15 lifts on Whistler. Of these 32 lifts, 13 are high-speed quads or gondolas. Operation hours are from about 8:30 am to 3:30 pm (depending on the day and time of year). So it's wise to get yourself to the top before the lifts close for the day if you think your legs can hold up for another 1.5 kms (1 mile) of vertical.

Unlike most other resort villages in North America, Whistler Village is particularly aesthetically pleasing. The architecture and paved walkways have a relaxing feel about them. After a hard day's riding, it's great to just wander through the village and do some window-shopping.

Right: *Adam Dawes the jibber.*
Below: *When the weather is bad, stick to the trees. Shane descends into Whistler Valley.*

TERRAIN

FREERIDING

BLACKCOMB

Powder Turns: The best place to find powder is the Blackcomb back bowls. Take the Glacier Chair up, then make the traverse to Spanky's Ladder. It is a short hike to climb over Spanky's Ladder. Here you will find four different bowls (Garnet, Diamond, Ruby and Sapphire Bowls). They all funnel down into the Blackcomb glacier and have great trees and cliffs.

Trees: Head off the top of the Crystal Chair where there are numerous gladed runs waiting for your enjoyment.

Steeps: The Jersey Cream Bowl offers a large area of double black runs with some nice cornices.

Bad Weather: Head down Rock 'n' Roll and Ridge runs, which are accessed by the Crystal Chair. These runs are great for cruising and have some nice banks on the side to pull some maneuvers.

Above: *A big mountain calls for big moves. Mic Larkin answers the call of duty in the Blackcomb back bowl. Photo—Gavin O'Toole.*

Avoiding Crowds: It is not the base lifts that attract crowds; it is the mid-mountain lifts. The Excelerator Chair is definitely one to avoid.

Hiking: The best hiking exists in the four back bowls of Blackcomb – Garnet, Diamond, Ruby and Sapphire Bowls. These are accessed through Spanky's Ladder.

Beginners: Some good beginner slopes lie around the Excalibur Gondola.

WHISTLER

Powder Turns: Head down the Whistler Bowl off the top of the Peak Chair and be greeted with heaps of rocks to drop and lips to slash. For a better guarantee of powder, head out to Bagel Bowl, which lies next to the area boundary.

Trees: The West Bowl offers extensive gladed runs. If you are feeling adventurous and know the mountain well, you could head into the unopened area directly below West Bowl. Just make sure you know where you are going as the area is pretty heavily treed.

Steeps: Anywhere off the top of the Peak Chair offers a great variety of steeps for the advanced rider.

Bad Weather: All the runs off the Black Chair include protected areas that still offer great riding.

Avoiding Crowds: Like Blackcomb, it is the mid-mountain lifts that attract crowds. Lifts to particularly avoid are the Big Red Express and the mid-station of the Whistler Village Gondola.

Hiking: The best hiking exists to skiers' left of the Bagel Bowl.

Beginners: The Emerald Express probably has the best beginner runs on the mountain.

FREESTYLE

BLACKCOMB

Halfpipes: The Catskinner Chair gives access to the two halfpipes at Blackcomb (one for beginners and one for advanced). Blackcomb hosts two pipes sponsored by Nintendo, with one being maintained every day to a competition standard. Because the pipe is of such a high standard, it draws a large crowd, with many seasoned pros turning up for a session. Although the pipe is well groomed, and has good transitions, it tends to have slightly too much vert. This makes it difficult to boost super-huge airs. A major benefit of the pipe is that it is located close to trees, which aids visibility during bad weather.

Snowboard Parks: The Catskinner Chair also gives access to the large Blackcomb snowboard park known as the Nintendo 64 Terrain Park. The park actually consists of two parks – an intermediate park that runs down the left-hand side and an expert park that runs down the right-hand side.

The intermediate jumps are marked with blue signs and the expert jumps with black signs. This grading system gives you a good indication of how big the jump is going to be. Many pros and other top locals session it regularly, which certainly pushes up the level of riding. The park is continually growing in size. It offers rails, pipes, gaps, tabletops, spines and a large stereo to pump out your favorite tunes while riding. All this adds up to a very attractive set-up.

Natural Hits: The Blackcomb windlip is probably the most famous piece of natural terrain on the mountain. The beauty of the windlip is that you can go as big as you want and still have a good steep landing. The quarterpipe on Seventh Heaven is also good for a session or two.

WHISTLER

Halfpipes: The Whistler N64 halfpipe is located near the top of the Emerald Express. In past years its shape has been

Above: *Whistler/Blackcomb has the largest lift-accessed vertical in North America. Photo courtesy Whistler/Blackcomb and Paul Morrison.*

poor and it hasn't been regularly maintained. However, this has recently changed and the pipe is certainly getting close to the quality of Blackcomb's pipe. The pipe is relatively narrow, which means keeping speed is not an issue. The transitions are shaped well. The major problem with the pipe is that it is very exposed, and the bad weather that plagues Whistler wreaks havoc with visibility.

Snowboard Parks: The Whistler N64 Terrain Park is located on the Green Acres, to skiers' right of the Emerald Express. A blue/black grading system is used, as in the Blackcomb Park. The Whistler Park consists of tabletops, spines and rail slides.

Natural Hits: You can find large drops and cornices anywhere off the top of the Peak Chair.

BIG WHITE
CANADA

STATISTICS

Average Annual Snowfall

	750 cm	300 in

Elevations	(m)	(ft)
Top:	2286	7500
Base:	1508	4947
Vertical Drop:	778	2552

Lifts

Surface Lifts:	3
Double Chairs:	1
Triple Chairs:	1
Quad Chairs – Fixed Grip:	1
Quad Chairs – Express:	4
Six Chairs – Express:	0
Gondolas:	0
Cable Cars:	0
Funiculars:	0
Total:	10

Contact Details

Phone:	+1 250 765 3101
Fax:	+1 250 765 8200
Email Address:	info@bigwhite.com
Internet Site:	www.bigwhite.com

RESORT REVIEW

This fine snowboarding mountain is nestled in the heart of the Okanagan Highlands, roughly 40 minutes' drive from the mini-metropolis, Kelowna. The Okanagan Valley is a summer haven, with many lakes surrounded by rolling mountains, which in winter offer some amazing scenery and snowboarding terrain. At 2,318 m (7,605 ft), Big White is a large mountain with a medium-sized village resort, a third the size of the massive Whistler/Blackcomb. However, Big White does have the highest lifted point in British Columbia.

A fantastic feature of Big White is that it receives plenty of snow but few visitors relative to nearby Whistler/Blackcomb. Further, it is much cheaper to visit Big White than Whistler, in terms of accommodation and food. Whistler may have more terrain, but you certainly pay a premium for it.

The frontside of the mountain holds most of the resort's lifts and accesses roughly seven different areas of varying difficulty. Large expansions at the resort in recent years mean that queues and time spent on lifts are short. There are now four high-speed quad chairs boosting you up the mountain in no time. An impressive feature is that from the busiest detachable quad (Ridge Rocket Express) any other lift on the entire mountain can be accessed. Further, Gem Lake Express – 2,438 m (8000 ft) long, which makes it bigger than any detachable at Whistler/Blackcomb– has opened the doors to an incredible amount of steep terrain.

Above: *The cliff riding at Big White isn't for the faint-hearted. Thanks to recent heart surgery, Adam Dawes takes on some of Big White's best.*

TERRAIN

FREERIDING

While only 26% of terrain is classified as advanced, the majority isn't gentle. In fact, 56% is classified as intermediate. There are a few flat spots around the middle half of the mountain but it is not necessary to unstrap. By contrast, in the Back Bowl there are some very steep sections. Generally speaking, the runs across Big White are fairly long and uncrowded outside of weekends and school holidays.

Many of the lower runs are cut through pines straight down the fall-line, and there is some amazing riding through the trees off to the sides of the pistes. The best terrain can be found in the Back Bowl. It has spectacular cliffs punctuated with steep chutes. These chutes can be dropped but there is not much room for error. The Back Bowl is deservedly double black, so be prepared. The Back Bowl is often closed due to avalanche risk, and it's a good idea to check conditions before riding out there.

Powder Turns: Interestingly, Big White doesn't receive the huge powder dumps that characterize some other resorts in the area (such as Whitewater and Fernie). But what it lacks in short-term dumps it makes up for in consistency. During January and February, the resort generally receives snow 4-5 nights a week, providing enough fresh snow to create that wonderful floating sensation. Big White, like any other resort, definitely has its dumps, too, and they are not to be missed!

Generally, as the mountain moves from east to west, the pitch of the runs increases. Therefore, the best powder turns can be had on the Powder, Falcon and Gem Lake Chairs. The 'Playground' (between Gem and Falcon) probably covers the steepest pitch on the hill (excluding the cliff area).

Bad Weather: Unfortunately, Big White is referred to colloquially as Big Whiteout. If there is one drawback to this place, it's the presence of Clarence – the cloud that sits over the top of the resort so often that it now has a name. It means that sunny days are less likely than in other places and that visibility can be severely restricted. The many gladed runs, however, provide some form of shelter against this and create sufficient definition to escape the white-out conditions that occur at the higher parts of the hill.

Avoiding Crowds: During the week, the only people you'll be fighting for freshies are the locals who have managed to get the morning off work, and some German tourists (but they'll stick to the groomed runs). On weekends and any public holidays, however, the whole town of Kelowna (about 100,000 people) appears to be on the hill. But, it's not that bad. Usually lift lines will be a maximum of 10 minutes and the slopes will be fairly crowded. In these circumstances, the places to avoid are the runs serviced by the Ridge Rocket (busiest chair on the hill) and the places to head for are the higher areas – Powder and Falcon. The area can get cut up quite quickly on days like this and it may be a good time to practice your moves in the sensationally big pipe or the excellently maintained terrain park.

Hiking: Big White is basically constructed on one face of a ridge that faces predominantly south-west. This means that there is another side of the ridge that has no lifts on it. While it can provide unparalleled terrain and powder for anyone willing to take the plunge, unfortunately there is no easy way out but to walk back up the hill. Alternatively, the escarpment that forms the cliff area has a saddle in its ridge line. This means that fresh tracks can be taken off the high points on either side of the saddle (again, down the back face of the ridge) and the walk out is only up through the centre of the saddle. With a slightly longer walk (15 minutes), the east peak of the cliff area can be reached. This is definitely worth the effort as it provides almost 180 degrees of steep face that lasts for around 200 vertical meters (600 ft). The walk out from the bottom of this is flat, across a frozen and snow-covered lake, and takes about 5 minutes.

Beginners: Big White is definitely a wonderful place to learn to ride. Voted the best groomed hill in all of Canada by *Ski Canada* magazine, the beginner areas resemble wide-open highways. Further, Big White has one extra bonus for beginners in that their bunny hill is serviced not by a rope tow or poma or t-bar but by a quad chair. This provides relief for many trying to stay upright on the way down instead of trying to avoid becoming downright on the way up.

FREESTYLE

Halfpipes: The Big White pipe and park set-up are fast becoming world renowned, with the big-name pros from all around North America regularly sessioning their transitions. The Big White halfpipe is perfectly maintained with a Snow Turbo Grinder grooming machine every second day (weather permitting), and gets up to 4.6 m (15 ft) walls at peak season.

Snowboard Parks: The snowboard park increases in size as the season progresses and is meticulously groomed, especially in spring. It has a boardercross track and tabletop jumps of differing sizes to challenge beginners to pros.

Above: *In a past life, Adam Dawes was a lumberjack. Here he returns to his roots with a tree slide.*

FERNIE
CANADA

STATISTICS

Average Annual Snowfall

875 cm	350 in

Elevations

	(m)	(ft)
Top:	1925	6315
Base:	1068	3504
Vertical Drop:	857	2811

Lifts

Surface Lifts:	4
Double Chairs:	0
Triple Chairs:	2
Quad Chairs – Fixed Grip:	2
Quad Chairs – Express:	1
Six Chairs – Express:	0
Gondolas:	0
Cable Cars:	0
Funiculars:	0
Total:	9

Contact Details

Phone:	+1 250 423 4655
Fax:	+1 250 423 6644
Email Address:	info@skifernie.com
Internet Site:	www.skifernie.com

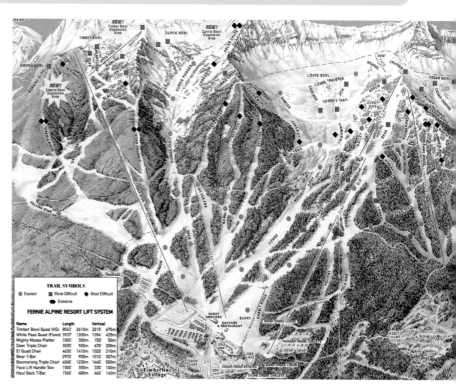

RESORT REVIEW

Upon driving into the Canadian town of Fernie, you can't help thinking that you have entered a world of days gone by. Old brick buildings, which appear to date back to the days of gun-slingin' cowboys, line the main street, slowly crumbling away. Beaten pick-ups with gun racks trundle aimlessly by. In amongst all this is a brand new supermarket called, wait for it, 'Overwaites Food Stores'. You could be forgiven for wondering how any type of quality mountain could possibly be located anywhere near such a strange town. First impressions are often deceiving, though and this must be the case with Fernie, since it was recently rated by *American Men's Journal* the 7th best town to live in in North America. One can only wonder what criteria were used to make this choice. In any event, it is the resort of Fernie that is important, not the town, and it is a resort not to be missed. Fernie consists of six large alpine bowls that contain some of the most amazing in-bounds terrain.

Fernie is renowned for the quantity and quality of its powder and its unbelievable terrain. With over 8.8 m (29 ft) of snow every year, snow is definitely not a problem here. Many snowboarders have realized this and have started infiltrating the Fernie community during winter. Although Fernie receives an extraordinary amount of snow, its low elevation means that it is prone to receiving rain.

Right: *A lazy toeside turn in too much powder.*

In 1998/99 Fernie experienced a massive ski area expansion, with the installation of two new lifts that in effect doubled its skiable terrain. The two new lifts, one a high-speed quad, opened up three new bowls – Currie Bowl, Timber Bowl and Siberia Bowl. Previously these bowls were only accessible through some gut-wrenching hiking. Despite the addition of these new lifts, the Fernie lift system still remains fairly antiquated. All chairs except the Timber Bowl quad are fixed grip and super slow. But more often than not it's worth the wait, since the terrain is so amazing. The other major problem with the lift system is that it requires two and sometimes three lifts to reach the very top of the mountain.

Despite its major expansion, Fernie still remains a fairly cheap alternative to other major resorts in Canada. In fact, Fernie offers some of the cheapest snowboarding in the world. Little wonder that it's home to the majority of the world's snowboarding bums.

TERRAIN

FREERIDING

The terrain at Fernie is extraordinary. There are wide-open powder bowls, gladed tree runs, awesome gullies and cruising groomed runs.

Powder Turns: Some of the best powder turns can be found in Currie Bowl – use the White Pass Quad Chair for access. There are also some awesome gladed tree runs in this area.

Early Morning: If the sun is out, head straight up to Face Lift and enjoy the early morning sun in Lizard Bowl.

Bad Weather: In bad weather it's best to stay away from Lizard Bowl as visibility deteriorates significantly. The runs directly off the Boomerang Triple Chair and the Haul Back T-bar offer the protection of trees, thus improving visibility.

Avoiding Crowds: The Timber Bowl Quad tends to be the most crowded lift on the mountain. To really avoid the crowds you need to head over into Cedar Bowl.

Hiking: One of the best hikes at Fernie is the one up to the 2,100 m (7,000 ft) Polar Peak. To get there, take the traverse to skiers' right of the Face Lift all the way to the edge of Lizard Bowl. Then hike up the ridge between Lizard Bowl and Currie Bowl. Another great hike is into Fish Bowl. Take the traverse out to skiers' left of the Face Lift and head up the ridge between Cedar Bowl and Fish Bowl.

Beginners: The runs around the Deer Chair are best.

FREESTYLE

Halfpipes: Traditionally, Fernie has offered little in the way of halfpipes and snowboard parks. This has recently changed and a reasonable halfpipe set-up exists on the Bambi run, accessed by the Deer Chair. It is a shallow pipe, with 1.5 m (5 ft) walls, shaped by a Pipe Dragon.

Snowboard Parks: As with the halfpipe set-up, little has been offered in the past in the way of snowboard parks. The park

Above: *Rick Hunte finds a nice cliff to drop and styles a nice method to match the moment. Photo—Alex Guzman.*

now maintained at Fernie is located on the Deer Run. It has two tabletops and a spine, all of an intermediate standard.

Natural Hits: Fernie is a freestyle snowboarder's heaven, with the best natural hits money can buy. One of the best natural gullies on the mountain is located in Cedar Bowl and is best accessed by the Face Lift. By veering off the Cruiser Run, you eventually enter a natural gully with hips, banks and quarterpipes the whole way down. Some other great gully runs are located right next door and are known as the KC Chutes.

A notorious spot at Fernie is a natural jump known by the locals as 'Air Canada'. It is located at skiers' right of the Face Lift and is basically a huge knoll with a nice smooth run in and transition, and a super-steep landing – perfect for going big on a powder day. It's also heaps of fun to go sliding the pine trees that have been bent over by the weight of the snow and launch off the cat tracks that zigzag their way down to Lizard Bowl.

RED MOUNTAIN
CANADA

STATISTICS

Average Annual Snowfall

	750 cm	300 in

Elevations	(m)	(ft)
Top:	2040	6693
Base:	1187	3894
Vertical Drop:	853	2798

Lifts

Surface Lifts:	1
Double Chairs:	1
Triple Chairs:	3
Quad Chairs – Fixed Grip:	0
Quad Chairs – Express:	0
Six Chairs – Express:	0
Gondolas:	0
Cable Cars:	0
Funiculars:	0
Total:	5

Contact Details

Phone:	+1 250 362 7384
Fax:	+1 250 362 5833
Email Address:	redmtn@wkpowerlink.com
Internet Site:	www.ski-red.com

RESORT REVIEW

Red Mountain is held in high regard by those who have been there and has a reputation as being a powder junkie's paradise. Its ample vertical rise and massive amount of advanced terrain make it an ideal destination for those wishing to pursue death-defying feats. If you are into steep tree runs, chutes, and backcountry, then Red will suit you to a T. As it is located in the British Columbia interior, some seven hours' drive from Vancouver, it rarely becomes crowded. The nearest town, Rossland, 5 km (3 miles) from Red, is a snowboard bum's hangout, with many Australians, Americans and Canadians shacking up in the cheap accommodation and riding just about every day of the season. With so many snowboard bums about, competition for early morning freshies after a large dump is fierce.

Red Mountain actually consists of two peaks side by side, with Red Mountain being the smaller, accessed by a double chair. The second and larger peak, Granite Mountain, is where all the action is. This is accessed by the Motherlode Triple Chair, which ascends some 850 vertical meters (2,788 ft). The terrain accessed by this chair is some of the most mind-blowing lifted terrain in Canada.

Right: *Tom Burt uses Mitch Large as his pin-up boy! This is Mitch Large boning gracefully at Red.*

Above: *A lone rider takes in the view of Mt Roberts, Rossland BC.*
Right: *Frank Desrosiers finds some space in the trees at Red to put down a powerful carve. Photo—Alex Guzman.*

TERRAIN

FREERIDING

Basically, the whole of Red Mountain is a freerider's dream. Of the 445 hectares (1,100 acres) of rideable terrain on offer, 283 hectares (700 acres) is covered in trees, so as you can imagine, it takes a while to get tracked out. Most of the trees are widely spaced, allowing for easy navigation even on the worst white-out days.

Steeps: For those who are looking for steep, adrenalin-pumping runs, the best places to check out are Beer Belly Bowl, Cambodia, Chutes of Pale Face, and the Powder Fields.

Bad Weather: Bad weather means good snowboarding at Red. With the large expanse of trees covering Granite and Red, there is a wealth of runs that will be fun in the worst conditions. Of course, if it rains or goes bullet-proof, go catch a movie at the cinema in Trail.

Avoiding Crowds: Like any other mountain, when the snow comes and you've got over a foot of fresh, you will get crowds. On the powder days, the whole town of Rossland and nearby Trail seems to stop work and go to the hill for their fair share of powder. But don't let that put you off. With the number of trees hiding all the secret spots, you can still get fresh tracks days after a dump. Weekends are more crowded, but compared to Whistler, the crowds aren't too bad, with a long wait at a chair being 10-15 minutes.

Hiking: If you do get sick of the crowds and terrain at Red, you can get stuck into the nearby backcountry. Mt Roberts, overlooking the Paradise Chair, is well worth the hike. Gray Mountain is also well worth the short hike although, it isn't as challenging as Mt Roberts.

Beginners: For those wanting some mellow fun runs, check out the trails that are accessed by the Paradise Chair.

FREESTYLE

Red Mountain is not renowned for its park or pipe so if that's what you are after, look elsewhere like Big White or Whistler/Blackcomb. They do manage to get a pipe or park happening occasionally, but it's not world class. There is great terrain for building kickers, just watch out for the numerous trees!

LAKE LOUISE
CANADA

STATISTICS

Average Annual Snowfall

	370 cm	148 in

Elevations	**(m)**	**(ft)**
Top:	2591	8501
Base:	1646	5400
Vertical Drop:	945	3100

Lifts	
Surface Lifts:	3
Double Chairs:	2
Triple Chairs:	2
Quad Chairs – Fixed Grip:	1
Quad Chairs – Express:	3
Six Chairs – Express:	0
Gondolas:	0
Cable Cars:	0
Funiculars:	0
Total:	11

Contact Details	
Phone:	+1 250 423 4655
Fax:	+1 250 423 6644
Email Address:	info@skilouise.com
Internet Site:	www.skilouise.com

RESORT REVIEW

Lake Louise is located 184 km (114 miles) west of Calgary and 60 km (37 miles) west of the town of Banff, just off Highway 1, right in the middle of Banff National Park. Offering some 1,620 hectares (4,000 acres) of rideable terrain, Lake Louise is one of the largest ski resorts in North America, and with more than four mountain faces, it takes days to really get to know the ins and outs of the resort. The American skiing magazines have poured accolades onto Lake Louise, giving it gold awards for terrain, difficulty and value for money. And they are not far off the mark.

Being so far away from the coast and close to the North Pole, Lake Louise receives some terribly cold weather, which can really turn you off your riding. It is not uncommon for the mercury to fall below –30°C (–22°F). Despite such low temperatures, Lake Louise does not receive huge quantities of snow. It has an average annual snowfall of about 355 cm (140 in). In contrast, Sunshine Village, which is located just 50 km (31 miles) away, receives in excess of 9 m (30 ft) of snow a year. The reason is that Sunshine is located in the main range of the Canadian Rockies, whereas Lake Louise is located in the foothills. Due to its meagre snowfall, Lake Louise is especially reliant on snow-making. This ensures that the season lasts well into April.

Despite the lack of snowfall, the amazing mountains that surround Lake Louise offer some incredible hiking and fresh tracks, weeks after the in-bounds terrain has been churned.

Further, because of the low temperatures, the powder remains super dry and light.

Above: *Neil Hardwick kickin' a lazy 20-foot stash in Lake Louise. Photo—Gavin O'Toole.*

TERRAIN

FREERIDING

The terrain at Lake Louise is as varied as the fish in the sea. There is terrain to suit every boarding ability and style. Groomed corduroy to wide-open powder bowls, huge killer cliffs to tree runs, backcountry hikes to high-speed GS runs. Lake Louise also has its fair share of cornices. Some of these cornices have featured in *Transworld Snowboarding*. Further, the runs at Lake Louise are long, with the mountain boasting nearly a kilometer (.6 mile) of vertical. The longest run at Lake Louise is 8 km (5 miles).

Powder Turns: After a fresh dump, it's best to track out as much in-bounds terrain as possible, before even thinking about going hiking. The best place to head in such a situation is straight out to Mt Whitehorn (if it is open). This is accessed by taking the Summit Platter. Then traverse out to skiers' left and follow the signs to Brown Shirt. Straight after Brown Shirt follow the ski-out trail to the Paradise Chair. Take the Paradise Chair up and drop into Paradise Bowl. The best place to drop in is slightly to skiers' left of the lift. There is a good cornice and some small rock drops on the way down. Next, head down to the Ptarmigan Chair and either take a run directly under the chair (if it is not tracked out) or follow the ridge off to skiers' right of the chair and drop in when you hit the power lines. The Larch Area is also a good place for fresh tracks, but it tends to be a bit flat and you're likely to get stuck unless you know where you're going.

Bad Weather: In bad weather it's best to stick to the lower elevations of the mountain. The Larch Area is the perfect place when the storms roll in. This area has been made even better with the recent installation of a high-speed quad.

Avoiding Crowds: To avoid the crowds you really need to avoid the two main high-speed quads, Friendly Giant and Top of the World. On extremely busy days it's best to stay away from the front side of the mountain and to ride the Paradise Chair (an incredibly slow triple chair) or the Larch Chair.

Hiking: After a few days it will be impossible to find any fresh tracks on the mountain, so the best option is to go backcountry. The easiest backcountry hike is out to West Bowl. Take the Summit Platter to the peak and then traverse out to skiers' right as you look back down the front side of the mountain. You have to traverse a fair way out before you actually hit West Bowl. But once out there, the options are endless. Just be aware that the traverse back in from West Bowl is rated as a Jedi Traverse – super hard. You will be very lucky if you don't get any bruises from hitting trees on the way through.

Beginners: Wiwaxy, on the front side of the mountain, is accessed by the Olympic, Friendly Giant and Glacier Chairs. It is a long wide cat track with a gentle slope – perfect for those learning.

Above: *Mic Larkin dropping to his heart's content. Photo—Gavin O'Toole.*

FREESTYLE

Halfpipes: Lake Louise has two halfpipes. Because of the freezing temperatures experienced during most of the season, it would be wise to stay away from the pipes until about the beginning of March. Before then the snow in the pipe is far too icy to be safe. One pipe is tucked away at the base of the Summit Platter T-bar. It is not easily accessible by lifts. If you intend to ride this pipe for the day you would be better off hiking it than riding the lifts. The other pipe is found just above the Temple Lodge, in the larch area. It has a similar story to the first pipe and is best left for late in the season.

Parks: During the peak of the season the terrain parks are small and at beginner standard. They are located under the base of the Friendly Giant Chair and next to the Larch halfpipe. As with the pipes, the parks are best left for late in the season.

Natural Hits: For a cornice drop take the Paradise Chair and at the top, immediately on skiers' right, you will find the Paradise Cornice. Otherwise, traverse to skiers' left and drop in on plenty of chutes and rock drops followed by the double black Pika Trees to return you to the base of the chair. For other cliff hits take Saddle Back on the back side of the mountain and detour through Hourglass, where there is a huge drop.

NORQUAY
CANADA

STATISTICS

Average Annual Snowfall

	300 cm	120 in

Elevations

	(m)	(ft)
Top:	2134	7001
Base:	1636	5367
Vertical Drop:	498	1633

Lifts

Surface Lifts:	2
Double Chairs:	2
Triple Chairs:	0
Quad Chairs – Fixed Grip:	1
Quad Chairs – Express:	1
Six Chairs – Express:	0
Gondolas:	0
Cable Cars:	0
Funiculars:	0
Total:	6

Contact Details

Phone:	+1 403 762 4421
Fax:	+1 403 762 8133
Email Address:	info@banffnorquay.com
Internet Site:	www.banffnorquay.com

RESORT REVIEW

Norquay is by far the smallest of the three resorts that surround Banff but it is the closest, being only a 10-minute drive from the town centre. Its proximity to Banff is a blessing, because you can sleep in and get up to the resort in no time, buy a snowboard pass and ride the park and pipe until closing. Norquay also offers night riding on Fridays. Even better, Norquay offers a free bus service, so it costs you absolutely nothing to get there.

To compensate for its meagre snowfall – a pitiful 340 cm (120 inches) per year – Norquay boasts snow-making on 90% of its terrain. You can therefore be guaranteed snow, even through long dry spells.

Norquay has recently constructed a new 2,580 sq m (24,000 sq ft) day lodge, complete with sundecks. This means you can sit outside, catch a few rays and watch the pipe action, as the pipe is located just above the day lodge.

Norquay is the perfect place to go if you like the pipe or the park, as the mountain is renowned for building quality table-tops and great halfpipes. In fact, they have two halfpipes, both located on the Cascade Run. Also, if you are working late nights in Banff, Norquay is close enough to get enough runs in to make it worthwhile. Norquay has really become the home of freestyle snowboarding in the Banff area.

Right: *Not so famous for having the deepest powder, Norquay can still put on a show if you know where to go.*

TERRAIN

FREERIDING

The natural terrain at Norquay is steep. This is reflected in the fact that only 11% of the runs are beginner runs and 44% are rated as experts-only. In fact Norquay has one of the steepest lift-accessed runs in North America. The only problem is that most of the runs are short. With a vertical of only 500 meters (1,640 ft), the runs don't last long and with only one high-speed quad, you tend to spend a lot of time on lifts rather than on snow.

In addition, Norquay doesn't receive substantial amounts of snow, so although the terrain may be steep it is usually a mogul field, making it a health hazard for snowboarders. The resort also lacks the cliffs and cornices offered by nearby Lake Louise and Sunshine. Norquay is more of a freestyle mountain because of the time and effort put into its pipe and park.

Powder Turns: Norquay is not the mountain to head to if you are searching for some powder to ride.

Bad Weather: The runs are well protected by trees and are low on the mountain. Thus, snowboarding during bad weather is not a complete nightmare.

Avoiding Crowds: Norquay is rarely crowded, so tactics for avoiding crowds need not be considered.

Beginners: The area suited to beginners on this mainly steep mountain is under the Cascade Chair. This is also the night riding area.

FREESTYLE

Halfpipe: Norquay has two pipes that are maintained five times a week using a Snow Turbo Grinder. One pipe is their expert pipe; the other is smaller, designed for kids and beginners. The expert pipe has excellent shape, gradient and transition. It is probably the best pipe in the Banff area. It is positioned well, not too far from the sundeck of the Norquay Base Lodge, and has a good fall-line. It is certainly a great place to spend the sunny afternoons in spring or days when the powder at Lake Louise and Sunshine has been tracked out.

Snowboard Parks: The snowboard park at Norquay matches the quality of the pipes. There is a good combination of small and large hits to suit everyone's needs. Most importantly, the landings on the tabletops are long and steep, which helps you avoid those nasty compression landings.

Natural Hits: The best natural hits at Norquay are cat track jumps. These can be found all over the mountain, especially in the Pathfinder Express area. However, be sure to check for moguls on the landing. Freestyle snowboarding is really where Norquay comes into its own. So, on a sunny day, stick to the snowboard park and halfpipe.

Top left: *Shane Stephens lays one back for the camera.*
Left: *Adam Dawes doing a bit of bush bashing deep in the Norquay forests.*

SUNSHINE VILLAGE
CANADA

STATISTICS

Average Annual Snowfall

	1025cm	410in

Elevations	(m)	(ft)
Top:	2730	8954
Base:	1660	5440
Vertical Drop:	1070	3514

Lifts	
Surface Lifts:	2
Double Chairs:	3
Triple Chairs:	1
Quad Chairs - Fixed Grip:	0
Quad Chairs - Express:	3
Six Chairs - Express:	0
Gondolas:	1
Cable Cars:	0
Funiculars:	0
Total:	10

Contact Details

Phone:	+1 403 760 5200
Fax:	+1 403 762 8765
Internet Site:	www.skibanff.com

3 Mountain Overview

RESORT REVIEW

Above: *Richard Hegarty stretches his arms and takes a deep breath, ready for the drop below him. Photo—Gavin O'Toole.*

Located atop the breathtaking Continental Divide in the Banff region of Alberta, Sunshine Village is a resort that lacks reputation but not terrain. It boasts the highest annual average snowfall in the Banff area (over 10 m/400 in per season, or 33 ft). Unfortunately, as it snows so much Sunshine does not often live up to its name. Nonetheless, the resort certainly offers the goods for snowboarders, especially with the recent expansion into Goat's Eye Mountain. Unlike nearby Lake Louise, Sunshine does not rely on manufactured snow, and is open for snowboarding more than half the year, from November to May. Sunshine, in fact, boasts 100% natural snow. You won't find a single snow gun here. It is rumored that it snows every day at Sunshine.

Sunshine Village dates back to 1928, when the Trail Riders of the Canadian Rockies built a log cabin close to the location of the current Sunshine day lodge. From that day, people began to experience the abundant natural snow that Sunshine has to offer.

Sunshine comprises three main mountains: Goat's Eye Mountain with an altitude of 2,806 m (9,200 ft) and a vertical of 580 m (1,900 ft); Lookout Mountain with an altitude of 2,739 m (8,954 ft) and a vertical of 442 m (1,450 ft); and Mt Standish with an altitude of 2,398 m (7,875 ft) and a vertical of 215 m (705 ft). Sunshine's advertizing slogan is 'three mountains, three high-speed quads and three times the snow', and it is pretty much spot-on. Although Goat's Eye and Lookout Mountains are both well serviced by high-speed quads, Mt Standish is still serviced by an antiquated fixed-grip double chair, triple chair and t-bar. This is a pity since, despite its short vertical, Mt Standish has some excellent freeriding terrain.

TERRAIN

FREERIDING

Since the expansion of lift-accessed terrain into Goat's Eye Mountain, the skiable terrain at Sunshine is an impressive 1,283 hectares (3,168 acres). The terrain consists of groomed trails, undulating powder runs, cat tracks, cornices, cliffs and gullies. Although Sunshine boasts over 1,000 m (3,333 ft) in vertical, almost half of this is represented by a relatively flat cat track that winds its way from the village of Sunshine down to the car park 400 m (1,312 ft) below. Therefore, the quality vertical at Sunshine is really only about 600 m (1,968 ft). There are some great steeps at Sunshine, but the terrain is mostly moderately steep and best suited for intermediate riders. Riders who are looking for the steeps should really consider Lake Louise.

The best freeriding terrain at Sunshine is located on Lookout Mountain and Goat's Eye Mountain. The terrain around the Strawberry Chair on Mt Standish is probably a little too flat for advanced riders. However, located off to riders' right of the Standish Chair is a long and large cliff known as Headwall. The actual size of the drop varies according to your launch point; you can choose whether you want to do a huge or small drop. Most of the terrain on Lookout Mountain and Goat's Eye offers quality freeriding.

Above: *The Rockies of Alberta are amongst the most picturesque in North America. Photo courtesy of Sunshine Village Ski Resort.*

Powder Turns: The chutes off the Goat's Eye Express generally offer some good powder turns. For secret stashes, head to the Wawa T-bar and the trees far on skiers' left of the Wawa T-bar.

Bad Weather: Both Goat's Eye and Lookout are too exposed in bad weather. The best options are the runs around the Wawa T-bar. The Wheeler Double Chair offers some good protected runs, the only problem is that they are fairly flat.

Avoiding Crowds: The lifts to avoid, if possible, are the Angel Express and the Gondola.

Above: *The open bowls of Sunshine collect over 1,016 cm (400 in) of light dry powder each year. Photo—Sunshine Village Ski Resort.*

Hiking: The hiking off the top of the Continental Divide Express gives access to an area known as Delirium Dive. It is super steep, with gnarly chutes. Avalanche beacons and a shovel are a requirement for riding this area. Nevertheless, it is definitely a place to check out even if you aren't going to take the drop.

Beginners: The best beginner runs are located around the Wheeler and Fireweed Double Chairs.

FREESTYLE

Halfpipes: The Kokanee Halfpipe is located under the Strawberry Triple Chair. The main problem is that in bad weather, visibility approaches zero. It is quite a short pipe with a relatively steep fall line. It is not exceptional and is certainly not a distinctive feature of Sunshine.

Snowboard Parks: Sunshine has constructed a boardercross course to skiers' right of the Wawa T-bar. It is a fun course and a great place to hone your boardercross skills. The Kokanee Terrain Park is located on the Creek Run at the ski boundary on Mt Standish. It is quite a flat area and a very exposed position. The tabletops are giant and also rock hard. The park is not particularly pleasant to ride on unless fresh snow has fallen, the hits have been shaped, there is no wind and visibility is excellent. It includes three tabletops and a quarterpipe.

Natural Hits: On Lookout Mountain, search the area between the Tee Pee Town and Angle Express Chairs for rock drops and natural launching spots. This area is gladed, making it an interesting place to get airborne. On Goat's Eye Mountain, the lower area amongst the trees offers many hidden hits to be discovered. Boosting off the Sunshine Coast cat track is a cool way to kick off this descent. On Mt Standish, try the Headwall cliffs drop or explore the trees around the Wawa T-bar.

AUSTRALIA

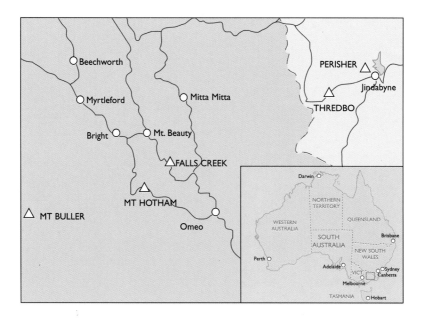

Everyone around the world seems to know Australia for its beaches, sun, surf and kangaroos. But few people are even aware that Australia has its own 'Alps'. With at least three good solid months of snow, Australia is a viable destination for Northern Hemisphere travelers looking for somewhere to go over their summer. Yes, that's right – when it's summer in USA and Europe, it's winter in Australia!

THE AUSTRALIAN ALPS

The alpine region of Australia spans a significantly large area. The Great Dividing Range winds its way up almost the entire east coast of the country, beginning in Victoria in the south and heading north to Queensland. The Great Dividing Range is an ancient mountain range and unlike many international mountain ranges such as the Sierra Nevada in USA, it doesn't lie on a fault line. Hence, the range is very low lying, with the highest point being Mt Kosciuszko at 2,229 m (7,314 ft). To make matters worse for Aussie snow fans, Australia is some distance from the South Pole, and therefore a very warm country. Consequently, the only part of the country that receives snow is a tiny area in the south eastern states: Victoria, New South Wales, and Tasmania. The snow line in winter is at about 1,400 m (4,593 ft), meaning that the Australian resorts don't have a lot of vertical. Further, the warm climate ensures that seasons are short by international standards.

SNOW CONDITIONS IN AUSTRALIA

The Australian snow season begins in mid-June and ends at the start of October. However, rarely have resorts been able to open the season with natural snow. Rather, they rely on man-made snow for the first few weeks of the season. The Aussie resorts average approximately 200–300 cm (80–120 in) of snow per season. Although it may seem strange, Australia can offer powder conditions even though the powder is generally very heavy.

Different weather patterns affect resorts in Australia according to their geographical location. There are three common weather patterns which will bring the snow to Australian resorts. The first, and the best scenario for big dumps, is when a deep low pressure system floats from west to east, crossing the island of Tasmania, and pumping cold, wet, southerly air into the Alps. The system will explode into light, dry powder and can accumulate to well over 30 cm (12 in) in 24 hours – a big dump by Aussie standards.

Right: *Paul Jones finds solitude in the twilight on Sentinel Ridge. Photo–Alex Guzman.*

Above: *See, there is snow in Australia! The slogan is 'Switzerland with gum trees'. Yeah, right!*
Opposite: *Heavy snow, gum trees and rocks. This is snowboarding in Australia. Adam Dawes finds an untracked slope in the New South Wales backcountry.*

The second scenario is when a low-pressure system floats further north over Victoria rather than Tasmania and brings a big wet dump from the north onto the bigger resorts such as Mt Hotham, Falls Creek, Thredbo and Perisher Blue. These northerly dumps will often bring rain to the southern resorts such as Mt Buller and Mt Baw Baw.

A third snow pattern brings more moderate snow falls to southern resorts. It occurs when a southwesterly air flow, generated by a slow-moving high-pressure system located over the Great Australian Bight, pumps very cold Antarctic air onto the coastal ranges. This pattern will occasionally bring snow to most of Victoria, Tasmania and southern New South Wales.

SNOWBOARDING IN AUSTRALIA

Australian resorts recognized the potential of snowboarding in the early days and opened their doors. However, even though all Australian resorts have openly accepted snowboarding, they are still very behind in providing quality freestyle facilities. Resorts have promised halfpipes and parks but noy yet delivered.

Australian resorts are often very crowded, especially on the weekends, as desperate Aussies try to utilize the limited snow season. Further, accessing the Aussie snow resorts is a hassle, as they are perched on top of peaks at or above 1,200 m (3,937 ft), requiring long winding drives up the hill, especially at the Victorian resorts.

ACCOMMODATION

All Australian resorts provide both off and on-mountain accommodation. The on-mountain accommodation is always more expensive, but it is generally the way to go as you get the real alpine atmosphere. If you choose to stay off the mountain, you lose the convenience of sleeping next to the slopes, the atmosphere is not the same and the half to one-hour drive up the mountain every morning is a hassle.

As a snowboard travel destination, Australia has advantages over summer snowboarding in the northern hemisphere. The snow is better than summer slush, the terrain is fun and the people are the coolest in the world. Consider it!

MT BULLER
AUSTRALIA

STATISTICS

Elevations	(m)	(ft)
Top:	1781	5843
Base:	1368	4488
Vertical Drop:	413	1355

Lifts	
Surface Lifts:	20
Double Chairs:	1
Triple Chairs:	4
Quad Chairs – Fixed Grip:	5
Quad Chairs – Express:	3
Six Chairs – Express:	0
Gondolas:	0
Cable Cars:	0
Funiculars:	0
Total:	33

Contact Details

Phone:	+61 3 5777 6077
Fax:	+61 3 5777 6219
Email Address:	mbresort@mansfield.net.au
Internet Site:	www.mtbuller.com.au

RESORT REVIEW

Mt Buller is the so-called 'Mountain of Fun' and with the second-greatest lifting capacity in the Southern Hemisphere, it certainly has the ability to ensure that you get the most hits for your dollar. The resort has been developed heavily, and has a huge array of lifts and on-mountain accommodation. In addition, millions of dollars have been thrown into snow-making. A good vibe exists amongst the Buller snowboard population. Many of Australia's best unknown riders come from Buller – probably because it's so close to Australia's second biggest city, Melbourne (only about 2.5 to 3 hours' drive). This proximity makes it a mecca for weekend skiers and snowboarders, which means it gets extremely crowded on weekends. However, with a bit of mountain knowledge it is usually possible to minimize wait times in queues.

One of Mt Buller's biggest drawcards is its lift capacity – over 30 lifts lifting 40,000 people per hour across 180 hectares (446 acres) of rideable terrain. Unfortunately, due to the fickle conditions at Mt Buller, many lifts are closed for most of the season. This makes the other lifts far more crowded.

Right: *With determination, you too can build a kicker this big. Bear Agushi lofts one over a cat track at Mt Buller.*

TERRAIN

Above: *It's not often the Buller pipe looks this good! Will Ekselman is lucky to lein this air into the pipe.*

FREERIDING

Mt Buller is a large cone-shaped mountain with all its rideable terrain falling around the peak. This ensures a variety of snow conditions and weather around the resort. The vertical rise at Buller is comparable to those of the other big Aussie resorts so when there is good snow, the runs are quite long and enjoyable. Most of the runs are below the tree line. After a dump (which doesn't occur too often), there is usually good snow stashed in the gum trees.

There are a few bad aspects of riding at Mt Buller. Firstly, Buller is well known for its bad weather. Fog, rain and drizzle frequent the mountain throughout the season. Secondly, the snow at Buller is most often very wet and dumps are infrequent. Thirdly, Buller has one of the lowest average annual snowfalls out of all the Australian resorts. And finally, snowboarders are required to skate for large distances if they wish to move around the mountain because of the many flat spots around the top.

Powder Turns: When a big dump comes, the first place to head is the Bull Run area. Here you will find a large, steep bowl containing plenty of little rock drops, cat tracks, gullies and powder.

Cliffs and Drops: For the big mountain cliff jumpers, the sickest cliffs at Buller are found on a rock band known as The Bluff. The drop here will challenge any legend freerider.

Trees: If you are into trees, the best tree riding at Buller (providing there is enough snow) is on the north face around the Cow Camp and Tirol Runs. In this area the gum trees are tall and spread out.

Beginners: Beginners should head over to ride Burnt Hut Spur. The slopes around here are often less crowded and there is usually a beginner snowboard park.

FREESTYLE

Halfpipes: Mt Buller has been trying to build halfpipes and parks since 1994 and hasn't really succeeded. Their marketing brochures continually promise two halfpipes, but they struggle to push up a single halfpipe during the season. What is lacking is not snow, but commitment. Resorts in New Zealand manage to provide excellent halfpipes even when the snow is very lean because they are committed to providing good freestyle facilities. So if you are looking for a halfpipe in Australia, don't believe what you read in the Mt Buller marketing brochures.

Snowboard Parks: Mt Buller has always had a problem with building decent parks. Beginners to early intermediates are catered for with parks consisting of small kickers and spines. However, for those riders who like bigger jumps and want to progress, Mt Buller generally fails to deliver. Even kickers built at big air competitions are often poor quality, lacking decent landings and size. You are far better off bringing your own shovels and building your own kicker. The best spot for this is on an old freestyle aerial jump next to the Spurs Restaurant.

Above: *Adam Dawes finds the right place to build a kicker and style this old school mute.*

FALLS CREEK
AUSTRALIA

STATISTICS

Elevations	(m)	(ft)
Top:	1752	5748
Base:	1500	4921
Vertical Drop:	252	826

Lifts	
Surface Lifts:	20
Double Chairs:	0
Triple Chairs:	0
Quad Chairs – Fixed Grip:	4
Quad Chairs – Express:	2
Six Chairs – Express:	0
Gondolas:	0
Cable Cars:	0
Funiculars:	0
Total:	26

Contact Details	
Phone:	+61 3 5758 3100
Fax:	+61 3 5758 3337
Email Address:	info@fallscreek.net
Internet Site:	www.fallscreek.net

RESORT REVIEW

Falls Creek is home to some of Victoria's best back-country terrain. Situated in the Snowy Mountain range, opposite Victoria's highest peak, Mt Bogong, it is surrounded by an awesome amount of snowboarding terrain. In-bounds, Falls has 20 lifts spread out over more than 162 hectares (450 acres). Snow-making covers an amazing 41 hectares (100 acres). This extensive snow-making system is a big drawcard for Falls and enables it to offer a snow guarantee. It is always one of the first resorts in Australia to open and maintains plenty of rideable terrain even when there have been poor natural snowfalls.

The resort offers plenty of on-mountain accommodation, which allows you to snowboard in and out of your lodge.

The lift system at Falls is a mixture of the old and the new. T-bars and pomas are still relatively common. Although Falls has recently installed three new quad chairs, they are all fixed grip and are annoyingly slow, except for the Ruined Castle Quad, which has a magic carpet. The resort would have been much better installing just one new lift and ensuring that it was a high-speed one.

Left: *A fresh dump and a fresh-looking air. Stalefish in the gum trees at Falls Creek.*

TERRAIN

Above: More action in the Headwater Park. A local grabs the tail and heads for the hills.

Hiking: On those frequent icy days, look to the trees near International Poma for some softer stuff or go for a hike out to Mt McKay or up the Rocky Knolls. These can be accessed easily from the top of the Ruined Castle Chair Lift. Mt McKay is an easy 4 km (2.5 mile) hike. Once you get there you will find excellent rocks, a sick cornice and plenty of spots to build kickers.

FREESTYLE

Halfpipes: In typical Aussie resort fashion, a good halfpipe has never existed at Falls Creek. The resort owns no decent equipment to shape and maintain a good international standard halfpipe.

Snowboard Parks: Falls Creek has begun to shine in recent years with the construction of some excellent snowboard parks. In comparison to nearby Mt Hotham and Mt Buller, Falls Creek is definitely the leader in snowboard parks and the spot to go if you want to enjoy a good freestyle set-up. The park is usually located next to the Headwater Poma and contains about four or five tabletops as well as the best quarterpipe in Australia.

Above: Marcus Wehrle enjoys the freshly groomed Headwater Park.

FREERIDING

Falls Creek has some excellent freeriding, and if you check the mountain out for a few days, you will find heaps of secret spots where the crowds don't go. There are plenty of cat tracks, rocks and cornices and a few nice places to put in some big turns after a dump. The mountain has a vast range of terrain, from the flat, short, intermediate slopes of Sun Valley to the sick tree trails and open bowls surrounding the Summit and the Valley of the Moon ridge.

Powder Turns: After a big dump, head to the International Poma in the Village Bowl. Once at the top, go to skiers' left toward Valley of the Moon. Here you will find an array of some of Australia's longest and steepest tree runs. A bit of ori-enteering and you can take a super-long run down to Howman's Gap, 6 km (3.7 miles) from the village. Just make sure you watch out for the aqueduct.

Cliffs and Drops: For the cliff jumpers, try the Summit. It has a good mixture of small and large rocks, Then there's 'Chair Air', an 18.3–21.3 m (60–70 ft) gap jump. Be very wary: the Summit area at Falls is one of Australia's biggest mogul fields and all drops and jumps should be done after a dump – unless, of course, you want to blow out both your knees.

Beginners: If you're looking for quick groomed runs or a fun place to learn to ride, head on over to Sun Valley. The runs around Scott Chair and Ruined Castle are excellent for practicing turns.

Above: Headwater is the home for tabletops at Falls Creek. A local launches a frontside 360 on a perfect spring day.

MT HOTHAM
AUSTRALIA

STATISTICS

Elevations	(m)	(ft)
Top:	1850	6069
Base:	1450	4757
Vertical Drop:	400	1312

Lifts	
Surface Lifts:	5
Double Chairs:	1
Triple Chairs:	1
Quad Chairs – Fixed Grip:	8
Quad Chairs – Express:	0
Six Chairs – Express:	0
Gondolas:	0
Cable Cars:	0
Funiculars:	0
Total:	15

Contact Details	
Phone:	+61 3 5759 4444
Fax:	+61 3 5759 3692
Internet Site:	www.hotham.net.au

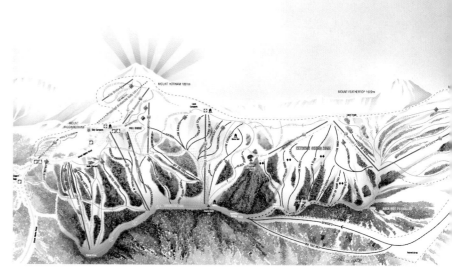

RESORT REVIEW

Mt Hotham was once called the sleeping giant of Victorian resorts. However, the resort is no longer in a deep slumber; it is stretching its arms. Recent years have seen enormous expansion at Hotham with the re-location of the Summit T-bar to Australia Drift, a Skier Bridge to link the Summit to Heavenly Valley, the addition of three quad chairs in the Mary's Slide area and the first alpine airport in Australia.

Split into two distinct sections by the Ovens Highway, the upper mountain hosts most of the resort's beginner runs, while the bottom section is home to some of Australia's most challenging terrain. It is little wonder Hotham's advertizing slogan is 'Get serious, get to Hotham'. Some of the terrain is certainly worthy of this slogan.

Hotham has the highest average snowfall of any Australian resort and reputedly the best powder in Australia. Although it does have snow-making, it is not as reliant on it as nearby Mt Buller.

The Mt Hotham lift system has improved in recent years with the installation of three new quad chairs and the upgrade of a double chair to a quad chair. However, the majority of lifts are fixed grip, so the lift system can be painfully slow at times.

Right: *As the sun drops on a late spring day, Bear Agushi finds a cliff to launch deep in the Mt Hotham backcountry.*

TERRAIN

Above: *Brett Archer finds a nice gully at Hotham.*
Photo—Alex Guzman.

FREERIDING

Mt Hotham is arguably Australia's best resort when it comes to freeriding, and this can be credited to two main factors. First, Mt Hotham receives the most snow in Australia, with an average season having quite a few dumps of over 30 cm (1 ft). The second factor is that Hotham has the best advanced terrain. The terrain is long, by Australian standards, and consistently steep. There are also many cornices and rocks to drop and Hotham's lift system offers easy access to some of Australia's best backcountry terrain. About 80% of the terrain at Hotham is intermediate to advanced, and some of the black runs are steeper than double black diamond runs overseas.

Powder Turns: The pick of the freeriding after a dump is a big open bowl area known as Mary's Slide. This run begins with a large cornice at the top and narrows to a steep chute-like section as it approaches the valley floor. Previously accessible only by foot, Mary's Slide is now accessible by lift and is sensational on a powder day.

Bad Weather: When the weather is bad, head to Blue Ribbon (if there is enough snow on it), which is sheltered from the wind and offers plenty of trees to provide definition in the fog.

Steeps: The steepest run on the mountain is a tree run known as 'Southern Cross', which is about 200 m (660 ft) long. It is marked on the trail map but not easy to find. Stick to the Heavenly Valley and Mary's Slide areas for the best steeps.

FREESTYLE

Halfpipes: Hotham was one of Australia's first resorts to have a halfpipe, and has hosted some big competitions. Some of Hotham's better-known guests include Matt Cummins and Tina Basich. However, since 1994, Mt Hotham's pipes have slowly deteriorated in quality. Following a change in management, the commitment by the lift company to providing a well-shaped halfpipe has waned. Much time and money has been spent in recent years on the massive lift upgrade as well as on other capital works, and snowboarding has been neglected. For this reason, Hotham is no longer a breeding ground for Australia's best snowboarders. They now travel to other resorts and overseas.

Snowboard Parks: In typical Australian resort style, nothing significant has happened at Mt Hotham by way of snowboard parks, and this doesn't look like changing. As with the halfpipe situation, Hotham hasn't provided a good park since 1994.

Natural Hits: Mt Hotham is a rad resort to use as a natural snowboard park. Many of the steep runs have cat tracks cutting across them so there are plenty of spots to get air into powder landings. In addition, the numerous ridges and spurs running down the fall line of the hill offer natural kickers into steep landings. Hotham is probably the best natural snowboard park in Australia.

PERISHER BLUE
AUSTRALIA

STATISTICS

Elevations	(m)	(ft)
Top:	2034	6673
Base:	1605	5266
Vertical Drop:	429	1407

Lifts	
Surface Lifts:	38
Double Chairs:	4
Triple Chairs:	2
Quad Chairs – Fixed Grip:	6
Quad Chairs – Express:	0
Six Chairs – Express:	0
Gondolas:	0
Cable Cars:	0
Funiculars:	0
Ski Carpet:	1
Total:	51

Contact Details

Phone:	+61 2 6459 4495
Fax:	+61 2 6457 5485
Internet Site:	www.perisherblue.com.au

RESORT REVIEW

Perisher Blue is Australia's biggest snow-board area, with 51 lifts and 1,250 hectares (3,099 acres) of rideable terrain spread across four distinct areas – Perisher, Smiggin Holes, Blue Cow and Guthega. It is Australia's answer to the North American and European mega-resorts. However, don't be deceived by the statistics. Sure there is a vast amount of terrain available to ride at Perisher Blue, but the vertical doesn't stack up to its northern counterparts.

Perisher Blue offers an extensive snow-making system covering some 35 hectares (80 acres) of terrain. This, coupled with its altitude (the highest resort in Australia), means that Perisher Blue is usually the first resort in Australia to open and the last to lose its base.

The lift system at Perisher Blue is huge and includes Australia's only alpine railway, the Skitube. The main problem with the lift system is that it mainly consists of t-bars and fixed-grip chairlifts. Thus, actually moving around the mountain can be a very slow affair.

Right: *Digging it deep at Perisher Blue. Photo courtesy Perisher Blue Resort.*

TERRAIN

FREERIDING

Perisher Blue is truly a vast resort, and the terrain varies immensely. Whilst the Front Valley of Perisher and Smiggins offers little in the way of lengthy runs and steeps, Blue Cow and Guthega make up for it.

The runs off to skiers' left of the Ridge Quad Chair provide the longest quality freeriding runs in the resort. Off the Mt Perisher Double Chair there are some good steeps through lightly treed areas. The problem is that this area is prone to being moguled out pretty quickly. If you really want to find some quality freeriding terrain, you need to go exploring.

Trees and Bad Weather: Leichhardt T-bar, Lawson T-bar at Perisher and Blue Calf T-bar at Guthega offer good tree riding. These are the best places to be when the fog rolls in.

Beginners: The runs under the Pretty Valley Double Chair offer the perfect terrain for beginners – long, open, groomed runs with a gentle gradient.

Avoiding Crowds: If you want to try and escape the crowds, the Guthega slopes are always a good option, as they are difficult to reach. Stay away from the Perisher Express Quad – this tends to get pretty packed.

FREESTYLE

Halfpipes: Perisher offers a commitment to snowboarding that is lacking at many other Aussie resorts, and this is evident in their halfpipe, which is excavated from the earth and is the first to open each season in Australia. The pipe is located directly under the Sundeck Restaurant on Front Valley. If you drive into the main car park you won't miss it.

Snowboard Parks: Perisher Blue offers two parks. They are located at Blue Cow near the Summit Quad Chair and at Perisher beside the Leichhardt T-bar. The problem with the parks in the past has been that they have been aimed at intermediate riders. Thus hits for the more advanced riders are sadly lacking. The parks could easily be improved by providing larger hits for experienced riders who want to progress their freestyle riding. There is a Big Air jump located next to the halfpipe (near the Sundeck Hotel). This is an excellent jump for advanced riders. However, it is rarely open to the public and is really only used during competitions. The best advice is to take your own shovel and build your own kicker.

Natural Hits: Lack of vertical does not affect freestyle riding and Perisher is no exception. Perisher has some great rolling terrain and cat tracks to practice all the latest freestyle moves.

Above: *. Under dark skies Bear Agushi finds the courage to method into the Australian wilderness. Fortune favors the brave.*

Right: *This is what you live for—an untouched open face. Dan Kneitel shot by Alex Guzman.*

THREDBO
AUSTRALIA

STATISTICS

Elevations	(m)	(ft)
Top:	2037	6683
Base:	1365	4478
Vertical Drop:	672	2204

Lifts	
Surface Lifts:	5
Double Chairs:	2
Triple Chairs:	1
Quad Chairs – Fixed Grip:	0
Quad Chairs – Express:	4
Six Chairs – Express:	0
Gondolas:	0
Cable Cars:	0
Funiculars:	0
Total:	12

Contact Details	
Phone:	+61 2 6459 4100
Fax:	+61 2 6459 4101
Internet Site:	www.thredbo.com.au

RESORT REVIEW

Located in the New South Wales Snowy Mountains, Thredbo is the closest thing that Australia can offer to an international standard resort. With nearly 700 m (2,310 ft) of vertical and heaps of lift-accessed terrain, the only thing that stops Thredbo from being comparable with the world's best resorts is its lack of snowfall. Thredbo boasts Australia's highest lifted point at 2,037 m (6,683 ft) and also Australia's longest run (5.7 km/3.5 miles). This is no coincidence, given that Thredbo is located close to Australia's highest mountain, Mt Kosciuszko (2,228 m/7,310 ft).

Thredbo Village is located at 1,365 m (4,478 ft) on the valley floor. It is probably the best designed and constructed village in Australia. This is not surprising considering that Thredbo management has pumped over AUD$100 million into developing the mountain and the village in recent years. The village has cool shops, cafes, restaurants and nightclubs. But of course they're not cheap. Thredbo is rather like the Vail of Australia – big and glitzy.

Most of Australia's best riders call Thredbo home, and have perfected their style on the awesome terrain the mountain offers. Also, Thredbo is home to Australia's two major snowboard competitions each year – the Sprite Sessions (mid-August) and the Quicksilver Boardriderz (late August).

The major advantage that Thredbo has over other Australian resorts is its lift system. It has four high-speed quad chairs, all in excellent locations. These lifts ensure that you are not stuck on the seat of your pants for most of the day.

Above: *The village of Thredbo is one of the most appealing in Australia. When the snow comes the village turns into a winter wonderland. Photo courtesy Kosciuszko-Thredbo.*

TERRAIN

Left: *Jae Pengelly launches a nice stalefish at Thredbo. Photo— Alex Guzman.*

FREERIDING

When it comes to freeriding, Thredbo rules. The massive vertical (670 m/2,200 ft) can almost all be accessed by one high-speed quad (the Crackenback Quad), meaning that top-to-bottom laps can be done all day. Tons of the terrain at Thredbo is steep, particularly around Antons and Sponars, and there are plenty of rock drops, rollers, natural tabletops and hips for big airs. The resort offers a few high-speed quads which are over 1 km (3,200 ft) in length, and they access the best in-bounds riding in Australia. Some great freeriding runs are Cannonball and Golf Course, located off the Crackenback Express.

Backcountry: Thredbo offers some great backcountry hiking. Short hikes are possible from the top of Karels. Alternatively, take the Cruiser Lift and start hiking out to skiers' left towards an area known as the Twin Valleys. This area offers some of the best backcountry runs in Australia, not to mention some great rock drops.

Cruising: For intermediates and beginners, Thredbo offers an array of 'Super trails' to get your thighs burning.

Bad Weather: In bad weather, the best places to ride are probably the runs around the Cruiser Lift. There are plenty of trees in this area, which aid visibility. The Crackenback Chair, Sponars T-bar and Antons T-bar (especially the tops of these t-bars) all tend to be more exposed than the Cruiser Lift. Better still, simply ride the park and pipe located near the base of the Merritts area as these are well protected from the weather.

Beginners: Friday Flat is the perfect learning ground for beginners. It supposedly has the perfect gradient for learning on and a very fast high-speed quad to get you to the top, rather than t-bars or pomas.

Avoiding Crowds: The best way to avoid the crowds at Thredbo is to take the slower lifts. For example, rather than taking Crackenback, try out the Ramshead Chair or the Snowgums Chair. Definitely stay away from the Cruiser Chair as this is always crowded.

FREESTYLE

Halfpipes: Thredbo's halfpipe is located next to the base of the Cruiser Lift in the Merritts area. It is the only halfpipe in Australia to have a base shaped out of dirt. It is about 70-80 m (230-260 ft) long and has its own t-bar, which is a blessing. The t-bar allows you to ride through the park then into the pipe. The pipe is shaped by a shaping blade and finished off by hand. This all sounds pretty good, but in reality the pipe at Thredbo is not what it's cracked up to be. There are several reasons for this. First, the gradient of the pipe is too shallow. In fact it's built across the fall line of the mountain rather than down the fall line. Second, the pipe is located at a relatively low altitude on Thredbo, meaning the snow is generally wet and slow. Finally, the pipe is not properly maintained. It's shaped on an irregular basis by the shaping blade and on an even less regular basis by hand. These three factors make it extremely difficult to maintain speed. The bottom line is that although the pipe is fun, it's far from world class.

Snowboard Parks: Located at the base of the Cruiser Lift, just above the halfpipe, the snowboard park at Thredbo is usually one of the best in Australia. Traditionally, there has been a combination of three or four hits that cater for all abilities as well as one 'super kicker' for those wanting to try more progressive freestyle tricks. In addition, the boarder-cross track that can be found snaking its way around and under the Cruiser Lift that is always great to ride and race your friends on.

Natural Hits: A similar story to the freeriding – Thredbo rules because the runs are long and the terrain offers a lot for getting air. There are plenty of cat tracks to launch from. In fact there are some spots where you can do 'double cat tracks' if you build a big enough kicker and have the guts.

Above: *Ishibashi Hajime dominates the Sprite Sessions with a boned out indy.*

NEW ZEALAND

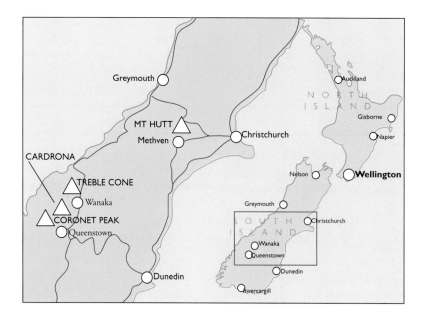

New Zealand is a tiny country of about 3.4 million people and made up of two main islands: the North Island and the South Island. Over recent years, the focus on snowboarding in New Zealand has become more intense as the snowboarding media seem to be taking plenty of interest. And rightfully so, because there is a lot on offer in New Zealand. However, don't expect the ultra-modern resorts and lift systems that you will find in Europe or North America. New Zealand is a little bit behind the rest of the world when it comes to high-tech lift systems, mostly because the country doesn't really have the population to support it. The bonus is that New Zealand has some beautiful mountain ranges that provide some of the most incredible snowboarding terrain around.

The North Island of New Zealand has a handful of resorts, most of which are situated on the still-active volcano known as Mt Ruapehu. The rest of New Zealand's ski areas are situated in the Southern Alps on the South Island. There are more than 22 snowboard destinations in the South Island. Most are privately owned club fields. These offer little more than one or two rope tows and endless powder. The five largest resorts on the South Island attract the vast majority of snowgoers in New Zealand and offer snowboarders the comforts that can make your snowboarding trip perfect. These resorts are slowly but surely making a concerted effort to upgrade old lifts with the latest in lift technology. And all of the 'big five' resorts are offering snowboarders fantastic halfpipe and snowboard parks, having recognised the big dollars in the snowboarder market.

SNOW CONDITIONS IN NEW ZEALAND

Despite the fact that New Zealand is known as the land of the long white cloud, snowboard conditions are more often than not sunny during winter. This is because the cloud is attracted to taller surrounding peaks that dominate the Southern Alps. New Zealand's location, deep in the South Pacific, means that it has a reasonably cool climate during winter. In general, both islands lack the extreme temperatures that are experienced by Northern Hemisphere landmasses which lie at a similar latitude. Occasionally it does snow down to near sea level in winter.

The North Island tends to get battered more by heavy storms, which can bring big dumps to the snowfields. However, rain is also likely due to its closer proximity to the equator. Weather conditions in the South Island snowfields can vary greatly. Resorts in the north of the South Island, such as

Opposite: *Richard Hegarty upside down above Lake Wanaka. Photo—Gavin O'Toole.*

Mt Hutt, tend to get the best deal when it comes to consistency of snowfalls. However, although they receive less snow, resorts in the south, such as Treble Cone, Cardrona and Coronet Peak, generally get lighter and drier snow.

When snowboarding in New Zealand, don't expect the regular 60 cm (2 ft) dumps often experienced in Europe and USA. However, often you will wake up to find a fresh 15–30 cm (6–12 in) of powder. Overall, the best powder in New Zealand is found by using a helicopter.

In this resort guide we are going to take you through the four major resorts on the South Island – Mt Hutt, Cardrona, Treble Cone and Coronet Peak.

ACCOMMODATION

Most of the skifields in New Zealand are situated within 30 minutes' drive of a small town. There is ample, cheap accommodation in these towns. There is virtually no on-mountain accommodation in New Zealand ski areas. Accordingly, it is necessary to drive, catch a bus or hitch your way to the resort each day. Nonetheless, the resort towns offer a good variety of accommodation and places to eat.

New Zealand is very affordable when compared to Europe and Japan, making for the perfect snow-bum lifestyle.

GETTING TO THE NEW ZEALAND RESORTS

If you are traveling to the resorts in the South Island, your best bet is to fly into Christchurch. From here you basically have three options to get to the resorts – catch a bus, hire a car or hire a motorhome. Hiring a motorhome is the cheapest and most effective way of seeing all the resorts of the Southern Alps. Most resort towns have large motorhome parks. Further, the motorhomes run on diesel, which is cheap in New Zealand.

Opposite: *The mountains of New Zealand are unique in their lack of vegetation and their volcanic origins.*
Below: *The typical way of enjoying the spectacular New Zealand scenery, a Maui motorhome.*

MT HUTT
NEW ZEALAND

STATISTICS

Elevations	(m)	(ft)
Top:	2075	6808
Base:	1585	5200
Vertical Drop:	490	1607

Lifts	
Surface Lifts:	8
Double Chairs:	0
Triple Chairs:	1
Quad Chairs – Fixed Grip:	1
Quad Chairs – Express:	0
Six Chairs – Express:	0
Gondolas:	0
Cable Cars:	0
Funiculars:	0
Total:	10

Contact Details
Phone:	+64 3 308 5074
Fax:	+64 3 308 5076
Email Address:	service@mthutt.w.nz
Internet Site:	www.mthutt.co.nz

RESORT REVIEW

Mt Hutt is one of New Zealand's best-developed resorts. It lies about one hour's drive southwest of Christchurch. Mt Hutt has one of the largest verticals in New Zealand and some of the best powder bowls in the country. However, it often experiences some very harsh weather conditions. During these times it is impossible to reach the resort, as the road passes over an extremely exposed and dangerous ridge.

Mt Hutt has invested heavily in snow-making, and pumps out tons of snow onto the main trails as required. Although it does have an extensive snow-making system, Mt Hutt receives some of the heaviest snow-falls amongst all the resorts in the South Island. One of the major benefits of the snow-making is that it allows Mt Hutt to be the first resort open for winter in the Southern Hemisphere. It consistently opens in mid-May. Further, the snow-making system feeds snow into the Mt Hutt pipe.

Mt Hutt has a small base lodge and amenities area, which has a cafeteria and restaurant. It also offers an extensive ski and snowboard school and a Burton Tech Centre where you can demo all the latest Burton gear. As in other New Zealand resorts, the lift system at Mt Hutt is relatively antiquated. Lifts are either fixed grip or t-bars.

Left: *Bear Agushi blowing minds with a backside air in an early season Mt Hutt pipe.*

TERRAIN

Above: *A lone rider enjoying the powder on top of one of Mt Hutt's many ridges. Photo—Gavin O'Toole.*

FREERIDING

Mt Hutt is a huge mountain, offering some of New Zealand's best freeriding terrain. There are long steeps and big rocks. As Mt Hutt receives some of New Zealand's biggest dumps, the powder riding here can be amazing. Everything is on offer at Mt Hutt, ranging from long powder runs to lengthy groomed runs. There are also plenty of big cliffs and easily accessible backcountry for those willing to hike. Also, a heli-boarding service operates from the resort and you can purchase single ride runs.

Early Morning: Most of Hutt is in the shade in the mornings, so the snow can take a little while to soften up on hardpack days. To avoid the ice early in the day, head up to the summit and traverse to skiers' left. It is not only the first to be exposed to the sun, but it is steep and fun for freeriding.

Bad Weather: When the wind is strong, stick to the runs below the car park. Your best bet is to ride the triple chair to the mid station. If it's a complete white-out, you may as well head back down to one of the cool pubs in Methven. If you still want to ride, try the pipe.

Beginners: Head straight for the double chair which accesses a long, gentle green run. For the more adventurous beginners, try the little hits scattered all over this run.

Avoiding Crowds: On busy days, go straight for the Triple Chair. The Quad Chair leaves straight out of the base of Mt Hutt and thus gets extremely busy. During school holidays and weekends, be prepared to wait at least 15-20 minutes at the Quad Chair.

FREESTYLE

Halfpipes: Mt Hutt was not one of the first resorts in New Zealand to embrace snowboarding, but the mountain has seen a major a transformation in recent years. Mt Hutt now offers one of the best pipes in New Zealand. Earthworks have ensured that the Mt Hutt pipe can be ready early on in the season. The resort has employed a crew of riders to shape and maintain the pipe. The beauty of the Hutt pipe is that it is far less crowded than the pipes at Cardrona. Further, unlike Cardrona, when the pipe isn't going off, there is plenty of brilliant freeriding available. However, the major drawback of the Hutt pipe is that it is shaped with a blade rather than with a proper shaping machine such as a Pipe Dragon. Therefore, the condition of the pipe is not guaranteed and often it can be downright terrible.

Snowboard Parks: Unfortunately there is not much on offer at Mt Hutt. Whilst the pipe is usually great, the park is average and you're better off building your own kickers.

Below: *The Mt Hutt Base Lodge on a superb winter's day.*

CARDRONA
NEW ZEALAND

STATISTICS

Elevations	(m)	(ft)
Top:	1894	6214
Base:	1504	4934
Vertical Drop:	390	1279

Lifts	
Surface Lifts:	2
Double Chairs:	1
Triple Chairs:	0
Quad Chairs – Fixed Grip:	2
Quad Chairs – Express:	0
Six Chairs – Express:	0
Gondolas:	0
Cable Cars:	0
Funiculars:	0
Total:	5

Contact Details

Phone:	+64 3 443 7341
Fax:	+64 3 443 8818
Email Address:	info@cardrona.co.nz
Internet Site:	www.cardrona.co.nz

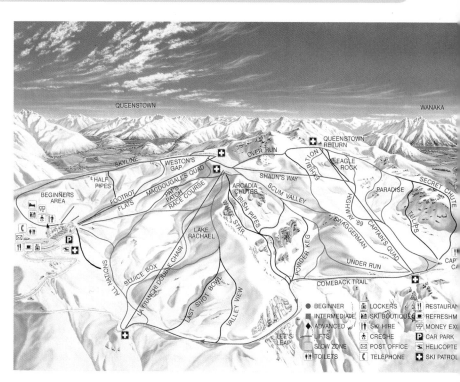

RESORT REVIEW

Cardrona skifield is a 30-40 minute drive from Wanaka on New Zealand's South Island and has traditionally been the home of freestyle snowboarding in New Zealand. The resort has been far ahead of its competitors in offering the very best in snowboard facilities, such as halfpipes and snowboard parks.

Cardrona is not a huge resort by international standards. However, it does make extremely good use of its terrain.

It does not have a snow-making system, which has occasionally been a problem in lean seasons. However, Cardrona tends to get more snow than some of its neighboring resorts. It is able to offer riders, especially freestylers, an extraordinary snowboarding experience. Due to its excellent freestyle facilities, hundreds of Japanese riders make Cardrona their home during the Southern Hemisphere winter.

The resort has a modern day lodge facility. What really lets the mountain down is its lift system. All lifts are fixed grip and slow. Another major problem is the weather. The resort is often plagued by fog and wind from which there is no escape, as there are no trees at Cardrona.

Right: *Frontside air by a touring Japanese rider in the Cardrona Pipe. Photo—Gavin O'Toole.*

TERRAIN

FREERIDING

The terrain at Cardrona is flat when compared to Treble Cone, Coronet Peak and other Kiwi resorts. It is largely a beginner and intermediate mountain. The natural terrain offers little for freestylers, and for freeriders there is very little in the way of steep powder runs. However, for those who enjoy dropping cliffs, Cardrona is the place to be. The resort offers more in-bounds cliffs and drops than most other New Zealand resorts. Even the best freeriders would be scared at what they can easily find at Cardrona. Apart from the cliffs, the in-bounds terrain at Cardrona is boring. It simply doesn't offer the terrain that can be found at Treble Cone and Coronet Peak. However, the hard-booters out there shouldn't be too disappointed with the reasonable-length groomed runs Cardrona offers.

Beginners: Beginners would have plenty of fun at Cardrona with a vast range of groomed runs with friendly gradients to learn and progress on.

Intermediates and Advanced: Head out to Captain's Basin for some of the better riding.

FREESTYLE

Halfpipes: Cardrona is arguably the home of halfpipe riding in New Zealand, with at least two halfpipes (sometimes there are up to four pipes) available for most of the season. In addition, all Cardrona's pipes are dug out of the earth and they are all shaped by a Pipe Master. The major benefit of the Pipe Master is that it is able to provide prefect transitions in low snow conditions. Unlike most resorts, which place priority on providing groomed trails for the mass market, Cardrona places an emphasis on providing halfpipes and snowboard parks. Each pipe caters for people of different abilities, ranging from beginner to pro. When there are fewer than three pipes open, they tend to get very crowded, and you have to be a master at snaking if you want to get a ride.

Above: *Cardrona is famous for its halfpipes and hosting the New Zealand Snowboard Championships.*

Snowboard Parks: Not only does Cardrona make excellent pipes, it also invests plenty of time in its snowboard parks. This certainly helps the resort make up for its lack of natural hits. The park generally consists of an array of tabletops and spines, varying in size to suit all standards.

Natural Hits: If you look hard you will find some natural hits around Captain's Basin. However, you are better off sticking to the pipes and parks or building your own kicker in the easily accessible backcountry.

Above: *The back side of Cardrona is the perfect place to build kickers. Mouse Beuchat enjoying one of his creations.*

Above: *The continuing search for powder in Captain's Basin pays off for this snowboarder.*

TREBLE CONE
NEW ZEALAND

STATISTICS

Elevations	(m)	(ft)
Top:	1860	6102
Base:	1200	3937
Vertical Drop:	660	2165

Lifts	
Surface Lifts:	3
Double Chairs:	1
Triple Chairs:	0
Quad Chairs – Fixed Grip:	0
Quad Chairs – Express:	0
Six Chairs – Express:	1
Gondolas:	0
Cable Cars:	0
Funiculars:	0
Total:	5

Contact Details

Phone:	+64 3 443 7443
Fax:	+64 3 443 8401
Email Address:	tcinfo@treblecone.co.nz
Internet Site:	www.newzealand.com/TrebleCone

RESORT REVIEW

Once upon a time, this not-so-well-known New Zealand resort was a club field, and contained the very basics in resort infrastructure. Today, Treble Cone (or TC, as it is known to the locals) is vastly different. With extensive snow-making, grooming machines, halfpipes and high-speed lifts, Treble Cone is arguably the best snowboarding destination in New Zealand.

Principally dominated by intermediate to advanced terrain, Treble Cone has been expanding its runs to cater for beginners. Perched high up in the Harris Mountains just outside Lake Wanaka and Mt Aspiring, Treble Cone is accessed by one of the sketchiest roads in New Zealand. Hairpin follows hairpin and beside the road, the mountain drops sharply away to the valley floor, some 1,000 m (3,300 ft) below.

Treble Cone has a medium-sized day lodge that is a great place to grab a snack or just hang out. However, the best thing about Treble Cone's infrastructure is its six-person high-speed chair, which accesses one of the largest verticals in New Zealand – 660 m (2,165 ft).

Left: *Andrew McNamara in the Treble Cone backcountry – deaf, dumb and MUTE.*

TERRAIN

FREERIDING

Treble Cone has definitely got some of New Zealand's best freeriding and freestyle terrain. The mountain is littered with natural tabletops and rock drops. A run directly under the high-speed chair enables a rider to get anywhere from 5 to 12 hits off the cat track and other natural rollers. On a powder day, TC goes off. Although not super extreme, the runs are some of the longest in New Zealand. TC gets smaller crowds compared to other resorts, meaning that powder can stay untracked for longer. TC is also home to some of the best gully runs in New Zealand. The gullies contain awesome quarterpipes, hips and spines.

If you're after real steeps, there isn't much on offer in-bounds at TC. But if you take a 30-minute hike directly above the Summit T-bar, what you will find will make your hair stand on end. Cliffs, chutes and any other type of terrain that an extreme rider would fancy are all accessible from the peak.

Powder Turns: When the powder comes, the place to be is the Summit T-bar. Here you will find some of the best powder bowls and gullies in New Zealand and the runs will melt your thighs.

Early Morning: Sundance Bowl, on skiers' right of the mountain, has the most sun in the early morning, so it is a good place to hit for some warm-up runs.

Bad Weather: When it's windy at TC, there aren't many places to hide. However, the gullies off the Summit T-bar usually offer the best protection. If it's a white-out, you'll struggle to see much as there aren't any trees for definition.

Above: *Aussie Sasha Ryzy enjoys some Kiwi air in Treble Cone. Photo—Gavin O'Toole.*

Beginners: Triple Treat, the cat track under the six-person high-speed chair, is the best run for beginners. It winds its way all the way down the front face of TC.

Avoiding Crowds: Due to the lack of lift capacity at Treble Cone, occasionally the lift lines get a little crowded. However the six-person high-speed is fast, and you'll never queue for more than 5-10 minutes. When the powder has been tracked, head to Sundance and Powder Bowls as these areas are expansive with plenty of hidden gullies and they often hold powder days after the last dump. Stay away from the Summit T-bar on busy days – you'll probably queue for up to 30 minutes.

FREESTYLE

Halfpipes and Snowboard Parks: TC doesn't specialize in halfpipes and snowboard parks. Most riders go to TC for the natural freeriding terrain. However, the mountain does offer a halfpipe that has been excavated out of dirt to ensure that it is operational even when the snow cover is bad. The pipe is shaped with a blade and a pipe-shaping machine. It is rarely in A-grade condition, so it is far better to go to either Cardrona or Coronet Peak if you are after some quality pipe action. The natural terrain at TC offers awesome kickers and windlips so you can get some serious air time. A super fun run is Triple Treat, which offers tons of little hips and lips for practicing backside and frontside re-entry airs.

Left: *Bear Agushi worked out quickly that the summit bowls of Treble Cone hold all the goods.*

CORONET PEAK
NEW ZEALAND

STATISTICS

Elevations	(m)	(ft)
Top:	1649	5410
Base:	1200	3937
Vertical Drop:	449	1473

Lifts	
Surface Lifts:	1
Double Chairs:	1
Triple Chairs:	1
Quad Chairs – Fixed Grip:	0
Quad Chairs – Express:	1
Six Chairs – Express:	0
Gondolas:	0
Cable Cars:	0
Funiculars:	0
Total:	4

Contact Details

Phone:	+64 3 442 4620
Fax:	+64 3 442 4624
Email Address:	service@coronetpeak.co.nz
Internet Site:	www.coronetpeak.co.nz

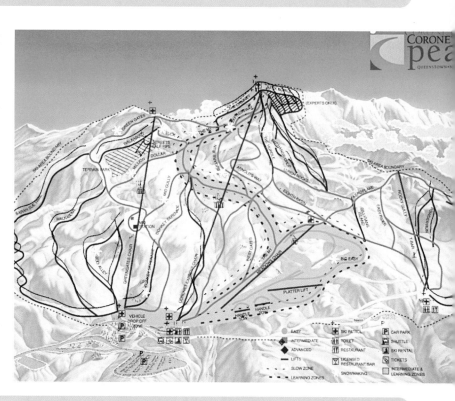

RESORT REVIEW

Coronet Peak is probably New Zealand's premier tourist destination for international skiers and snowboarders. The major reason for this is its proximity to Queenstown – only a 25-minute drive. Queenstown is the adventure capital of New Zealand. People come from all around the globe to the 102 m (336 ft) Pipeline Bungie. There are also heaps of package deals available for travelers to Queenstown, so the slopes of Coronet Peak are probably some of the busiest in New Zealand.

Coronet Peak has one of the best lift systems in New Zealand, with a high-speed quad rising from the base lodge to the very peak of Coronet. From this lift you can access just about all the terrain that Coronet has to offer. Coronet lacks good natural snowfalls, so it relies heavily on manmade snow. There is extensive snow-making throughout the resort. What Coronet lacks in natural snow, though, it makes up for in the terrain and snowboard facilities available to riders.

WEATHER AND SNOW

Coronet Peak tends to get the least powder of all the New Zealand resorts. The storms that bring the most snow here come directly from the south (ie Antarctica). And when they come, they can bring some decent snowfalls. However, don't expect to see the same quantities of snow as are received further north, at resorts such as Mt Hutt and the Canterbury club fields.

Above: *No matter how bad the weather, you just have to go big. Mouse Beuchat flying headlong into some imposing clouds above Queenstown.*

TERRAIN

FREERIDING

The snowboarding terrain at Coronet Peak is simply awesome. Coronet is just one massive snowboard park. The resort offers long, groomed, hardpack pistes for the beginners and intermediates, and rolling, tabletop-style terrain for freestylers. The in-bounds terrain is characterized by gullies and small bowls that line the main ridges. If you are after serious steeps and chutes, you'll have to walk a few minutes out-of-bounds (which you are allowed to do in New Zealand without losing your pass). The in-bounds terrain is more suited to the freestyle rider who enjoys natural terrain park-style riding and the intermediate freerider who likes long cruising bowls.

Cliffs and Chutes: Take a very short hike out behind of the summit of Mt Coronet. There you will find some sick chutes and freeriding terrain. The only bad thing is the hike out – it's a tough uphill climb, but it is well worth it.

Early Morning: Most of Coronet Peak is in the shade in the mornings, so the snow can take a little while to soften up. However, head over to the t-bar far on skiers' left of the mountain for the best early morning terrain. Not only is it the first to be exposed to the sun, but it has some nice natural hits.

Bad Weather: When the wind is strong, head straight for the t-bar and surrounding terrain – it is more sheltered than the rest due to its lower altitude. Or head to the top left of the t-bar and into the dunes where you can build a nice wind-protected kicker. If it's a white-out, there aren't many places to go because of the lack of trees to give you visual definition.

Above: *Richard Hegarty cranking out a powder turn in the upper elevations of Coronet Peak. Photo—Gavin O'Toole.*

Perhaps try the pipe or the day lodge. On these days, it's all the same wherever you are on the mountain.

Beginners: Head straight for the double chair which accesses a relatively long green run. For the more adventurous beginners, try the high-speed quad and enjoy the long groomed trail to the base lodge.

Avoiding Crowds: On busy days, go straight for the Triple Chair or the t-bar. The high-speed quad is the first to get busy on school holidays and weekends. Once you take these lifts, the terrain is so abundant that you'll be bound to find untracked snow or at least fewer moguls and people.

FREESTYLE

Halfpipes and Snowboard Parks: In recent years, Coronet Peak has committed to snowboarding in a big way and has upped the ante on the traditional home of freestyle riding in New Zealand, Cardrona. Coronet Peak offers two halfpipes, side by side, both of which have been excavated out of the earth. This means that the pipes can be operational even on a less than 20 cm (8 in) base. It appears that the management of Coronet are fully focused on the snowboarding dollar and this means better facilities for all riders. Unlike in the past, where the only freestyle riding at Coronet was cruising the off-piste slopes, nowadays the pipe and park provide as good, if not better, riding for the freestyler. Coronet has recently invested in a Pipe Shaper. This will ensure that the shape of the pipe is more consistent.

JAPAN

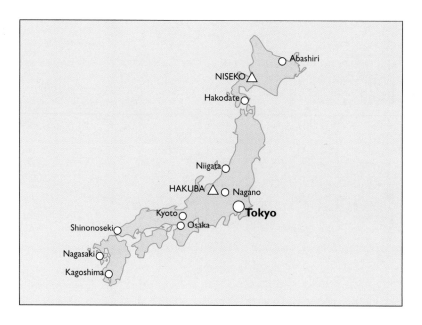

Although skiing has existed in Japan since the beginning of the 20th century, it is only since the early 1980s (the so-called bubble era) that the Japanese have fallen in love with snowboarding. The result is that more money has been flowing into the Japanese ski industry than anywhere else in the world. With a population of around 125 million, the market for skiing and snowboarding is huge. As the Japanese have a tendency to embrace the latest trends with gusto, snowboarding has taken off in a huge way in Japan. However, some resorts still only give limited access to snowboarders, with the steepest sections of many resorts often being closed to snowboarders.

Since the beginning of the Japanese ski boom, the number of Japanese resorts has exploded. There are over 700 ski resorts throughout the Japanese archipelago. With its massive investment in resort infrastructure, Japan now boasts around ten world-class resorts that rank with the likes of Vail, Verbier, Tignes and Ischgl. Japan is now a recognised and highly recommended destination for the traveling snowboarder. Japan's success in establishing itself as a major destination for skiing and snowboarding has been reflected in the fact that it has hosted two Winter Olympic Games. The first was held in 1972 on the Hidaka Mountains of Hokkaido. Most recently, the 1998 Winter Games were held around Nagano. These were the first Games to include snowboarding.

The majority of Japanese resorts are located either on the northern island of Hokkaido or on Japan's main island of Honshu. On Honshu, most resorts are built in the Japan Alps, a rugged mountain range that runs like a spine down the island, separating the west coast from the east coast. The Japan Alps are certainly spectacular, rising over 3,000 m (9,900 ft) above sea level. The traditional Japanese name for these mountains is the Hida Mountains, but British explorers were so reminded of the Swiss Alps when they saw the mountain range that they named it the Japan Alps. Colloquially, the range is still known as the Japan Alps. In terms of steepness and snowfall, these mountains are easily comparable with the Swiss or French Alps. The Japan Alps and the Hidaka Mountains receive more snow than almost any other place in the world with similar latitude.

With Japan's population and its love affair with skiing and snowboarding, it is not surprising that the slopes become extremely packed. In fact, on weekends and public holidays there are so many people on the slopes that you may as well be in the Tokyo subway. However, while the slopes may be

Opposite: *Damo Liddy at home in the light, dry powder of Kijimadaira.*

Above: *The mountains of Hakuba are painted pink as the sun reveals a gorgeous day.*

crowded, the lift lines are typically not long. Why? Because of the massive investment in the Japanese ski industry, there are usually several lifts servicing one area of the resort.

The 700 or so resorts in Japan are located in five geographical clusters: Hokkaido, Tohoku, Joetsu, Shinetsu and Hakuba. In this guide we shall review resorts at three of these clusters – Hokkaido, Shinetsu and Hakuba.

TRANSPORT

To Japan: Most major airlines fly into Narita, which is the major airport, about 1.5 hours out of Tokyo. It is highly recommended that you use a travel agent that specialises in Japanese travel.

Around Japan: Don't even bother trying to hire a car in Japan. Not only is it damn expensive to rent, but petrol is expensive and there are toll roads everywhere. Furthermore, traffic is heavy and road signs are not always in English. Parking at the resort is also a hassle. Buses and trains are a more viable option.

Japan's public transport system is equal to any in Europe. It is so large and sophisticated that it just about reaches every corner of the Japanese archipelago. You literally do not need a car to go anywhere in Japan.

Two types of trains provide access to the mountains from the major cities. The bullet trains (Shinkansen) are by far the fastest and most expensive trains in Japan. If a bullet train is not available there are usually express trains (usually known as Azusas and Super Azusas) running to the resorts. The cheapest way to use the Japanese train system is to purchase a rail pass. If you are traveling to a resort, the best pass to buy is a flexible pass that allows unlimited travel for a specified number of non-consecutive days over a one-month period on most of Japan's major trains. You can buy rail passes at most of the large train stations and airports.

Although buses do operate from the major cities to the resorts, the best plan of attack is to use the train system to get to the resort and then use the local bus system to get around. Catching buses during the day from the major cities to the resorts is certainly a slower and more frustrating affair than catching the bullet or express trains. However, if you catch an overnight bus it can be a cheap and efficient alternative to the train system.

WEATHER IN JAPAN

Japan is famous for its large and consistent snowfalls. When the cold, dry winter air moves down from Siberia, and heads south over Japan, it meets the moist air moving up from the Pacific. The resulting precipitation causes Japan's vast range of mountains to get smothered in meters of quality snow.

HINTS AND TIPS

- Be polite and respect the Japanese culture. The Japanese are very friendly people and are always willing to help foreign travelers.
- Take a long board to Japan – it is essential for those huge snowfalls that are common from December through to March, especially in Hokkaido.
- Don't expect to use your credit card with ease, especially in the resorts. Although Japan may be technologically advanced in many areas, financial service is not one of them. So be prepared and bring cash.
- Make sure you try an onsen. An onsen is a large bathing pool filled with hot natural spring water from below the mountains. Apparently the water is filled with minerals that have great healing properties. Whatever is in the water, it certainly revitalizes your body and is a great way way to end an awesome day of riding the powder or the pipe. Tradition dictates that you bathe naked. However, there are separate men's and women's onsens.
- Try to avoid snowboarding on weekends and public holidays as the slopes become extremely packed.
- Unlike the typical green, blue, red, black system used by resorts elsewhere in the world to grade runs, Japanese resorts have not adopted a consistent grading methodology. So beware before you head off down a blue run that it may turn out to be a double black.

Above: *The sun goes down but Bear Agushi keeps riding in the Land of the Rising Sun.*

HAKUBA
JAPAN

OVERVIEW

Hakuba, which hosted some of the events for 1998 Winter Olympics, is probably one of the best-known ski destinations in Japan. The name Hakuba literally means 'white horse'. The name comes from a patch of glacier snow that lasts all year round; when viewed from the valley floor, it looks like a horse. Seven major resorts stretch over 30 km (19 miles) along the Hakuba Valley. At the southern end is the medium-sized resort of Sun Alpina. In the centre are the resorts of Goryu-Toomi, Hakuba 47 and Hakuba Highlands. At the northern end of this magnificent valley are the three sister resorts of Happo-one, Iwatake and Tsumgaike. Although each resort has its own village, the main village is the town of Hakuba. All the villages are connected by buses so if you are staying in Hakuba you can get from resort to resort.

Hakuba is home to some of the highest peaks in Japan, with Mt Shiroumadake towering 2,932 m (9,675 ft) above Hakuba village. Both Goryu and Happo-one have peaks over 1,500 m (4,950 ft). It is a shame that the resorts in the Hakuba Valley do not reach higher elevations since there are over 50 peaks in the area above 2,500 m (8,250 ft).

In Hakuba, it is almost required that you visit one of the many onsens in the area. An onsen is the perfect way to relax the body and restore the energy after a hard day of riding the powder or the pipe.

WEATHER IN HAKUBA

Siberian storms, rolling in off the Sea of Japan, bring consistent snowfalls to the Hakuba region. The quantities of snow are not as large as in Hokkaido, and blue-sky days occur more often. The climate is generally temperate, with few extreme days during the season, unlike what can be experienced in Hokkaido.

ACCOMMODATION IN HAKUBA

The best place to stay in the Hakuba Valley is in the town of Hakuba rather than one of villages below the resorts. This is because Hakuba has all the facilities of a modern resort town – supermarkets, convenience stores, fast-food outlets, restaurants and plenty of accommodation.

Below left: *Bear Agushi feels privileged launching a backside 360 above the picturesque Hakuba Valley.*
Below: *The mountains of Hakuba dwarf this classic Japanese lodge.*

GORYU-TOOMI & HAKUBA 47
JAPAN

STATISTICS

Elevations	(m)	(ft)
Top:	1676	5498
Base:	763	2503
Vertical Drop:	913	2995

Lifts	
Surface Lifts:	0
Double Chairs:	12
Triple Chairs:	0
Quad Chairs – Fixed Grip:	2
Quad Chairs – Express:	4
Six Chairs – Express:	0
Gondolas:	2
Cable Cars:	0
Funiculars:	0
Total:	20

20 lifts are available in the Goryu Toomi/Hakuba 47 area

Contact Details
Phone:	+81 261 75 2101
Fax:	+81 261 75 3926
Internet Site:	www.cnet-nf.ne.jp/goryu47

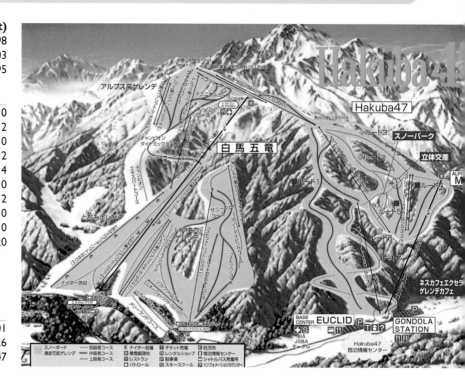

RESORT REVIEW

Goryu-Toomi and Hakuba 47 recently combined to form the resort of Hakuba-Goryu. The amalgamation of the two resorts created a resort that is one of the largest in Japan, with two gondolas, four high-speed chairlifts, 14 other lifts and over 100 hectares (40 acres) of skiable terrain. The Goryu base area sits below a magnificent open bowl with jagged peaks rising up to Mt Goryu (2,814 m/9,285 ft). The base lodge at Goryu is also impressive. It is a three-story modern structure that comprises restaurants and shops and is probably one of the best base lodges in the Hakuba region. Surprisingly, the basement of the base lodge contains a large open room where you can sleep on the floor for 1,000 yen a night. This is certainly the snowboarding bum's heaven.

The great thing about Hakuba-Goryu is that it is extremely snowboard-friendly. It is one of the few mountains in the Hakuba region that actually allows snowboarding all over the mountain, including the high alpine regions and the steep sections. This commitment to snowboarding is also reflected in the halfpipe set-up. Hakuba-Goryu have a special hut located below the halfpipe complete with seats, music and vending machines that actually serve hot coffee.

Right: *Light and dry, that's how it comes at Hakuba 47. Mouse Beuchat puts down yet another bottomless turn.*

TERRAIN

FREERIDING

Before you keep reading, you must remember one critical point: riding off-piste at Goryu-Toomi and Hakuba 47 is strictly illegal, and if you are caught off the marked trails, you will lose your pass and may be taken by the police. Having said this, the best riding at this resort is often in the trees, so you will have to make your own risk assessment about deciding where to ride.

Hakuba-Goryu consists of four areas – Toomi Gerende, Alps Daira Gerende, Iimori Gerende and Hakuba 47. Toomi Gerende is a great beginner slope just above the Goryu base lodge. It is the perfect area to learn to snowboard. Iimori Gerende is also a good beginner or intermediate area. It is located on skiers' left of the Goryu base lodge. The Iimori area actually has its own base lodge and car parking so there is no real need to go to Goryu if you want to ride at Iimori. The halfpipe is also located at Iimori, and it is probably one of the best halfpipes in the Hakuba region. If you are after steep, fast tree runs, 47 is the place to be. If you want some high alpine, above-tree line skiing, you will have to head up to the Alps Daira Gerende.

The substantial vertical at Hakuba-Goryu (close to 1 km [0.6 mile]), combined with the numerous pockets of trees, make it one of the premier freeriding mountains in the Hakuba Valley. Of course, like most Japanese mountains, it lacks the gnarly chutes and cliffs that are found in many of the top freeriding mountains in the USA and Europe. Any lines directly under the Line D Pair Lift and the Line C Quad Lift represent some of the best tree runs at Hakuba-Goryu. However, the trees are pretty tight so make sure you are wearing goggles, unless you want to lose an eye.

For some steep terrain, head up the Goryu Toomi Telecabin and then take the Alps No. 1 Lift to the peak of Goryu. If you get a chance, stop and check out the view from up here. It is an amazing sight – jagged rocky peaks, the backbone of the Japanese Alps, stretching out both north south, as far as the eye can see. One of the steepest runs at Goryu extends from the top of the Alps No. 1 Lift all the way back down to the base of the gondola – a thigh-burning 1 km (0.6 mile) of vertical. In typical Japanese fashion, the run is given the corny name of Champion Expert. The major problem with this run is that it is churned into moguls fairly rapidly, so the best time to hit it is early morning.

Powder Turns: Good powder can usually be found in the trees below the Line D Pair Lift at Hakuba 47. Another good alternative is the clump of trees between Routes 2 and 3. There is an awesome natural gully in these trees that always holds good powder.

Early Morning: Hit the Champion Expert Run directly under the Goryu Toomi Telecabin.

Bad Weather: In bad weather it is best to take to the trees directly under the Line D Pair Lift. The trees here offer good protection and the elevation is relatively low, ensuring good visibility.

Above: *Damo Liddy gets all tangled up with a roast beef in the Goryu pipe.*

Avoiding Crowds: The best way to avoid the crowds is to stay away from the Goryu Toomi Telecabin during peak times, ie 9 am to 12:30 pm. Hakuba 47 tends to be less crowded than the Goryu area of the mountain, so it is a good choice on a busy day.

Beginners: The slopes around Toomi Gerende are the best for beginners. An alternative is to try the Panorama course at the top of the Telecabin Gondola.

FREESTYLE

Snowboard Parks and Halfpipes: The halfpipe is the major hangout for freestylers at this resort. The halfpipe is located in the Iimori area of the mountain. If you drive up to the Iimori car park you can almost see the pipe from the base lodge. The pipe is not long, but it has excellent shape and transition and just enough vertical to allow you to boost some sizeable airs. Hakuba-Goryu's commitment to maintaining the pipe is demonstrated by the fact that they close the pipe between 12 pm and 1 pm each day for hand maintenance and salting when required. It is shaped a few times per week with a Pipe Dragon.

HAPPO-ONE
JAPAN

STATISTICS

Elevations	(m)	(ft)
Top:	1831	6007
Base:	760	2493
Vertical Drop:	1071	3513

Lifts	
Surface Lifts:	0
Double Chairs:	26
Triple Chairs:	4
Quad Chairs – Fixed Grip:	3
Quad Chairs – Express:	0
Six Chairs – Express:	0
Gondolas:	1
Cable Cars:	0
Funiculars:	0
Total:	34

Contact Details	
Phone:	+81 261 72 3066

RESORT REVIEW

Happo-one is the king of the Hakuba Valley. It is a big mountain by both Japanese and world standards: over a kilometer of vertical, a fancy gondola, three high-speed quads and 30 other lifts across some 175 hectares (71 acres) of skiable terrain. The place is not small by any stretch of the imagination. To accommodate the 1998 Nagano Winter Olympics, the facilities at Happo-one received a substantial upgrade, including a new base lodge. The fact that Happo-one hosted the men's Olympic downhill in 1998 provides some indication of the gradient and length of the terrain. It also has one of the highest lifted points in the Hakuba Valley at 1,831 m (6,042 ft).

Although there is an immense amount of terrain at Happo-one, there are two main problems with the resort. First, snowboarders are only allowed on the lower portions of the mountain. The high alpine areas of Happo are not accessible by snowboarders until late in the season thanks to resort regulations. This significantly cuts down the amount of vertical available to snowboarders. Second, Happo is extremely popular with the Japanese, and this means only one thing – crowds. It is the cool and hip place for the younger generation Japanese to hang out.

Right: *Happo-one equals trees, powder and dropoffs. Damo Liddy loves his new-found home with a stalefish off a nice rock.*

TERRAIN

FREERIDING

As with other resorts in the Hakuba Valley, riding off-piste at Happo-one is strictly illegal, and if you are caught you will lose your pass. The decision is really up to you – pass or powder.

Although not all of Happo-one is open to snowboarders, the terrain available is still pretty amazing. After all, 80% of its runs are for intermediate/advanced riders. If you want beginner terrain you're better off heading to Hakuba Highlands or Iwatake. Unlike many other Japanese resorts, Happo-one has some interesting natural obstacles. There are small drops, cliff bands and cornices. There are even some small gullies and log slides through the trees. The best thing about the natural terrain at Happo-one is that it is located just off the ski runs, so you pretty much have it all to yourself since the Japanese prefer to stick to the groomed.

The best freeriding terrain accessible to snowboarders is located off the Sakakitaone Quad Chair. An excellent tree run is located just to skiers' left of the Sakakitaone Quad. This tree run has a nice gully, a log slide and even a good-sized cornice. Alternatively, head far over to skiers' right of the Sakakitaone Quad and follow the tree run down here. There are some avalanche barriers along this run.

Powder Turns: A little-known tree run is located on the back side of Happo-one. Take the Sakakitaone Quad and traverse hard under the Kitane Triple Chair until you reach the edge of the ski run, then simply drop into the trees. This run is seldom tracked because of the lengthy traverse out to it. However, it is well worth it, since there is some nice rolling terrain. You will need to traverse hard right when you near the bottom of the run. Another good alternative is to drop directly off the base of the Kitane Triple, into the trees.

Early Morning: As snowboarders cannot ride the top portions of Happo-one, there are not really any good early morning runs, as most of the lower parts of the mountain are in the shade.

Bad Weather: The trees around the Sakakitaone Quad provide excellent shelter from the weather.

Avoiding Crowds: Happo, particularly the Adam Gondola, becomes very crowded on weekends. Further, as Happo has so many lifts servicing the same runs, the problem is compounded. Happo is not really a place you want to visit on a weekend. You would be better off getting drunk in a Japanese karaoke bar.

Beginners: The Sakibana slope has several good, short, beginner runs.

FREESTYLE

As snowboarding is fairly restricted at Happo-one they do not provide any freestyle facilities. If you want pipes and parks, you are beter off going to Hakuba Highlands or Hakuba-Goryu.

Above: *Happo-one was the site of the 1998 Olympic downhill and is one of the most famous resorts in Japan, thanks to its sheer size.*

Above: *Look closely – Mouse Beuchat is concealed deep in the trees of Happo-one.*

HAKUBA IWATAKE
JAPAN

Elevations	(m)	(ft)
Top:	1289	4229
Base:	730	2395
Vertical Drop:	559	1834

Lifts	
Lifts:	23
Total:	23

Contact Details	
Phone:	+81 261 72 2780

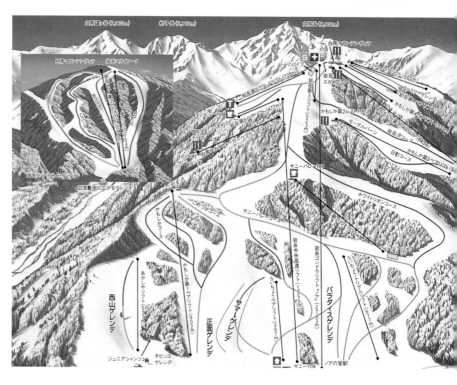

RESORT REVIEW

Iwatake is the sister resort to Happo-one. The same companies operate both lift systems. Although Iwatake is not as large as Happo and the terrain is not quite as challenging, it does have two big advantages over Happo. First, snowboarders are allowed on all marked trails (pistes) on the mountain. This certainly opens up the amount of freeriding terrain. Second, Iwatake is generally less crowded than Happo, so it is definitely a good alternative on weekends.

Although Iwatake is smaller than Happo it is still a sizeable resort with close to 1 km (.6 mile) of vertical, one express gondola, a high-speed quad and 18 other chairlifts. The great thing about Iwatake is that it has a good mix of freeriding and freestyle terrain. However, facilities at the base of Iwatake are limited; instead, Iwatake has built a sizeable and modern restaurant and rest facilities at the peak of the mountain.

Left: *That's not a pipe — this is a pipe. The 16-foot walls of the Iwatake halfpipe would scare any rider.*

TERRAIN

FREERIDING

Iwatake has enough vertical to be a good freeriding mountain, and there are plenty of trees to explore. As in most other Japanese resorts, it is illegal to ride off-piste, so be wary when you start exploring. There is a good variety of medium and steep terrain which is all on-piste. Iwatake lacks the natural obstacles of Happo, but if you look hard enough there is still some interesting terrain to be found in the trees off the Noah Gondola and next to the Family No. 2 Lift. Although Iwatake doesn't quite match Happo when it comes to freeriding, its freestyle facilities are far superior. Iwatake is totally committed to providing quality halfpipes.

Powder Turns: Try the trees directly under the Noah Gondola. But don't get caught in the huge gully that runs down the side of the mountain. Alternatively, check out the trees on the back side of the mountain directly under the Iwatake View Lift. The trees on skier's left of the D Course are super fun and have good fall-line riding.

Early Morning: In the early morning it is great to do top-to-bottom runs of the Noah Gondola.

Bad Weather: In bad weather it is best to stick to the lower elevations of the mountain. A good lift to ride in bad weather is the Kamushika No. 1 Double Lift.

Above: *Mouse Beuchat loses his board as he dips another grandiose powder turn.*

Avoiding Crowds: The best way to avoid the crowds is to take the Noah Gondola to the top then stick to the lifts at the top of the mountain. In this way you avoid the crowds that congregate at the base of the gondola and also the crowds on the main run from the top to the bottom.

Beginners: There is a great beginner slope near the peak of Iwatake, right next to the Iwatake No. 5 Quad Lift.

FREESTYLE

Snowboard Parks and Halfpipes: Iwatake has one of the biggest pipes in the Hakuba Valley. In fact, the pipe stands out so much that on a clear day you can actually see it from just about anywhere in the valley. The pipe is really too big to be of any use. The walls tower close to 4.3 m (14 ft) with about 1 m (3 ft) of vert, yet the gradient of the pipe is relatively shallow. A pipe with walls this big really needs a steep slope to allow more speed and bigger airs. If Iwatake simply shaved about 60 cm (2 ft) of vert off their pipe it would be perfect, since the transition and grooming are excellent.

Above: *Bear Agushi lays down a signature powder carve in the Iwatake trees.*

KIJIMADAIRA
JAPAN

STATISTICS

Elevations	(m)	(ft)
Top:	1351	4432
Base:	751	2464
Vertical Drop:	600	1969

Lifts	
Lifts:	18
Total:	18

Contact Details

Phone:	+81 269 82 4404
Fax:	+81 269 82 4606
Internet	
Site:	shinshu.online.co.jp/resort/kijima

RESORT REVIEW

SHINETSU

The Shinetsu area is located in the rugged mountain peaks of the Japan Alps in the Nagano Prefecture. There is some awesome riding in this area at the resorts of Nozawa Onsen, Shiga Kohgen, the Tagara-Madaro combination, Kijimadaira, Togari and many other resorts. In this guide we will concentrate on the resort of Kijimadaira. Unlike the Hakuba region, which has a central town around which the seven resorts are based, there is no central town for the resorts in the Shinetsu area. Hakuba is the better option if you want to spend a season in Japan and live in a nice-sized town. Of course you can always do day trips to the Shinetsu area.

Kijimadaira is the home of freestyle snowboarding in Japan, with the resort management firmly embracing snowboarding. It is constantly ranked by Japanese snowboarding magazines as the number one snowboard resort in Japan, and it is easy to see why. It has three halfpipes and two parks that are meticulously maintained. It also has close to 1 km (0.6 mile) of vertical, which provides some relatively long runs. Snowboarders are allowed everywhere except on the No. 3 Sanshoo (Summit) Pair Lift, which accesses the mountain's summit. This is a bit disappointing, since the No. 3 Sanshoo Pair Lift provides access to some of the steepest and best terrain on the mountain.

Above: *Kijimadaira has some awesome powder. Mouse Beuchat samples some of the finest.*

TERRAIN

Above: *With three halfpipes, a park and powder, Kijimadaira has it all.*

FREERIDING

Kijimadaira is a low-elevation resort, with its peak at 1,351 m (4,460 ft) and its base at 500 m (1,650 ft). For this reason, it is not surprising that most of the runs are cut out of the trees. The mountain is of medium gradient. There are not many natural hits off rollers on the groomed runs. You really need to head into the trees to find natural hits or session the park if you want man-made hits. The runs are groomed extremely well and are great for cruising around on and practicing flatland or jibbing tricks.

Kijimadaira has some awesome freeriding terrain off the No. 3 Sanshoo Pair Lift. There are great tree runs filled with natural banks and small rock drops. The problem, of course, is that this lift is not open to snowboarders, so most of the top area of the mountain is left untracked. If you're prepared to hike, you'll be more than rewarded. There are plenty of incredible tree lines off the peak of Kijimadaira. Unfortunately this is not the resort for steep chutes and cliff bands.

Powder Turns: Some great powder in the trees can be found off to skier's left of the No. 7 Pair Lift.

Bad Weather: As the resort has very low elevation, it is not often plagued by low-lying cloud, so there is normally good visibility on most of the runs. The trees on skiers' left of the Number 9 Run are a good choice in bad weather

Avoiding Crowds: The main lift to avoid is the Ikenodaira No. 1 Chairlift that serves the main car park. Most other lifts handle the crowds reasonably well.

Beginners: The best beginner runs on the mountain are found next to the No. 8 Sky4 Lift.

FREESTYLE
Snowboard Parks and Halfpipes: What Kijimadaira lacks in freeriding terrain it certainly makes up in man-made freestyle terrain. Forget about looking for natural hits and head straight to the parks and pipes. One park and pipe is located just up from the main base of Kijimadaira and the other two pipes and the park are located far on skiers' left of the resort. All three pipes are first shaped by a backhoe then finished with a Pipe Dragon. The main two pipes are located next to a hut that pumps out all day. The parks have nicely shaped tabletops. All freestyle facilities are maintained regularly.

Above: *A classic method above a classic town. Mouse Beuchat enjoying the park at Kijimadaira.*

NISEKO HIRAFU
JAPAN

STATISTICS

Elevations	(m)	(ft)
Top:	1200	3937
Base:	300	984
Vertical Drop:	900	2953

Lifts	
Quad:	13
Gondolas:	1
Total:	14

Contact Details

Phone:	+81 136 220 109
Fax:	+81 136 222 821
Internet Site:	www.niseko-tokyu.co.jp

RESORT REVIEW

HOKKAIDO

Hokkaido is the coldest and most northernly of Japan's four main islands. The major resorts in this region are located in the Hidaka Mountains, close to the centre of the island. The six major resorts on Hokkaido are Kiroro, Niseko, Rusutu, Furano, Sahoro and Tomamu. The first three are located to the west of Sapporo, the major city of Hokkaido, and the latter three are located to the east. In this guide we shall concentrate on the resort of Niseko.

Niseko is located about 100 km (62 miles) from Sapporo. It actually consists of six resorts. There are four major resorts and two small resorts (Niseko Weiss and Niseko Kokusai Moiwa). Locals typically only visit the latter two resorts. The four major resorts are Niseko Higashiyama, Niseko Annupuri Kokusai, Niseko Kohgen and Niseko Alpen. The last two areas are typically known under a single name, Niseko Hirafu, and only a single lift pass is required for the two. The infrastructure is huge across the three resorts of Niseko Higashiyama, Niseko Annupuri Kokusai and Niseko Hirafu. There are three gondolas, six high-speed quads and 29 other lifts. In this review we will concentrate on Niseko Hirafu.

Left: *The sun finally comes out after a severe Siberian storm. Adrian Deffert is more than happy to enjoy the leftovers. Photo—Gavin O'Toole.*

Niseko Hirafu has a reputation as a resort for the intermediate to advanced rider. One of Niseko's strongest features is its consistent low temperature range that ensures the snow stays dry and doesn't melt too often during winter. The sheer volume of snow enjoyed here means that avalanche danger is often high – the ski patrol is always busy. Not surprisingly, the freeriding here and the quantity of fresh snow are second to none.

WEATHER IN NISEKO

Niseko Hirafu is the place to experience the light and dry snow that falls on northern Japan between November and March every year. This snow is a result of very cold air that pushes across Siberia, gains moisture as it crosses the Sea of Japan and then dumps on Niseko. During the day, the temperature rarely rises above –10°C (14°F) and on most nights it hovers around –25°C (13°F). If you can tolerate freezing weather and very few sunshine days, then head to Niseko.

TERRAIN

FREERIDING

Trees: Contrary to popular belief it is not illegal to ride the trees in all of Japan. Niseko is one place in Japan where the ski patrol turns a blind eye to off-piste riding. Japanese skiers seem to prefer the groomed slopes and generally stick to the main runs. Try Miharashi, a short hike to the right at the top of the gondola, or the Strawberry Fields area on the back side of the resort.

Cliffs and Chutes: While Niseko offers limited double black runs or the extremes associated with big European or American resorts, short steep chutes can be found after hiking from the top of the resort.

Powder Days: This is when Niseko comes into its own. You will often find it snows for days with only momentary breaks, when a patch of blue sky will appear for a short period. Head into the trees and you'll have a blast. Most runs will have a trail that will take you back to a chair. Better still, find a local and follow.

Above: *Beneath the volcano of Niseko, Sasha Ryzy pumps out a gigantic plume. Photo—Gavin O'Toole.*

Bad Weather: Try the trees on the front face under the gondola. The gondola will give you some respite from the constant snow and a chance to clear your goggles.

FREESTYLE

Halfpipe: As you are heading up the gondola, look to your right and you will find the halfpipe, which is approximately 150 m (492 ft) in length. The Japanese are totally obsessed with halfpipe riding and this is reflected in their skills. Even on the best powder days they can still be found hiking the pipe. Unfortunately, the pipe is not maintained well, which often leads to excess vert and rutted walls. The pipe does get crowded on the weekends. Niseko management have recently purchased a pipe groomer, which should definitely improve the daily condition of the pipe.

Snowboard Parks: Traditionally, Niseko has not offered a snowboard park, but the popularity of freestyle riding and the fact that 50% of the patrons at Niseko are snowboarders indicates that a park can't be far off.

Natural Hits: Niseko lacks the large cornices and chutes that characterize the more mountainous European or North American resorts. There are, however, some good cornices located at the back of the resort. These cornices can be accessed by hiking from the single chair at the top of the front face. This area is only accessible on clear days and only available after it has been cleared by the ski patrol. On a clear day you will see people hiking towards Niseko's peak. Alternatively, try the rock garden in Strawberry Fields. This is a great short, steep run, with numerous boulders to launch off. This area is often closed by the ski patrol.

Left: *Grant Quinn with a huge powder spray and a huge smile, Niseko. Photo—Peter Murphy.*

EUROPE

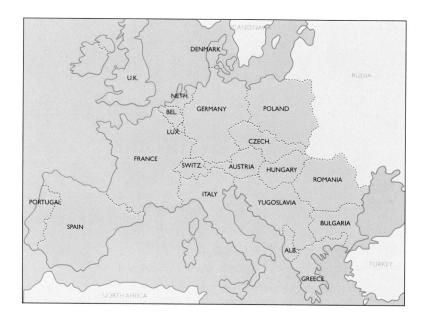

Continental Western Europe is home to 14 countries and over 300 million people. Combined, Western Europe is similar in economic size and population to the USA. However, when it comes to culture the similarities between Europe and USA end. The cultures in Europe have been evolving over the past 2,000 years whereas the dominant American culture has only existed for some 200 years.

When it comes to snowboarding, the mountains in Europe are second to none. No amount of infrastructure development in the USA or anywhere else in the world could re-create a mountain range as impressive and majestic as the European Alps. The mighty Alps rise over 4,000 m (13,200 ft) and spread across France, Switzerland, Austria and Italy. The peaks and resorts located on this amazing geographical formation are countless. It is often said that it is impossible to place another lift in the Alps. Austria itself has some 1,000 lifts, France has over 500 resorts and Switzerland – well, there are just too many to count.

Whilst most European resorts once led the world in resort infrastructure, things have changed. The North American and Japanese resorts have been pumping large amounts of money into new lifts and resort villages. And it has worked, with some of the European resorts losing valuable clients to North American and Japanese resorts. European resorts are beginning to realize that skiers and snowboarders alike are sick of queuing in long lift lines, waiting in badly catered cafeterias and paying big bucks for a cheesy night out on the town. Only now are European resorts ploughing money back into their lift systems. And it is showing – more and more high-speed lifts are appearing at the bigger resorts.

European resorts do offer something that really can't be found in USA, Canada or Japan, though, and that is size, both vertically and horizontally. Places such as Chamonix, with 3 km (1.8 miles) of vertical, and Les Portes du Soleil, with 219 lifts amongst a dozen different villages, put the North American giants to shame. With so many snowboard destinations so close to each other, Europe really is a snowboarder's paradise.

Snowboarding in Europe is a totally unique experience and incredibly different from riding in North America, Japan, Australia or New Zealand. The mountains are huge, the lift systems are expansive and the culture is fantastic. Sit back and enjoy the ride as we take you to some of the best resorts on offer in Austria, Switzerland and France.

Opposite: *The mountains in Europe are big. Mouse Beuchat scaring the wildlife with this monster carve in Ischgl.*

TRAVELING AROUND EUROPE

Europe has one of the largest and most efficient train and bus systems in the world. Every single corner of continental Europe can be reached by train or bus. What's more, the train system runs like clockwork – no matter what the weather, the trains are always on time.

If you are traveling by yourself around the European resorts, the best option is to buy a Eurorail Pass. This pass pretty much gives you unlimited access to most of the trains in Europe. Eurorail Passes can be purchased from most reputable travel agents around the world. If you are traveling with a group of three or more friends and are planning to stay in Europe for more than 17 days, then contrary to what you may think, it's actually cheaper to rent a car. As the distances you will travel in Europe are small, the high cost of petrol is not really an issue.

ACCOMMODATION

Unlike the USA and Canada, where youth hostels are a fairly normal occurrence, in Europe the whole backpacker thing is only just starting to take off. Accommodation in most European resorts is basically confined to pensions and chalets. The best option is really the small family-run pensions, which cost around USD$25 per day. These are rather like bed and breakfast places but with a particularly European feel. In some resorts, such as Laax and Davos there are cheaper options but these are rare. If you are in a group of four or more and you are staying in a resort for more than five days, the best option is to rent an apartment.

Apartments are very reasonably priced. To organise accommodation, go straight to the local tourist office. It will have information about all the accommodation options in the area.

HINTS AND TIPS

- Surprisingly, most people speak some English in the Western European countries. But it is polite to learn a few French, German or Italian phrases.
- MasterCard tends to be more widely accepted in Europe than Visa.
- The best sources of information are the local tourist offices. There is a tourist office in just about every town and resort across France, Switzerland and Austria. The tourist office can help you with just about any question you have – directions, accommodation, telephone numbers, resort information etc.
- Eating and drinking at restaurants and bars is not cheap. Even fast-food places such as McDonalds are expensive. The best option is to stick to the supermarkets. Food is reasonably priced and beer is super cheap.

Opposite: *Sometimes it's worth traveling to a resort just to check out the view. Le Brévent is one of those places.*
Below: *The crew hangin' out on some disused airplane seats at Jakobshorn in Davos.*

AUSTRIA
EUROPE

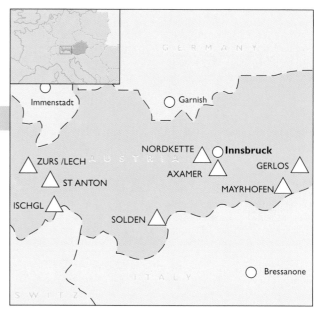

OVERVIEW

Austria is a small republic in central Europe that is bounded on the north by the Czech republic, on the northeast by Slovakia, on the east by Hungary, on the south by Slovenia, Switzerland and Italy, and on the west by Liechtenstein, Switzerland and Germany. Austria is in fact only 580 km (360 miles) long, so most of the resorts are located close to each other.

The Austrian people, who number around 8 million, are extremely friendly and love to party. It is not often that you will go into an Austrian town and not be able to find a bar that has a swinging vibe. Over one third of the Austrian population live in the five major cities of Vienna, Graz, Linz, Salzburg and Innsbruck. The principal tongue in Austria is German despite an ethnic mixture that includes Croats, Czechs and Slovenes.

THE AUSTRIAN ALPS

Austria is an extremely mountainous country. In fact, the country has an average elevation of about 910 m (3,000 ft). In general, the major mountain ranges of Austria run in an east–west direction. The northernmost line of ranges includes the North Tyrol Alps and the Salzburg Alps. The largest resorts, such as St Anton and Ischgl, are located in these mountain ranges. The highest peak in Austria is the Grossglockner, which soars some 3,797 m (12,457 ft) into the stratosphere. One of Europe's largest glaciers, the Pasterze Glacier, descends from the Grossglockner peak. The southernmost ranges include the Ötztal Alps, the Zillertal Alps, the Carnic Alps, and the Karawanken Mountains.

Below: *Austria has over 1,000 lifts and peaks above 3,500 m (11,483 ft). Little wonder snowboarders travel from all corners of the world to explore its many resorts.*

SNOW CONDITIONS IN AUSTRIA

The Northern Tyrol Alps are subject to moderate Atlantic conditions and generally experience greater snowfalls than the eastern lowlands, which are under continental influences. When a deep Altantic storm moves in, it can dump mountains of snow on the Northern Tyrol Alps. On average they receive a healthy 6 m (20 ft) of annual snowfall. Further, most resorts employ a significant amount of snow-making to top up their bases. The ski season is usually ended by the föhn, a warm, dry wind that comes in from the south and rapidly melts the snowpack, thus creating high avalanche danger.

Mean annual temperatures range from about 6.7– 8.9°C (about 44–48°F) throughout the country. In mountain ranges, the average annual rainfall can be between 154 and 203 cm (about 60–80 in), which translates into a lot of snow.

SNOWBOARDING IN AUSTRIA

The best place for snowboarding is the Tyrol region, which is located in the west of the country, on the border with Switzerland. In this area there are some extremely large resorts that offer some of the best freeriding in Europe. The snowboarding is characterized by long, groomed runs, and steep chutes located between jagged peaks and sizeable cliffs. An amazing amount of extreme terrain is located in-bounds at Austrian resorts. On the freestyle side, most Austrian resorts have grandiose plans to build the best pipes and parks. However, the reality is that although most Austrian resorts do put pipes and parks in place during the season, they are not what they are cracked up to be in the glossy marketing brochures.

ACCOMMODATION

The best places to stay are the family-run pensions. These usually run at about ATS300-400 per person per night and include breakfast. Generally, the more expensive the pension, the better the breakfast. If you are stuck for accommodation it is best to visit the local tourist office, as the people will have plenty of contacts.

GETTING TO THE AUSTRIAN ALPS

If you are traveling to the mountains in the Tyrol regions the best option is to either fly into Zurich in Switzerland or Innsbruck in Austria. From these major cities, depending on which resorts you are visiting, it is only a few hours' drive to the mountains. Alternatively, it is possible to hop off the plane and on to a train. Trains go to most of the resorts in Austria. If you are traveling in a group, the best method is to lease a car from Renault Eurodrive.

HINTS AND TIPS

- Like most of Europe, Austrian businesses typically close for lunch between 12 and 2 pm, so be prepared to do your business outside these times.
- Credit cards are accepted throughout Austria but MasterCard tends to be preferred.
- The Austrian telephone system is not as advanced as some other systems in Europe, so be prepared for some frustration. Alternatively, buy a phonecard – these tend to work well.

Above: *Zürs is the place for freeriding in the Tyrol Mountains. Mouse Beuchat is more than happy to oblige.*

- Roads in the Tyrol region are often closed due to heavy snow, so check with the local tourist office to see whether the road you want to travel on is open.
- There are several toll roads in Austria, so be prepared to pay.

ST ANTON
AUSTRIA

STATISTICS

Elevations	(m)	(ft)
Top:	2811	9222
Base:	1304	4278
Vertical Drop:	1507	4944

Lifts	
Surface Lifts:	20
Chairs:	11
Gondolas:	2
Cable Cars:	2
Funiculars:	1
Total:	36

Contact Details	
Phone:	+43 5446 22690
Fax:	+43 5446 2532
Email Address:	st.anton@netway.at
Internet Site:	www.tiscover.at/st.anton

RESORT REVIEW

St Anton, located in the Arlberg region of Austria, is probably one of the best-known Austrian resorts worldwide. The setting is stunning: the picturesque St Anton

Above: *Just a sample of what's available in St Anton. Justin and Damo dwarfed by the 2,811 m Valluga Peak.*

village, located at 1,300 m (4,300 ft) is dwarfed by the twin peaks of the Valluga (2,811 m/9,300 ft) and the Weisschrofenspitz (2,752 m/9,081 ft) that tower above it. Not only is the setting stunning, the amount of terrain in this area is massive. When combined, the resorts of St Anton, St Christoph, Stuben, Lech and Zürs cover an amazing 84 cable cars and ski lifts and 260 km (162 miles) of on-piste trails. If you so desire, you can ride all these areas on the one pass – 'Ski Pass Arlberg'.

The St Anton ski area actually consists of three villages – St Anton, St Christoph and Stuben. This area consists of 41 lifts and a vertical of over 1.5 km (1 mile). The longest run in the area is over 10 km (6.2 miles) – thigh-burning stuff. To ensure there is plenty of snow, St Anton has 53 snow guns that pump out snow when required.

The lift system at St Anton has improved over recent years. Fixed-grip chairs have been slowly replaced by high-speed chairs. Recently a six-person high-speed chair with a bubble was placed on the Kappel peak and a double chair was installed in Rendl to replace the groin-breaking Mass T-bar. Further, most of the high alpine areas on the Valluga are reached by cable cars, which is definitely a bonus. There is nothing worse than being on an exposed chairlift at 2,500 m (8,202 ft) during a blizzard.

Forget about the scenery and the mountains, St Anton is actually renowned for its night life. If you want to party the night away, St Anton is the place for you. The Austrians have a reputation as hard party-goers and the Austrian breed in St Anton is no exception. In clubs such as Club Amadeus and the Underground the schnapps flows freely and the music plays until the early hours. Be prepared to boogie.

TERRAIN

FREERIDING

As the freeriding terrain at St Anton is so huge, it is best to break it up into the different areas of the mountain. Most of the slopes at St Anton are south-facing, so they do get sun-affected relatively quickly. An exception is the Rendl area.

SCHINDLER AREA

This area has several natural pipes, which range in length from 100-300 m and in width from 5-30 m (16-98 ft). The natural pipes are controlled by the ski patrol and are relatively safe.

BACKSIDE AREA

This is a nice area with open-face riding on Galzig's north side. It offers short, steep and varied off-piste runs down Happy Valley. The sheer size of the area makes the riding very varied. The area faces north and is therefore colder and holds snow longer. After a snowfall, this is one of the most likely places to find powder the whole day, but it is also where most people go for off-piste riding, so the area is tracked out quickly.

SCHÖNGRABE AREA

It is here that you will find great forest riding. Take the ride through the forest from the bottom of the Schöngrabe Lift. Go straight down between the trees. Here you'll find varied forest and open terrain. Keep riding down and you will come to an uninhabited area with small houses. Keep going in the tracks down to the Nasserein Lift. This will bring you back to the main area of St Anton. This is a nice long run with plenty of powder stashes.

NORTH FACE AREA

This area down towards the town probably hides some of the best off-piste riding in St Anton. Start at the top by the Gampberg Lift. From here you'll have an hour's worth of off-piste riding in front of you. Here you probably need a guide, because of avalanche danger and cliffs. A wrong turn here could cost you your life, so be careful and ride with someone who knows the terrain.

LANGEN AREA (OUTSIDE THE TRAIL MAP)

This place is a St Anton classic. It is a short day trip and starts at Stuben. Start from the Albona Restaurant and traverse around the mountain to the west. Stay high at all times. After approximately 30 minutes you'll arrive at the Kaltenberg Cabin. When you see power lines, turn down towards the forest. You will find varied riding with lots of small jumps. When you arrive at the valley floor, go over a stone bridge and turn left. Go to Langen train station. Take the train back to St Anton. The trip takes approximately ten minutes and costs somewhere around ATS25.

STUBEN NORTH-SIDE AREA (OUTSIDE THE TRAIL MAP)

You can see this run from the Albona Lift. The avalanche danger here is extreme, so listen to the locals before you go, and take their advice. When you go, go down the fall line. This run is on the shadow-side and the snow stays cool for a

Right: *'Run to the Hills' is the catch-cry in St Anton when the snow dumps thick and fast. Somehow Sasha Ryzy manages to outwit the crowds. Photo—Gavin O'Toole.*

long time. Here you can find untouched powder 2-3 days after a snowfall.

Powder Turns: When the snow comes it really is a classic 'run to the hills'. The lifts are jam-packed and the powder gets tracked in hours. The best place to head on a crowded powder day is Rendl. People tend to avoid this area because of its slower lift system.

Avoiding Crowds: To avoid the crowds you really need to hang out in the lesser-known areas of Stuben and Rendl.

Beginners: The Gampen has plenty of slopes suited for beginners.

FREESTYLE

It is unfortunate but the freestyle facilities at St Anton do not match up with the freeriding. This is not surprising since the majority of the clientele at St Anton are skiers from the UK and Germany. If you are going to St Anton, go for the freeriding alone.

Halfpipes: The halfpipe is located at Rendl. It is on a relatively steep slope and is not maintained very often. The pipe at nearby Lech is a better option.

Snowboard Parks: The park is located right next to the pipe. Like the pipe, the park is maintained infrequently and the tabletops tend to be more dangerous than fun.

ZÜRS AND LECH
AUSTRIA

STATISTICS

Elevations	(m)	(ft)
Top:	2450	8038
Base:	1720	5643
Vertical Drop:	730	2395

Lifts	
Surface Lifts:	10
Chairs:	18
Gondolas:	0
Cable Cars:	5
Funiculars:	0
Total:	33

Lifts are for the combined Lech/Zürs area.

Contact Details	
Phone:	+43 5583 2245
Fax:	+43 5583 2982
Email Address:	zurs-info@zuers.at
Internet Site:	www.zuers.at

RESORT REVIEW

Zürs and Lech lie in the next valley across from St Anton, in the stunning Arlberg region of Austria. Although Lech and Zürs are distinctly different towns, they share the same lift pass. By purchasing the 'Ski Pass Arlberg' it is possible to ride Lech, Zürs, St Anton, Stuben and St Christoph in a day, although this would really be suicide.

When driving up from the valley floor, you first drive through the town of Zürs at 1,716 m (5,660 ft). Just 10 minutes further down the valley is the town of Lech, some 250 m (825 ft) lower in elevation at 1,450 m (4,780 ft). The mountain skyline around these two Austrian villages is totally amazing. Peaks such as the Mohnenfluh and Widderstein tower over 2,500 m (8,250 ft) above. Wide, open alpine bowls border Lech and Zürs on either side. There is a free ski bus that connects Lech and Zürs. This makes transfers between the two ski areas hassle-free.

In the Lech/Zürs area there are 33 lifts, including five cable cars. Like other Austrian resorts, they have begun to upgrade their lift systems. Recently, a new six-person high-speed chair was installed in Lech and a new quad chair replaced a t-bar at Zürs. These new lifts add to the extensive range of cable cars that already service the high alpine areas of Lech and Zürs.

Left: *Follow the signs and you shall find what you are looking for. Well, if you are looking for powder, Zürs and Lech will deliver.*

Lech's main claim to fame is that it has the highest casino in Europe. The casino is located at the peak of the Rüfikopf Cablecar, 2,362 m (7,790 ft) above sea level. Zürs' main claim to fame is that it offers the only heli-skiing in Austria. Heli-skiing takes place on the peaks of Mehlsack and Orgelscharte and is relatively cheap – about ATS4,000 for four people.

The beauty of Lech and Zürs is that their mountains and villages are totally different. Lech is the more sophisticated and expensive village. It tends to have most of the long, cruising groomers and gentle terrain as well as the halfpipe, boardercross track and park. Zürs, on the other hand, is slightly rougher around the edges. It has cheaper accommodation and more of a rustic feel. And it is home to the best freeriding – open bowls, cliffs and windlips can all be found at Zürs.

TERRAIN

FREERIDING

Although there is good freeriding off the Mohnenfluh Cablecar in Lech, Zürs is really the place to go freeriding. The lines accessible by the Trittkopf Cablecar in Zürs are amazing. Consistent gradient, steep chutes, windlips, gullies and cliffs – this area definitely has it all. Also it tends not to be as crowded as the slopes of Lech. Of course, if you want long groomers, then Lech is the perfect alternative. The runs off the Kriegerhorn and Petersboden are long and groomed to perfection.

Powder Turns: At Lech the best powder can probably be found off the Steinmahder Cablecar. You can actually ride all the way to the valley floor from this run. At Zürs, head straight to the Trittkopf Cablecar, as there are numerous good lines.

Early Morning: In the early morning it is fun to hit the groomers off the Petersboden Six-chair.

Bad Weather: As there are not many trees at Lech and Zürs, bad weather can be really annoying. On bad weather days you're probably better off trying something else, such as curling or indoor golf.

Avoiding Crowds: The lower lifts of Lech tend to attract the crowds. Avoid these and you should be right. The Hexenboden Lift at Zürs tends not to get too crowded.

Hiking: There are some excellent hiking opportunities in Lech and Zürs. In Lech the best hiking exists off the Salober Kopf peak. Take the Salober Kopf Chair up and then traverse to skiers' left. Drop in anywhere you choose. You will be able to ride some nice rolling terrain to the valley floor. At Zürs, take the Muggengrat Chair up and drop over the back onto the Zürser Täli. This run usually remains fairly untracked.

Beginners: Most of the beginner runs are located on the lower portions of Lech, especially around the Schlegelkopf Lift.

FREESTYLE

The freestyle facilities are all located at Lech. As well as a pipe and park, there is also a permanent boardercross track.

Above: *Peter Naporotti is a qualified stuntman. Do not try this at home. Photo—Alex Guzman.*

Above: *Classic Zürs – rolling hills and jagged peaks.*

Halfpipes: The halfpipe is located under the Schlegelkopf Lift. It has a good shape but tends to lack size. The major problem with the pipe is that it tends to be maintained on an irregular basis. It is shaped using a Snow Turbo Grinder.

Snowboard Parks: The park is small and is located close to the Schlegelkopf Lift. It is really a park designed for intermediates. There are no large kickers.

ISCHGL
AUSTRIA

STATISTICS

Elevations	(m)	(ft)
Top:	2864	9396
Base:	1377	4517
Vertical Drop:	1487	4878

Lifts	
Surface Lifts:	21
Chairs:	15
Gondolas:	3
Cable Cars:	2
Funiculars:	0
Total:	41

Contact Details	
Phone:	+43 5444 5266
Fax:	+43 5444 5636
Email Address:	tvb.ischgl@netway.at
Internet Site:	www.tiscover.com/ischgl

RESORT REVIEW

It's not very often that you find a resort that has freeriding terrain that is out of this world, a halfpipe that is kept to ISF standards and a lift system that is so efficient it puts the Swiss to shame. Ischgl is such a resort. Set in the Silvretta Mountains of Austria, even uperlatives can't convey the quality of this resort.

The Silvretta Ski Arena, which comprises the towns of Ischgl at 1,400 m (4,620 ft) and Samnaun at 1,840 m (6,072 ft), is one of the largest areas in the Alps. It has over 40 lifts, including three gondolas, two aerial cableways and 15 chairlifts, which are nearly all high speed. There are over 200 km (125 miles) of on-piste runs and a vertical of some 1,500 m (4,950 ft). If you're not convinced yet, wait till you hear that it has a 1.1 km (0.7 miles) snowboard park that incorporates tabletops, spines and a 100 m (333 ft) halfpipe groomed regularly by a Pipe Dragon. Ischgl is definitely a place that should be on your must-see list. If it is not evident already, Ischgl is totally committed to catering for snowboarders.

No expense has been spared to ensure that customers have the best holiday possible. Ischgl village has a totally relaxed atmosphere, with a continual stream of après ski events. Ischgl even has its own travelator that runs under the town. This saves you having to walk from one end of the town to the other.

If you thought the night life in St Anton was good, wait till you hit Ischgl. It has some of the best après snow antics in Austria. Bars such as the Kitzloch and Niki's Stadl all have schnapps specialties and go off. For some late-night techno,

Left: *Mouse Beuchat floats a stalefish over a white wave in the Ischgl backcountry.*

check out the Madlein Wunderbar. Alternatively, you could just go to bed and get some sleep before the next amazing day riding Ischgl.

Of course Ischgl is not completely perfect. The main problem with Ischgl is the crowds. Its proximity to Innsbruck and its reputation throughout Europe ensures that it is nearly always at capacity. Although the lift system can handle it, it usually means that the fresh snow gets tracked out pretty quickly. The bottom line – get up early.

TERRAIN

FREERIDING

Where do you start? The area around the Gampenbahn High-speed Quad offers some long, quality runs. The bonus about this area is the variety of terrain – small windlips, cliffs, trees and cat tracks. The open bowls on skiers' left of the Greitspitzbahn represent a freerider's heaven – open fields with small drops. For more challenging freeriding terrain, check out the runs from the top of the Pardatschgraft T-bar down to the Velillatal. In fact, anywhere across Ischgl's five massive bowls you will be able to find some quality freeriding terrain. Further, a lot of the faces at Ischgl are north-facing, which ensures the snow stays drier for longer.

Powder Turns: There are plenty of choices, but one of the best is the area below the Palinkopf Chairlift. It is north-facing and holds good snow for days.

Early Morning: In the morning it's good to warm up with some cruising runs down under the Idjoch Chairlift.

Bad Weather: One of the major downfalls of Ischgl is its lack of bad-weather riding. When the clouds roll in, the bars really start pumping, because the visibility on the slopes deteriorates. If you really want to go snowboarding, stick to the Paznauner and Bodenalm T-bars in the Fimbatal area.

Avoiding Crowds: The lifts to definitely avoid are the Flimjoch and Idjoch Chairlifts. A good choice on heavy days is the Velilleck Chairlift.

Hiking: There is really no need to bother with hiking at Ischgl since the in-bounds terrain is so awesome. If you really want to hike, a good option is to hike from the Palinkopf to the Piz Val Gronda. This gives access to an amazingly long run down to Fimbatal. However, this is a very tough day's hike, so make sure you're fit.

Beginners: The best beginners' area is under the Velill Chairlift. The slope is wide and well groomed, and serviced by a chairlift rather than an unfriendly t-bar.

FREESTYLE

The freestyle facilities at Ischgl truly are a snowboarder's dream. Located on skier's left of Idjoch Chairlift there is 1.1 km of pure heaven. Perfectly shaped kickers and spines are scattered throughout the run. It is aptly named the 'Boarder's Paradise'. And at the end, there is an ISF-standard halfpipe.

Above: *The powder and the glory. Damo Liddy knows the feeling.*

Halfpipes: The Ischgl pipe is one of the best in Europe. It is 100 m (333 ft) long, 15 m (50 ft) wide has 3.5 m (12 ft) walls and is meticulously groomed with a Pipe Dragon. On sunny days it is a tough choice whether to ride pipe or go freeriding.

Snowboard Parks: Just like the pipe, the park is kept in great shape. The kickers, tabletops and spines are all maintained regularly to ensure that the take-off and landing areas are always up to scratch. Check it out and be blown away.

SÖLDEN
AUSTRIA

STATISTICS

Elevations	(m)	(ft)
Top:	3250	10663
Base:	1650	5413
Vertical Drop:	1600	5249

Lifts	
Surface Lifts:	11
Double Chairs:	9
Triple Chairs:	5
Quad Chairs – Fixed Grip:	4
Quad Chairs – Express:	2
Six Chairs – Express:	0
Gondolas:	4
Cable Cars:	0
Funiculars:	0
Total:	35

Contact Details
Phone:	+43 5254 2361
Fax:	+43 5254 210120
Email Address:	oetztalarena@netway.af
Internet Site:	www.tiscover.com/oetzal-arena

RESORT REVIEW

Sölden is the largest resort in the Ötztal Valley and is located only 80 km (50 miles) from Innsbruck. Sölden is in fact made up of two huge mountains, Schwarzsekegi (2,885 m/ 9,520 ft) and Gaislachkogl (3,058 m/10,091 ft), which are separated by the Rettenbachferner Glacier. The scenery is breathtaking, with the 67 km (41 miles) Ötztal Valley running north–south and huge peaks rising up on either side.

Sölden really is huge. It takes a day to ride from one end of the resort to the other. There are 35 lifts, including four cableways and six high-speed quads. The Gaislachkogl Cableway is one of the longest bi-cableways in Europe. Despite its size, Sölden has an excellent system of express lifts that link the two mountains and the glacier. Further, you can actually drive from Sölden village at 1,377 m (4,544 ft), through a 1.7 km (1 miles) glacier tunnel, up to the Rettenbach and Tiefenbach Glaciers some 2,800 m (9,240 ft) above sea level. The road is open all year round, snow permitting, and free with any lift ticket. So if you only want to ride the glacier you can drive straight up there.

The village of Sölden is spread out along the Ötztaler River. The first thing you notice about the village is the number of neon signs. In fact, there are probably more neon signs in Sölden than anywhere else in Austria. Well, that's not really true, but it does indicate that Sölden is a relatively new resort, being less than 20 years old. Sölden is certainly a party town, and it attracts many of the young people from around Austria. Most nights the beer and schnapps flow freely.

The famous 'Glacier Man', the corpse from a prehistoric age that was found preserved by glacial ice, was actually found in the glaciers above Sölden. The locals know the 'Glacier Man' as Ötzi. Ötzi attracted world attention to Sölden.

Above: *The crew scans the view for the best line home.*

TERRAIN

Above: *Damo Liddy makes a turn before being apprehended by a ski patrol for being out of bounds at Sölden.*

FREERIDING

As a freeriding mountain, Sölden definitely has the goods. There are plenty of wide-open bowls, tree and cliff drops. There are also a lot of natural hits, but these are quite often in secret spots, so you need to know where to go. The best idea is to head to one of the local snowboard shops and see if you can hook up with a friendly local who may be kind enough to show you his or her daily hit lines. Alternatively, read on and we will try to give you some clues.

Powder Turns: For some early morning powder turns, take the Roßkirpl Chairlift up and hike out to skiers' left. There are some good steep slopes to drop here. Any lines that drop into the Rettenbachtal Valley off the back of the Glacier Lift or off the Stabele Lift are awesome, especially as they are north-facing.

Early Morning: It's good to do some speed runs under the Silberbrünn Chairlift and catch some early morning sun.

Bad Weather: The majority of riding at Sölden is located above the tree line, so when the cloud cover is thick, it is probably better to go curling.

Avoiding Crowds: The best place to avoid the hordes of Austrians that invade Sölden on weekends is on the Heide Chairlift. There are some good open bowls off this lift, so it is usually well worth it.

Hiking: The best hiking really exists off the Roßkirpl Chairlift. From here you can hike the ridges out to the Breitlehner and Roßkirpl peaks. Both peaks offer open-bowl riding and the short hikes are well worth it.

Beginners: The best lifted beginners' terrain is off the Giggijoch Triple Chair. The Rettenbachferner Glacier also has good beginners' terrain, but it is only serviced by a t-bar and it is located at the very peak of the mountain.

FREESTYLE

Freestyle facilities are provided at Sölden but the marketing brochures tend to hype them so much that it is impossible for the reality to live up to the expectations. During winter, Sölden usually has a halfpipe, park and boardercross track located next to the Hainbachkar Chairlift. In summer, the halfpipe is moved up to the Rettenbachferner Glacier.

Halfpipes: The pipe suffers from two major problems. First, the walls are far too small – they are not even 2.4 m (8 ft). Second, the pipe is not regularly maintained, so the shape is never consistent. You would be much better off going freeriding.

Snowboard Parks: The park does have several kickers, but the landings are far too short. Unless you enjoy landing on the flat, stay away.

Above: *If you want gnarly chutes. Austria delivers. Alex Kupprion gets his fix. Photo—Alex Guzman.*

INNSBRUCK
AUSTRIA

OVERVIEW

Innsbruck is the major city in the Tyrol region of Austria. It is home to some 128,000 people and it is also the home of snowboarding in Austria and perhaps even Europe. Why is this? Well, there are several reasons. First, Innsbruck is located close to some of the world-class resorts in Austria, such as Ischgl, Sölden and Hintertux. Second, there are six resorts all within 30 minutes' drive, including the huge Stubai Glacier which has a lifted point up to 3,150 m (10,400 ft). Third, Innsbruck is the European home to Burton Snowboards, the largest and most famous manufacturer of snowboards. Fourth, it is the headquarters for the International Snowboard Federation, the governing body for snowboarding. Finally, it is a cool place to live, so snowboarders hang out there. Thus, it's not surprising that Innsbruck's advertising slogan is 'The Boarder's City'.

Innsbruck is also famous for another reason – the Air & Style Contest (or as it is more commonly known, the Innsbruck Big Air). Every year in early December, around 30,000 people crowd into Innsbruck's Bergisel Stadium (the 1976 Olympic ski jumping site) to watch the world's best riders launch themselves off a massive kicker, stomping the landing then boosting off a huge quarterpipe. Riders of the caliber of Daniel Franck, Fabien Rohrer and Jim Rippey usually compete. Further, the crowds are treated to some of the best bands in the world, jamming the night away. The Innsbruck Big Air is probably one of the biggest nights on the snowboarding calendar.

Innsbruck is circled by six resorts. Together, the six areas (Stubai Glacier, Mutterer Alm, Patscherkofel, Glungezer, Axamer Lizum and Nordkette) have over 112 km of on-piste runs. There are nine cable cars, one funicular, 15 chairlifts and 28 t-bars. What's more, all the areas are accessible from Innsbruck via a free shuttle bus. Most of the areas are not small – the Stubai Glacier actually has a vertical of 1,400 m (4,620 ft) and goes up to 3,150 m (10,400 ft) on the Jochdohle peak. In this guide we will concentrate on the resorts of Axamer Lizum and Nordkette, as they are the best for snowboarding.

Innsbruck is also a cool place to hang out. There are plenty of bars and nightclubs. The centre of town has plenty of trendy shops and has a good Austrian feel about it. You just seem to feel at home and relaxed walking around Innsbruck, probably because you know you can go snowboarding anytime you want.

Left: *Innsbruck, 'the boarder's town'. Courtesy of Innsbruck Tourism and Schmeiderer.*
Opposite: *Head to the trees for some protection from poor weather.*

AXAMER LIZUM
AUSTRIA

STATISTICS

Elevations	(m)	(ft)
Top:	2343	7687
Base:	874	2867
Vertical Drop:	1469	4819

Lifts	
Surface Lifts:	4
Double Chairs:	4
Triple Chairs:	0
Quad Chairs – Fixed Grip:	1
Quad Chairs – Express:	0
Six Chairs – Express:	0
Gondolas:	1
Cable Cars:	0
Funiculars:	1
Total:	11

Contact Details	
Phone:	+43 5234 68 1780
Fax:	+43 5234 67 158
Email Address:	info@innsbruck.tub.co

Above: *Damo Liddy ollies his way through the pines in search of more powder.*

RESORT REVIEW

Axamer Lizum (or Axamer) is a medium-sized resort located about 30 minutes' drive west of Innsbruck. It is in fact located on two mountains, the Hoadl (2,340 m/ 7,722 ft) on one side and the Neue Birgitzköpfhtt on the other. Most of the intermediate and beginner runs are located on the Hoadl and the more challenging terrain is located off the Birgitzköpfl Chairlift on the Neue Birgitzköpfhtt. The only problem is that the Birgitzköpfl Chairlift is fixed grip and super slow. So it is best to stick to the Hoadl, which does have some fun terrain.

The vertical in the actual resort is about 800 m (2,640 ft) but when there is a lot of snow you can actually ride down to the valley floor at 878 m (2,890 ft). This provides a vertical of about 1,500 m (4,950 ft). Then it is simply a matter of catching a bus back up to Axamer.

TERRAIN

FREERIDING

The freeriding terrain located off the Olympia Funicular is fun, to say the least. There are some great gullies and rollers off the Olympia run, which is on skiers' right of the Funicular. However, one of the best gullies is located directly under the Kuppel High-speed Quad. After a dump, this gully is super fun.

Powder Turns: The Birgitzköpfl Double Chair is the area for powder turns. The slope is north-facing, which keeps the snow drier. Further, as the lift is old and rickety, it tends not to get crowded.

Early Morning: Catch the Olympia Funicular up and crank some wide-open turns down the fresh corduroy on the Olympia Run.

Bad Weather: Axamer is not great in bad weather, as the majority of the mountain is relatively exposed. However, the short Hoadl I Double Chair gives access to some good tree runs that offer good visibility when the weather turns sour.

Avoiding Crowds: The Olympia Funicular and the Kuppel High-speed Quad tend to attract the biggest crowds. Your best bet is to stick to the slow Birgitzköpfl Double Chair.

Hiking: Axamer does not offer a lot of good hiking. However, there are some great backcountry runs right off the lifts. From the top of the Pleisen Double Chair, head out to skiers' left and ride down through the trees to the valley floor. This provides an awesome run through the forest. It is known as the Axamer Run, as you ride down to Axams village. When you reach Axams, jump on the free bus back up to Axamer.

Beginners: The best beginner runs are located on the Kaserwald T-bars at the base of Axamer.

FREESTYLE

Axamer probably has the best halfpipe in the Innsbruck region. It regularly hosts the ISF European Snowboard Championships, so it needs to maintain a high standard.

Halfpipes: The halfpipe is right next to the Kaserwald T-bars. The t-bars are the perfect length – you ride straight out of the pipe onto the t-bar, which then deposits you right at the top of the pipe. Not one bit of hiking is required. The pipe is long – about 80–100 m (264–333 ft). It has good transitions and the perfect amount of vert. It is maintained regularly using a Snow Turbo Grinder. One of the best times to hit the pipe is on Wednesday nights. The pipe is lit up, freshly cut and super fast. All the local riders from Innsbruck come up to strut their stuff and the standard is pretty high. The major problem with the pipe is its low elevation – 1,583 m (5,220 ft). This means the snow is often slushy and the pipe is slow. So really the best time to hit the Axamer pipe is at night.

Snowboard Parks: There is a small park next to the halfpipe. It is great for beginners but if you are into big jumps, don't bother.

Below: *Mouse Beuchat had a smile from ear to ear after this powder turn.*

NORDKETTE
AUSTRIA

STATISTICS

Elevations	(m)	(ft)
Top:	2256	7402
Base:	868	2848
Vertical Drop:	1388	4554

Lifts

Chair Lifts:	2
Cable Cars:	2
Total:	4

Contact Details

Phone:	+43 512 29 33440
Fax:	+43 512 29 334413
Email Address:	nordkette.info@tirol.com
Internet Site:	www.tirol.com/nordkette

RESORT REVIEW

Nordkette is the closest resort to the centre of Innsbruck. In fact, the main cablecar, the Nordketten I Cablecar, almost comes right into Innsbruck.

Nordkette is famous for three things – its steep terrain, its quarterpipe and its view. Nordkette has some of the steepest lift-accessed terrain in Europe. There is a consistent steep gradient for almost two-thirds of the whole resort. It is definitely not a beginner's area. In fact, there is only one marked beginner run on the whole mountain. Nordkette maintains one of the best quarterpipes in the Innsbruck area. The quarterpipe is big, easily over 4.5 m (15 ft), and allows massive back side airs. With the city of Innsbruck in the background, the backdrop is truly amazing. The view from Nordkette is exhilarating – down in the valley is the city of Innsbruck, and across the valley is the mighty Stubai Glacier.

However, the major problem with Nordkette is that all slopes are south-facing, so when the sun comes out all the slopes get baked pretty quickly, making it very slushy.

Above: *Nordkette is famous for its massive quarterpipe. After two hours of shaping, Mouse launches large over Innsbruck below.*

TERRAIN

FREERIDING

There is one word for the terrain at Nordkette – steep. If you rode from the top of Nordketten II Cablecar at 2,256 m (7,444 ft) all the way to the base at 860 m (2,840 ft), you would experience 1,400 m (4,620 ft) of the steepest vertical drop you have ever ridden.

Powder Turns: For some steep and deep stuff, head straight down the chutes off the Nordketten II Cablecar. A good place to find untracked snow is far out on skiers' right of the resort, in an area known as Tobel.

Early Morning: Stick to the Nordketten II Cablecar, as this gets the sun first.

Bad Weather: In bad weather don't even bother coming to Nordkette – there are no lower-level lifts. Perhaps go bowling in Innsbruck.

Avoiding Crowds: With six resorts in the area, Nordkette doesn't get too crowded. The crowds tend to go to the Stubai Glacier. Thus Nordkette is a good choice on the weekend.

Hiking: There are some great backcountry runs right off the lifts. At the top of the Nordketten I Cablecar, traverse hard to skiers' left. You will have to hike a bit to get over a small ridge. In effect, you are hiking into the next gully, which is known as Bodenstein-Alm. This gully goes all the way to

Above: *Avalanche barriers protect this station from being wiped out by debris. Above the station is the steepest lift accessed run in Europe.*

the valley floor and is awesome. Make sure you check with the locals before you head out, as the avalanche danger can be high.

Beginners: In three words – go somewhere else.

FREESTYLE

Except for its quarterpipe, freestyle facilities are non-existent. Nordkette does not maintain a pipe. They do have a few kickers off the Frau-Hitt-Warte Chairlift, but they are pretty useless. However, what Nordkette does have is plenty of natural terrain for building kickers. Because the terrain is steep, there are plenty of good landings for jumps. Basically, anywhere on the front face of Nordkette provides good opportunities to build kickers. In fact, the front face of Nordkette is littered with kickers made on previous days. Just make sure the landings are not bombed out before you hit them.

Above: *Whilst the rest of Innsbruck prepared to evacuate owing to avalanche danger, Mouse Beuchat couldn't resist the temptation of this epic run.*

ZILLERTAL VALLEY
AUSTRIA

OVERVIEW

The Zillertal Valley, located some 80 km (50 miles) from Innsbruck, is home to an incredible 15 resorts. All resorts can be ridden on the one lift pass – the Zillertal Super Ski Pass. This pass gives access to some 154 lifts and over 455 km (284 miles) of on-piste runs. The resorts are connected by both lifts and buses. The buses are free with the Zillertal Super Ski Pass.

Mayrhofen, as well as being a resort, is one of the main towns in the Zillertal Valley. It has grown rapidly in recent years. The buildings in the town are almost all traditional Tyrolean chalet design, giving the resort a natural ambience and picturesque look, in common with its surroundings. It has one of the liveliest après scenes in the region, with a wide range of bars and nightclubs. Some places to check out are Niki's Schirmbar, the Ice-Bar and Mo's Bar. The local snowboard hangout tends to be the Scotland Yard Pub, probably because the beer's cheap. For some late-night dancing, go to the Disco Papageno.

Mayrhofen and the surrounding resorts in the Zillertal Valley are becoming more and more popular with snowboarders. Resorts such as Gerlos, Mayrhofen, Hintertux Glacier and Hochzitteral are attracting riders from all over Europe. In this guide we are going to focus on two of the resorts in the Zillertal Valley, Gerlos and Mayrhofen.

Opposite: *Trees and powder are a perfect combination when the weather isn't on your side.*
Below: *The view down the valley to Gerlos.*

GERLOS
AUSTRIA

STATISTICS

Elevations	(m)	(ft)
Top:	2315	7595
Base:	1245	4084
Vertical Drop:	1070	3510

Lifts	
Surface Lifts:	12
Double Chairs:	8
Triple Chairs:	0
Quad Chairs – Fixed Grip:	3
Quad Chairs – Express:	0
Six Chairs – Express:	0
Gondolas:	0
Cable Cars:	0
Funiculars:	0
Total:	23

Contact Details

Phone:	+43 5284 5244 0
Fax:	+43 5284 5244 24

Email Address:
    tourismusverband.gerlos@telecom.at
Internet Site: www.tiscover.com/gerlos

RESORT REVIEW

Gerlos is located above the Zillertal Valley at 1,246 m (4,111 ft). The highest lifted point is 2,315 m (7,640 ft) on the Königsleiten peak. Gerlos actually comprises three mountains: Braun-ellkogel (2,158 m/7,120 ft), Königsleiten (2,315 m/7,640 ft) and Isskogel (2,264 m/ 7,470 ft). Gerlos has some great intermediate terrain but when it comes to extreme stuff, it is lacking. However, the assets of the terrain are its rolling tabletops and natural hits.

One of the major problems with Gerlos is the lift system – most of the lifts are of the old, fixed-grip variety, making them slow. Further, the lifts do not connect the three mountains very well. For example, there is a t-bar on one of the major traffic points. Thus, it is almost better to rely on the free shuttle bus to get you from mountain to mountain.

Like Mayrhofen, Gerlos is a pretty big party town. When the sun goes down the people certainly come out. If you want to experience nightlife in a small resort town, this is the place to do it.

Right: *The Gerlos pipe is shaped regularly with a Pipe Dragon which ensures that it is in top condition for riding pleasure.*

TERRAIN

Above: *Gerlos is now a big name in Europe thanks to the Grand Slam Halfpipe competition, which has a prize pool of well over USD$100,000.*

FREERIDING

The best freeriding exists on the Braunellkogel. The top half of the mountain has nice rolling terrain with some good lofting jumps, while the lower half has some fun steep stuff. This part of Gerlos also has the longest runs.

Powder Turns: The best place for powder turns is on the Braunellkogel in the Ziel area.

Early Morning: Head up to the Königsleiten and catch the early morning sun. There are some nice cruisers here, off the Bergrest Königsleiten Lift.

Bad Weather: Gerlos is a good place for bad weather as there is a lot of riding available in the trees. Try the trees off the quad chair at the Bergrest Fürstalm.

Avoiding Crowds: Gerlos does get pretty crowded, especially on weekends. The best place to hang out is the t-bar that accesses the Arbiskogel peak.

Hiking: There is some awesome hiking off the Königsleiten and Braunellkogel – you just need to know where you are going. The best thing is to go and speak to the guys at the

Hot Zone Snowboard School, as they have all the inside lines and know the place extremely well.

Beginners: The best place for beginners is the Oberhof T-bars, near the base of Gerlos.

FREESTYLE

In terms of freestyle riding, Gerlos was placed on the map by the USD$100,000 Gerlos Grand Slam Halfpipe competition that happened in 1997. At the time, it was the richest snowboarding competition ever. From that day forward, Gerlos had a name as a place to ride pipe.

Halfpipes: The pipe is located just above the Umbrella Bar in the Sunnalm part of Gerlos. The pipe is about 80 m (260 ft) long with nicely shaped 3 m (10 ft) walls. It is maintained by a Pipe Dragon. After the Hintertux pipe, it is probably the best pipe in the Zillertal Valley. However, the pipe has two main problems. First, there is no lift, so you always have to hike. Second, the low elevation of the pipe and the fact that it receives sun all day means that it deteriorates extremely quickly, especially in spring.

Snowboard Parks: Contrary to its description on the trail map, the park is nothing to write home about. It is directly below the halfpipe. As a boardercross track it is great, but as a park, well, it falls well short of the mark. There really are no good kickers to session.

MAYRHOFEN
AUSTRIA

STATISTICS

Elevations	(m)	(ft)
Top:	2250	7382
Base:	630	2067
Vertical Drop:	1620	5315

Lifts	
Surface Lifts:	15
Chairs:	10
Gondolas:	3
Cable Cars:	1
Funiculars:	0
Total:	29

154 Lifts are available on the Zillertal Super Pass

Contact Details
Phone:	+43 5285 6760
Fax:	+43 5285 6760 33

Email Address: mayrhofen@zillertal.tirol.at
Internet Site: www.tiscover.com/mayrhofen

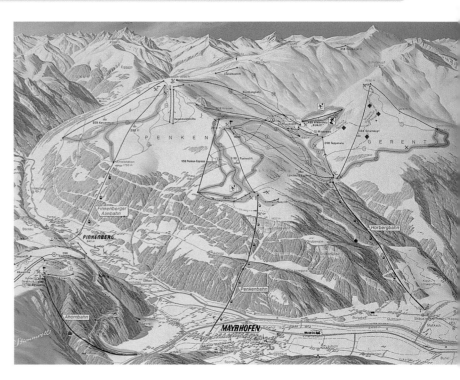

RESORT REVIEW

Mayrhofen's main riding is located on the Penken Mountain (2,095 m/6,910 ft). Mayrhofen is linked to the mountain via the Penken Gondola, which is probably one of the scariest gondolas you will ever ride. It rises out of Mayrhofen, goes across the main highway, then up and over a huge cliff. The scariest thing is that, at some points, it dangles some 50-60 m (165-200 ft) above the ground. Two other gondolas provide access to the resort from the villages of Finkenberg and Hippach. A free shuttle bus connects Finkenberg, Hippach and Mayrhofen.

In total, there are 29 lifts at Mayrhofen, including three gondolas accessing some 102 km (63 miles) of on-piste runs. However, as in Gerlos, once you are on the mountain, the lift system is fairly antiquated, with plenty of fixed-grip double and triple chairs. However, there are two express quads.

Left: *Mayrhofen at sunset. Photo courtesy of Mayrhofen Resort.*

TERRAIN

FREERIDING

Mayrhofen has good, wide, open-face freeriding. This is great when the sun's out, but is a big problem when the storms roll in.

Powder Turns: Some of the best powder turns can be found off the Gerent and Gspielkopf T-bars.

Early Morning: The Korren side of Penken Mountain receives the sun in the morning so it is the best place to head.

Bad Weather: Most of the riding is above the tree line. Although there are many trees at low elevations, they are filled with large cliffs, so it is not really a good idea to venture into them, unless you want to die. In bad weather, you're better off checking out the Mayrhofen Adventure Pool, which has a sauna, whirlpool and waterslide.

Avoiding Crowds: The Lärchwald Express tends to get pretty busy so it is a good lift to avoid. The Gerent T-bar tends to remain fairly uncrowded.

Hiking: The best hiking is off the Gspielkopf T-bar. Hike directly out behind the lift and drop into one of the bowls that leads back to the Nordhang Quad.

Beginners: The Ahorn area is popular with beginners as the slopes are all of a mild gradient.

FREESTYLE

Mayrhofen is gaining a reputation for providing quality freestyle facilities. Both the park and the pipe are located under the new Sunjet Quad Chair. As this chair is relatively short, it provides the perfect set-up for the pipe and park.

Halfpipes: The halfpipe is shaped by hand so the transitions tend to be a little inconsistent. To really put themselves on the map, Mayrhofen needs to purchase a Pipe Dragon.

Snowboard Park: The park contains a good variety of intermediate to expert kickers. It's worth checking out.

Below: *The town of Mayrhofen, nestled in the heart of the Austrian Alps. Photo courtesy of Mayrhofen Resort.*

FRANCE
EUROPE

OVERVIEW

With a staggering 320 resorts spread across the country, France is certainly heaven for snow-sport enthusiasts. French resorts easily match the size of the resorts in Switzerland and Austria. It is little wonder that travelers from around the world call the French Alps home during the winter months.

France, located in western Europe, is bounded on the north by the English Channel, the Strait of Dover and the North Sea; on the northeast by Belgium, Luxembourg and Germany; on the east by Germany, Switzerland and Italy; on the southeast by the Mediterranean Sea; on the south by Spain; and on the west by the Bay of Biscay. France is roughly hexagonal in shape, with a length from north to south of about 965 km (about 600 miles) and a maximum width of about 935 km (about 580 miles).

Below: *The Chamonix Valley is one of the most spectacular in the world. The mighty L'Aiguille du Midi towers above the mecca for extreme riders, the village of Chamonix.*

226

THE FRENCH ALPS

The massive French Alps form natural boundaries at the Italian and Swiss borders. With flanking chains and foothills, the Alps dominate the area east of the south central plateau. Many of the Alpine mountains extending across and along the French border are more than 3,962 m (13,000 ft) above sea level. Mont Blanc (4,807 m/15,771 ft) is the highest mountain in France and the second-highest peak on the European continent. The other major mountain range in France is the Pyrenees, which extend along the Franco-Spanish frontier from the Mediterranean Sea to the Bay of Biscay. Pic de Vignemale (3,298 m/10,820 ft) is the highest French peak in the Pyrenees.

The people of France, who number some 58 million, are extremely parochial. If you don't speak French, they may even consider not speaking to you. However, if you make the effort to experience the French culture, they are extremely helpful and friendly people. Unlike the Swiss, the French are far from conservative and more often than not are willing to try something new and outlandish. They are daredevils and love to party. And if you think they aren't slightly crazy, just try driving in Paris.

SNOW CONDITIONS IN FRANCE

Atlantic and Mediterranean storms are the main sources of snow in the French Alps. Although the French resorts don't receive the same quantities of snow as some of their North American counterparts, good conditions are usually guaranteed. Snow conditions in the far south of France, at resorts such as Isola 2000, tend to be the best.

An interesting factor in France's snow conditions is a meteorological pecularity known as 'the mistral'. It is a violent northerly wind from the Mediterranean central plateau and it plays havoc with snow conditions.

SNOWBOARDING IN FRANCE

Talk to different snowboarders and you are bound to get a mixed reaction about the quality of snowboarding in France. Some may argue that it is the only place in the world to ride. Others will advise you to head to nearby Switzerland or even that North American resorts are better. It all depends on the style of riding you are into. Freeriders are certainly not disappointed when they come away from a snowboarding excursion to France. The terrain is massive, with the vertical of many of the resorts exceeding any other place in the world. However, French resorts have fallen behind the rest of the world in catering for freestyle riders, with most resorts lacking quality pipes and parks.

Most of the French snowboard resorts are located in the southeast corner of the country. The French Alps offer some of the most picturesque views in the world, with the freeriding terrain to match. French resorts vary considerably, from the wide-open powder bowls of Tignes to the steeps of the resorts in the Chamonix Valley. As the resorts are so varied, it is possible to find any type of terrain you are looking for.

French resorts are still behind their Swiss and Austrian counterparts when it comes to upgrading their lift systems. Slow lifts mean you can spend as much time on a rickety double chair as you do actually coming down the mountain. However, the overall size and variety of terrain available at French resorts still makes France one of the best places in the world to ride.

ACCOMMODATION

Like Austria, youth hostels have not yet taken off in France. The best places to stay are the family-run pensions. These usually run at about FRF150-160 per person per night and include breakfast. Generally, the more expensive the pension, the better the breakfast. If you are stuck for accommodation, visit the local tourist office, as they have plenty of contacts.

GETTING TO THE FRENCH ALPS

As most of the French Alps are located in the south-east, it is best to fly into Geneva in Switzerland. From Geneva, most resorts are an easy two to four-hour drive away. Just remember that all major French motorways have tolls. Most French resorts are accessible by train. If you are traveling in a group, the best method is to lease a car from Renault Eurodrive. Visit their website at www.eurodrive.renault.com.

HINTS AND TIPS

- Like those in most of Europe, French businesses typically close for lunch between 12 and 2 pm, so make sure you remember to do your business outside these times.
- Learn some French if you want to have a good time in France, as the French appreciate it when you can speak their language.
- Credit cards are accepted throughout France, but MasterCard tends to be preferred.
- French baguettes are probably the best bread you will ever taste.
- All major motorways in France have tolls.

Above: *When the snow comes, Chamonix has the longest, deepest and steepest runs in the world. Mouse Beuchat tests out these superlatives and can't disagree.*

AVORIAZ
FRANCE

STATISTICS

Elevations	(m)	(ft)
Top:	2350	7710
Base:	1100	3609
Vertical Drop:	1250	4101

Lifts	
Surface Lifts:	14
Double Chairs:	0
Triple Chairs:	0
Quad Chairs – Fixed Grip:	20
Quad Chairs – Express:	0
Six Chairs – Express:	0
Gondolas:	2
Cable Cars:	1
Funiculars:	0
Total:	37

Contact Details

Phone:	+33 4 5074 0211
Fax:	+33 4 5074 1825
Email Address:	avoriaz@wanadoo.fr
Internet Site:	www.ot-avoriaz.fr

RESORT REVIEW

Avoriaz is one of the 12 resorts that make up the Les Portes du Soleil region. Les Portes du Soleil is the largest international skiing region in the world. Here are the numbers: two countries (Switzerland and France), 230 lifts including four cable cars and 11 gondolas, 12 villages, 550 instructors and over 640 km (400 miles) of on-piste runs. Bamboozled already? Well wait till you try riding the place.

A major downfall of Les Portes du Soleil is that all the resorts are very low in altitude (highest point is 2,360 m/ 7,708 ft). Therefore the area is far more susceptible to rain and wet snow. The lift system ranges from slow double chairs to pomas, to high-speed quads and cable cars. However, the majority of lifts are still fixed-grip or drag lifts which means slow rides and long queues.

The village of Avoriaz has a spectacular setting, perched above a sheer cliff high up in the Alps. The architecture is like something you might find on the moon. Towering hexagon-shaped apartments rise mysteriously out of the snow. And there are no cars, which adds to the moon-like atmosphere. In terms of nightlife, the best places to go are the Taraillion for drinking and Midnight Express for dancing.

Left: *Shane Stephens hit Avoriaz on the right day and was pleasantly surprised to be granted a powder licence.*

TERRAIN

Above: *Terrain to the power of infinity. Adam Dawes finds a small place for himself in the vast terrain of Avoriaz.*

FREERIDING

The terrain at Avoriaz varies from large steep bowls to flat groomed cruisers. The lift system accesses a lot of great terrain, so hiking for steeps isn't necessary. For beginners, there is a multitude of flat areas for learning and a few long intermediate runs for your progression. As is the case in most European resorts, a rider doesn't have to look too hard in Avoriaz to find awesome freeriding terrain. Cliffs and rocks can be found just off the pistes and the lifts access large bowls that, when full of powder, make a freerider's paradise. The only drawback of the freeriding terrain at Avoriaz is that the runs are short.

Powder Turns: For powder, go up to the Les Hauts Forts and traverse to skiers' left. Here you can drop into a natural gully that funnels into trees and ends up in Les Prodains. The top of this run is avalanche-prone, so check the conditions.

Early Morning: Head up to the Col du Fornet and crank some GS turns.

Bad Weather: In bad weather, head for the trees at Les Lindarets. The trails through this area have good natural obstacles.

Avoiding Crowds: Les Hauts Forts tends to be the most crowded – skiers love its fast groomers.

Hiking: With 12 resorts and over 230 lifts, why bother hiking? If you hike, you will probably be snaked by someone who caught a lift and traversed easily onto the slope.

Beginners: There is a great beginners' area off the south side of the Col de la Verte. The runs are serviced by a chairlift.

FREESTYLE

Avoriaz was one of the first French resorts to open up to snowboarders, and they have continued their commitment by providing good freestyle facilities.

Halfpipes: The pipe at Avoriaz is located right in the village at the bottom of the Arare Run. This is great when it comes to going back to the apartment/car for lunch or to change your gear. It has been dug out of the dirt, which means that it can operate on little snow (theoretically), and is very steep, which makes hiking a killer. Avoriaz does not use a pipe-shaping machine, so the pipe tends to lack finish. The main problem with the pipe is that it tends to be maintained infrequently.

Snowboard Parks: The park is a fun size and most suited for intermediates. Generally, the park at Avoriaz consists of a series of small hits and tabletops, including a Volkswagen Beetle for bonking. Overall, the park is usually good fun, especially if the snow isn't too firm. Other pluses of the park are that it is accessed by a poma and is not too far from the high-speed quad.

Natural Hits: The pistes at Avoriaz offer plenty of fun for riders who enjoy small hits and drops. However, the terrain is not particularly undulating, so natural kickers are not as readily available.

Above: *Adam Dawes, composed and in control as the mountain tries to swallow him.*

CHAMONIX
FRANCE

OVERVIEW

The Chamonix Valley is probably the most famous area in all of France. It has a reputation for extreme terrain unsurpassed by any other resort in Europe, and possibly the world. When there is snow, the reputation is well deserved, as you can ride from over 3,000 m (9,900 ft) down to the valley floor at 1,200 m (3,960 ft) through some of the most amazing chutes you will ever experience. The problem is that Chamonix does not receive a huge amount of snow, so there is rarely sufficient snow to ride to the valley floor. This significantly reduces the vertical at Chamonix.

There are four main resorts in the Chamonix Valley:

LE BRÉVENT

Le Brévent is a very steep resort where one step off the trails could permanently end your snowboard career. It is located directly above the town of Chamonix.

LA FLÉGÈRE

La Flégère has possibly the best natural terrain for freestyle snowboarding in all of the Chamonix Valley. La Flégère is located right next to Le Brévent. These two resorts have recently been linked by a high-speed gondola, which has significantly improved the area.

LES GRANDS MONTETS

Les Grands Montets is the most famous resort in the Chamonix Valley. It is famous for its spectacular views, long runs and extreme riding. The recent installation of a high-speed gondola has been a blessing. The resort is located about 20 minutes from Chamonix, above the town of Argentière.

LE TOUR

Le Tour is a great place to find natural hits and quarterpipes. The resort has recently installed a detachable quad to the Tête de Balme, which has doubled the skiable area.

In total there are 31 lifts spread across the four resorts, including five cable cars and four gondolas. Despite some recent additions, the lift systems remain relatively antiquated with an excess of fixed-grip chairs. The main downfall of the Chamonix Valley is its freestyle facilities. Good pipes and parks are sadly lacking. Whilst other resorts in Europe have been building up a freestyle scene, the Chamonix resorts have not. The reputation of Chamonix needs to be balanced against the fact that, in terms of freestyle facilities, it is years behind.

In this guide we will review Le Brévent, La Flégère and Les Grands Montets.

Located at the foot of Mont Blanc (the highest peak in Western Europe) at 4,807 m (15,750 ft), Chamonix is a decent-sized resort town filled with villas and hotels of varying age and style as well as a range of restaurants and shops. It also has a very lively nightlife. The best bars to check out are La Cantina, Wild Wallabies and Bar Savoia. Bar Savoia is a cool little bar behind the casino. The drinks are cheap and the atmosphere is relaxing. There is even Internet access.

It is almost obligatory when in Chamonix to check out L'Aiguille du Midi. It is one of the most famous peaks in the Alps, rising to 3,842 m (12,678 ft). The L'Aiguille du Midi Cable car takes you close to the top and then, after a series of caves, you catch a lift to the very peak. To say the view is breathtaking is truly an understatement. You can actually ride down through the glacier from the L'Aiguille du Midi on a run known as the Vallée Blanche, but most of the run is very flat and uninteresting.

Right: *Neil Hardwick was happy to escape Australia's summer to take a leisurely turn through Chamonix Valley's deepest and lightest powder. Photo—Gavin O'Toole.*
Below: *The town of Chamonix is a haven for big-mountain extreme riders.*

LES GRANDS MONTETS
CHAMONIX, FRANCE

STATISTICS

Elevations	(m)	(ft)
Top:	3275	10745
Base:	1035	3395
Vertical Drop:	2240	7349

Lifts

Surface Lifts:	0
Double Chairs:	0
Triple Chairs:	0
Quad Chairs – Fixed Grip:	6
Quad Chairs – Express:	0
Six Chairs – Express:	0
Gondolas:	1
Cable Cars:	2
Funiculars:	0
Total:	9

Contact Details

Phone:	+33 4 5053 2333
Fax:	+33 4 5053 3615

Email Address: contact@grandsmontets.com
Internet Site: www.grands-montets.com

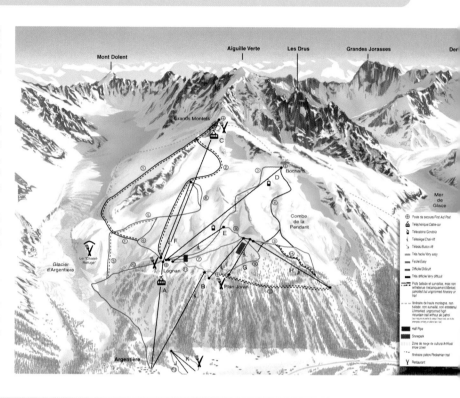

RESORT REVIEW

Les Grands Montets is the largest and most prestigious resort in Chamonix. The mountain is located directly above the town of Argentière. It is the only north-facing resort in the Chamonix Valley, and is more expensive than the other resorts in the Valley.

The major problem with Les Grands Montets is the lift system. Despite the recent addition of the Bochard Gondola, the lift system remains old and slow. Further, the placement of some of the lifts is ludicrous – they serve absolutely no purpose and give access to no new terrain. A good example is the Tabe Chair. Another silly thing about the lift system is the fact that you need to pay FRF30 every time you want to ride the top cable car. You could blow a lot of money if you wanted to ride circuits of the best terrain Les Grands Montets has to offer.

The great thing about Les Grands Montets is that it is north-facing, which means the powder is still dry days after the last snowfall. However, this can also be a problem, since the hard-pack never really softens up until late in spring. Wearing a helmet is a good idea.

Right: *Damo Liddy laying back and enjoying the view from one of the chutes of Les Grands Montets.*

TERRAIN

FREERIDING

Les Grands Montets is like a large pyramid, of which two faces can be ridden safely. The rest can also be ridden, but death is likely. The slopes of Les Grands Montets are a combination of open bowls, cliffs and chutes. Although it is expensive, it is worth riding the top cable car at least once. From here you can ride on the back side of Les Grands Montets next to the Argentière Glacier. The run is not extremely challenging but the glacier is spectacular.

The best freeriding terrain is located in the Combe de la Pendant, which is accessed using the Bochard Gondola. This area has natural gullies, chutes and drops. When the snow falls, you can ride all the way to the valley floor – it is one of the best runs in Chamonix.

Powder Turns: Pay the FRF30 for the Les Grands Montets Cablecar and drop in directly beneath it. Stick close to the cliff face on the right-hand side and you will definitely find some awesome powder.

Early Morning: Go to La Flégère as Les Grands Montets doesn't really receive sun until late in the morning.

Bad Weather: Don't even bother – the mountain is far too exposed. When the weather craps out, head for the Bar Savoia or Wild Wallabies.

Above: *Local snowboard bums are attracted to Chamonix like bees to honey. Now you can see why.*

Avoiding Crowds: As the Bochard Gondola provides access to most of the mountain, it gets extremely crowded. If you don't mind a super-slow lift, stick to the Herse Lift.

Hiking: There is some great hiking at Les Grands Montets but unless you want to die, you should hire a guide.

Beginners: The t-bars at the base service an excellent beginner area.

FREESTYLE

Until very recently, Les Grands Montets has ignored freestyle riders. However, they have now purchased a Pipe Master and installed a pipe near the base of the Logan Cablecar.

Halfpipes: The transitions of the halfpipe are smooth, but it lacks sufficient vert. Also, the slope of the pipe changes gradient halfway through. It starts with a good 20-degree gradient, then flattens out to about 5 degrees. This makes the bottom half of the pipe totally useless. However, the lower walls do work well for one-hit wonders. It is shaped using a Snow Turbo Grinder.

Snowboard Parks: There is no park at Les Grands Montets. Go to Le Tour instead.

LE BRÉVENT
CHAMONIX, FRANCE

STATISTICS

Elevations	(m)	(ft)
Top:	2525	8284
Base:	1035	3395
Vertical Drop:	1490	4888

Lifts	
Surface Lifts:	3
Double Chairs:	0
Triple Chairs:	0
Quad Chairs – Fixed Grip:	4
Quad Chairs – Express:	0
Six Chairs – Express:	0
Gondolas:	1
Cable Cars:	1
Funiculars:	0
Total:	9

Contact Details	
Phone:	+33 4 5053 2333
Fax:	+33 4 5053 3615

Above: *Steep, extreme and amazing. Dancing with death at Le Brévent.*

RESORT REVIEW

Le Brévent has an abundance of extreme terrain. Everywhere you look, there are steep chutes, cliffs and any other sort of obstacle that an adrenaline junkie would be looking for. The Brévent Cablecar rivals L'Aiguille du Midi as the scariest lift ride in the Chamonix Valley. It stretches across two jagged peaks and dangles over 150 m (495 ft) above the ground. The runs at Le Brévent are generally very steep. Make sure that you stick to them, as a wrong turn will send you straight off a cliff. The resort sits at 2000 m (6,562 ft), 1 km (0.6 mile) above the town of Chamonix, with the slopes all above this point. You can do a run back down to the town, but it requires a lot of snow.

Similar to Les Grands Montets, the lift system at Le Brévent is antiquated. All lifts are fixed grip. However, one lift does have a magic carpet, making it a bit quicker.

TERRAIN

FREERIDING

Steep, extreme and amazing are three adjectives you could use to describe the terrain, but the list could go on. Unless you are an extreme rider who likes to dance with death, you will need to stick to the marked trails. The problem is, if there is no fresh snow, these trails can become a little boring. They are super fast but lack natural obstacles. Extreme caution should be exercised off-piste during dry spells. However, when it does get powder, Le Brévent is awesome because of the length and steepness of runs.

Powder Turns: If there is a ton of new snow, the place to be is the Couloir du Brévent. You can ride this couloir all the way to the valley floor. It is dangerous, so wear an avalanche transceiver and speak to the locals before you attempt it.

Early Morning: The whole area is covered in sun from morning to afternoon. It is best to take the Brévent Cablecar in the morning before it gets busy.

Bad Weather: No hope in bad weather as the mountain is very exposed to the elements. The Brévent Cablecar will only run if there is little or no wind.

Avoiding Crowds: An old lift system and a single access point to the resort results in havoc when crowded. Avoid Le Brévent when it is crowded.

Beginners: Don't even bother trying to learn here unless you want to break an arm or a leg. There is a t-bar at the base but you are better off going to Le Tour.

FREESTYLE

There is no park or pipe available at Le Brévent. The only freestyle terrain that you will find is off-piste. Compared to other resorts, Le Brévent doesn't rate too highly on the freestyle stakes. Go here only if you are into extreme terrain.

LA FLÉGÈRE
CHAMONIX, FRANCE

STATISTICS

Elevations	(m)	(ft)
Top:	1894	6214
Base:	1035	3395
Vertical Drop:	859	2818

Lifts	
Surface Lifts:	0
Double Chairs:	0
Triple Chairs:	0
Quad Chairs – Fixed Grip:	4
Quad Chairs – Express:	0
Six Chairs – Express:	0
Gondolas:	1
Cable Cars:	0
Funiculars:	0
Total:	5

Contact Details	
Phone:	+33 4 5053 2333
Fax:	+33 4 5053 3615

Above: *A flying board takes Bear Agushi for a ride in the French Alps.*

RESORT REVIEW

La Flégère is a south-facing resort next to Le Brévent. The two resorts have recently been joined by a gondola, which means you can enjoy the steeps of Le Brévent in the morning and the natural rolling terrain of La Flégère in the afternoon. La Flégère is excellent in spring, as the snow is soft and there are natural kickers everywhere. Most of the freestylers from Chamonix hang out here, sessioning big kickers and spines. As in all the other Chamonix resorts, the lift system needs a serious upgrade.

TERRAIN

FREERIDING

La Flégère is one resort that doesn't get tracked out in a few hours. It's not renowned for its epic powder runs, but it does have some great bowls, windlips and cliffs. There are a few flat sections around the resort that are a pain if you get stuck. All the best runs are accessed from the Index Chair. The main runs down either side of the chair are fun. As you get off the chair, turn right. This leads to a few nice big bowls that wind their way down to the La Trappe Chair, which will take you back to the base of the Index Chair. Be careful going down these runs, as they are not frequently used. If you are unsure of your directions, look for someone else's tracks to follow, or traverse right and just keep going.

Powder Turns: There is plenty of powder to be had at La Flégère. Because it is less crowded than Les Grands Montets, it stays untracked for longer. The best run for powder turns is the Lachenal Bowl. It's big, wide and has a few small cliffs, but it is prone to avalanche. To get there, traverse left off the Index Chair. From here a chute provides access to the run. This bowl goes down to Evettes Chair, which links back to the base of the Index Chair.

Bad Weather: Like most other Chamonix resorts, La Flégère is not good in bad weather.

Avoiding Crowds: La Flégère does not get as crowded as the other resorts in the area. Lift queues tend to be around 5-10 minutes on weekends. The Index Chair gets the most attention.

Beginners: La Flégère is a good place for beginners. The nice easy slope that winds its way down from the Index Chair is excellent for learning.

FREESTYLE

La Flégère is possibly the best resort in Chamonix for non-pipe-riding freestylers. It has a wide assortment of bowls, windlips and small cornices that are ideal for launching. The Pic Janvier trail that winds its way down the front face has good walls and is super fun to jump off in the right conditions. There are also lots of good locations for kickers. However, for pipes you are better off heading to Les Grands Montets. If you are looking for or man-made kickers, head to Le Tour.

LES ARCS
FRANCE

STATISTICS

Elevations	(m)	(ft)
Top:	3226	1058
Base:	850	2788
Vertical Drop:	2376	7795

Lifts	
Surface Lifts:	31
Double Chairs:	0
Triple Chairs:	0
Quad Chairs – Fixed Grip:	27
Quad Chairs – Express:	4
Six Chairs – Express:	0
Gondolas:	3
Cable Cars:	1
Funiculars:	1
Total:	67

Contact Details	
Phone:	+33 4 7907 1257
Fax:	+33 4 7907 4596
Email Address:	wlesarcs@lesarcs.com
Internet Site:	www.lesarcs.com

RESORT REVIEW

Above: *Why does Stu Johnson love France so much?*
Photo—Gavin O'Toole.

Les Arcs, located about 45 minutes from Albertville (site of the 1992 Winter Olympics) and about two hours from Geneva, is home to the legendary Regis Roland. Roland starred in the epic snowboard trilogy *Apocalypse Snow,* and is founder of A Snowboards. Les Arcs actually consists of three 'Arcs': Arcs 1600, Arcs 1800 and Arcs 2000. You can buy a ticket for each of the areas, but it is recommended you get a ticket for all three, especially Arcs 2000. Arcs 1800 is the hub of Les Arcs. Arcs 1600 is located about 2 km (1.2 miles) down the road and has cheaper accommodation, while Arcs 2000 is 12 km (7.5 milses) up the road and is more expensive.

The mountain is extremely snowboarder-friendly, and it is easy to see why Axel Pauporté and his Belgian friends hang out here. Les Arcs actually has a separate snowboarder trail map, which highlights good snowboard areas.

When it comes to size, Les Arcs is no slouch. It has over 2,750 hectares (6,795 acres) of skiable terrain accessed by 77 lifts including a funicular, a cable car and two gondolas. However, most of the lifts are fixed grip or t-bars. In fact, some of the t-bars are the longest in Europe. Put up with the pain of the lift system, though, and you will be more than rewarded. The natural rolling terrain on the back side of Les Arcs is awesome.

Les Arcs is the site of the 'Piste de Vitesse', a run used for speed skiing and snowboarding. This run, near the summit, goes for 1,740 m (5,742 ft) at a gradient of 76 degrees and is where Australian Darren Powel set the world speed record on a snowboard (196.937 km/h/122.357 mph).

The place to be at night is Arcs 1800, as this is the focal point of the whole Les Arcs area. If you are after some jazz, head to the aptly named Blue Bar. Alternatively, if you want a snowboard atmosphere, check out the Carré Blanc in Les Villards. If you want something a bit cheaper, head down into the town of Bourg-St Maurice, which is linked to Les Arcs by a funicular.

TERRAIN

FREERIDING

Les Arcs offers every type of terrain you can imagine, from cat tracks to rocky chutes to cliffs and rolling powder bowls. This place is awesome after a big dump as there are plenty of runs with little drops, ledges and hits. At the base of the resort there are mainly groomed wide trails through trees and open bowls. These trails offer a range of fall lines for all types of skill levels. The main bowl of Arcs 2000 is littered with gullies and rolls. These trails start out with a good gradient but flatten out towards the bottom. As a result, there are a lot of bowls and jumps that are fun to ride into but require a traverse to get out of.

Powder Turns: The best powder run is located under Plan Bois 69. It is littered with small drop-offs and has banks on both sides.

Early Morning: Any of the runs on the front face of Les Arcs, above Arcs 1800, are good for early morning cruising.

Bad Weather: The lifts around Arcs 1600 are best in bad weather. The lower portion of this part of the mountain has good tree runs. Les Arcs is definitely a better mountain than Tignes/Val d'Isère in bad weather.

Avoiding Crowds: The lift to avoid is the gondola that comes out of Arcs 1800. The crowds here are particularly bad in the morning.

Hiking: There are some great hikes around the ridges of Les Arcs but you should really speak to a local first.

Beginners: Beginner terrain exists at all three Arcs. A few chairlifts have no beginner trail, so plan your route well.

FREESTYLE

There is a healthy freestyle scene at Les Arcs, so the pipe, which is located at the base of the Carreley Run, is well maintained. It has a good shape and a good gradient. The park is also kept in good shape. It is located between the Arpette Chairlift and Frettes Draglift and contains some nice-sized kickers. Further, at Arcs 2000 there are a lot of natural gullies and gunbarrels which provide excellent opportunities for frontside and backside hits. All the access trails and cat tracks generally have fun walls to ride.

Above: *Spring quarterpipe session at Les Arcs.*
Photo—SCALP DPPI (Les Arcs).

Above: *With a pillow of clouds to land on, a lone rider styles a stalefish in one of the massive bowls of Les Arcs.*
Photo—SCALP DPPI (Les Arcs).

TIGNES
FRANCE

STATISTICS

Elevations	(m)	(ft)
Top:	3450	11319
Base:	1550	5085
Vertical Drop:	1900	6233

Lifts	
Surface Lifts:	19
Double Chairs:	0
Triple Chairs:	0
Quad Chairs – Fixed Grip:	26
Quad Chairs – Express:	0
Six Chairs – Express:	0
Gondolas:	2
Cable Cars:	1
Funiculars:	1
Total:	49

Contact Details	
Phone:	+33 4 7940 0440
Fax:	+33 4 7940 0315
Email Address:	tignes@laposte.fr
Internet Site:	www.tignes.net

RESORT REVIEW

Tignes is huge! Super Tignes (as it is known) consists of 46 lifts, including a funicular and two cable cars. When combined with nearby Val d'Isère the area is referred to as Espace Killy (after the famous French downhill skier, Jean-Claude Killy) and has 96 lifts, including two funiculars and four cable cars. Further, the area has a whopping 1,900 m (6,270 ft) vertical drop from a height of 3,450 m (11,385 ft) down to a base of 1,550 m (5,115 ft). However, unlike a place like Saas Fee, this vertical is not available in one hit. You need to catch several lifts to benefit from the full extent of the vertical. Tignes and Val d'Isère can be ridden on a single lift ticket, but keep aside a week if you are thinking about attempting this.

Tignes is located at 2,100 m (6,930 ft) next to a large lake. It actually comprises three villages – Val Claret, Le Lac and Lavachet. A free shuttle bus connects these villages. However, at peak times the shuttle bus is packed. Like Avoriaz, Tignes is a purpose-built resort, and it shows. It lacks any of the atmosphere you associate with French mountain villages. Rather, large apartment complexes scar the Tignes landscape. This is in stark contrast to the beauty of the surrounding mountains. Who knows what sort of drugs they were on when they designed Tignes in the 1970s.

Although its lift system is ageing, Tignes is ahead of most other French resorts in upgrading. Recently it installed two new high-speed six-chairs at Le Lavachet. More still needs to

be done, though, because the majority of lifts that service the runs are of the fixed-grip variety.

Above: *The cliffs at Tignes are Damo Liddy's nemesis ... until now.*

238

TERRAIN

FREERIDING

The terrain at Tignes is incredible, ranging from cliffs and chutes to gentle green runs to wide-open powder fields. With such a variety of terrain, Tignes is certainly a world-class resort.

There is also some great hiking to be had around the towering peaks of Tignes. The pistes are always well groomed, allowing high-speed carving.

Powder Turns: The area between the Tichot Lift and the Chardonet Lift does not get tracked because you have to hike out along the road. This area is known as Lognan, and has guaranteed powder. The great thing about it is the rolling terrain. Good powder turns can also be found off to skiers' left of the Merle Blanc Lift.

Early Morning: The Palafour, Aiguille Percée and Grand Huit Lifts are the best places in the morning as they all receive the sun first. Fresh turns are often available off the Perce-Neige Run.

Bad Weather: A lack of trees above Val Claret makes riding difficult in bad weather. It would probably be better to stick

Above: *Peter Coppleson at home in the craters of Tignes. Photo—Gavin O'Toole.*

to the lower altitudes, especially the runs around the Sache Gondola, which leaves from the village of Les Brevieres.

Avoiding Crowds: The best way to avoid crowds is to stay away during the Christmas-New Year period, since nearly half of Europe is on holiday. The Aiguille Percee Lift is a particularly bad place for crowds, especially early in the morning.

FREESTYLE

Tignes has a very healthy freestyle environment. In fact, it has the largest snowboard park in Europe. It is located on the Palafour Coomb and has 600 m (1,980 ft) of vertical. The halfpipe is also in this area, and is serviced by the Millinex Draglift. Although the park is usually kept in good shape, the pipe tends to be maintained less regularly.

In summer, Tignes installs a park and pipe on the Grande Motte Glacier. Unlike many of the summer camps in the USA, where you have to pay to use the facilities, the summer park and pipe are free. Of course, the quality of the park and pipe is not quite as good as those at Mt Hood, Oregon.

SWITZERLAND
EUROPE

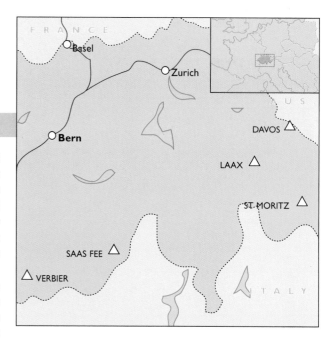

OVERVIEW

Switzerland is one of the smallest countries in Europe, with a total surface area of 41,293 sq km (15,943 sq miles). It is located in west-central Europe and is bounded on the north by France and Germany, on the east by Austria and Liechtenstein, on the south by Italy, and on the west by France. Unlike most other countries, it is neutral, meaning it does not have alliances with any other country. In fact, it is not even part of the European Community (EC).

Although about 60% of Switzerland's 6 million people are classified as urban, most live in small villages that are scattered throughout the countryside. Three main languages are spoken in Switzerland – French (20%), German (65%) and Italian (10%). The other language spoken is Romansh. Most Swiss can speak French, German and Italian, and

Below: *The Alps of Europe are huge. Damo Liddy takes in an incredible Swiss Alps panorama.*

also have a good command of English. The Swiss are conservative people and like things to be clean and efficient. Their transport system provides an excellent example of this – it is probably the most comprehensive and efficient in the world.

THE SWISS ALPS

Switzerland is one of the most mountainous countries of Europe, with more than 70% of its area covered by the Alps, in the central and southern sections, and the Jura, in the northwest. The Swiss Alps are part of the largest mountain system in Europe, and are famous for their jagged peaks and steep ravines. The highest peak in Switzerland is the Dufourspitze of Monte Rosa, which rises to 4,634 m (15,203 ft). The Jura (Celtic for 'forest') are much lower and smaller than the Alps. Most of the resorts are located in the Alps, with the Jura left for cross-country skiing.

SNOW CONDITIONS IN SWITZERLAND

The storms that brew over the Atlantic push deep into the Swiss Alps, depositing snow. The east of Switzerland tends to receive larger quantities and more consistent snow than the southwest. It is for this reason that the east of Switzerland is typically called the 'White Arena'.

The bise, a cold, northerly wind, predominates in the winter, and the föhn, a warm, dry southeasterly wind, predominates during the rest of the year. The beginning of the föhn usually spells the end of the snow.

SNOWBOARDING IN SWITZERLAND

Most of the resorts are located along the southwestern, southern and eastern borders of Switzerland. Resorts in Switzerland are big, even by European standards, so make sure you are fit. For example, Verbier and the Four Valleys is one of the largest resorts in the world, and has a 100-installation lift system that connects 15 mountain villages.

Unlike French resorts and some resorts in Austria, Swiss resorts are committed to continually upgrading their lift systems. The result is that Swiss resorts have some of the fastest and most efficient lifts in the world. High-speed quads tend to be the norm rather than the exception.

The freeriding in Switzerland is out of this world. Nowhere else in the world could you find so much in-bounds extreme terrain. Cliffs, cornices, chutes – you name it, at least one Swiss resort will have it in-bounds and accessible by lift. In terms of freestyle, the Laax, Davos, St Moritz triangle, in the Graubunden region of Switzerland, probably has the best halfpipes and parks in all Europe. Some of Europe's best riders, including Michi Albin and Fabien Rohrer, call this triangle home.

ACCOMMODATION

Unlike Austria, youth hostels are more common in Switzerland, both in the large cities and at the resorts. They usually cost around CHF30 per person per night. Although this is relatively expensive, they are always very clean and comfortable. If there is no hostel, the next best option is the bed and breakfast pensions, which run at about CHF40 per person per night. If you are still stuck for accommodation, go to the local tourist office.

GETTING TO THE SWISS ALPS

If you are going to resorts in the southwest corner of Switzerland (such as Verbier, Crans Montana, Saas Fee), your best bet is to fly into Geneva. From Geneva you can either get a train to the resorts or drive. On the other hand, if you are going to resorts in the east (such as Laax, Davos or St Moritz), it is better to fly into Zurich. If you are traveling in a group the best method is to lease a car.

HINTS AND TIPS

- Like those in most of Europe, Swiss businesses typically close for lunch between 12 and 2 pm. Do your business outside these times.
- Credit cards are accepted throughout Switzerland but MasterCard tends to be preferred.
- Almost all Swiss public phones use phonecards. Do not expect to be able to pump coins into the phones.
- There are no tolls on the Swiss motorways. The Swiss pay an annual fee of CHF120 to drive on the major motorways.
- If you have any questions or queries, go straight to the local tourist office.

Above: *Going ...down! Mouse Beuchat drops 40 feet into bottomless Euro powder.*

VERBIER
SWITZERLAND

STATISTICS

Elevations	(m)	(ft)
Top:	3330	10925
Base:	1500	4921
Vertical Drop:	1830	6004

Lifts	
Surface Lifts:	46
Double Chairs:	0
Triple Chairs:	0
Quad Chairs – Fixed Grip:	32
Quad Chairs – Express:	0
Six Chairs – Express:	0
Gondolas:	5
Cable Cars:	12
Funiculars:	0
Total:	95

This includes the Four Valleys lift system.

Contact Details

Phone:	+41 27 775 3888
Fax:	+41 27 775 3889
Email Address:	verbiertourism@verbier.ch
Internet Site:	www.verbier.ch

RESORT REVIEW

Verbier is the Whistler/Blackcomb of Switzerland. It is simply huge; in fact, it is one of the world's largest ski areas. There are 400 km (250 miles) of on-piste runs and over 90 lifts. The area is known as the 'Four Valleys', and the lifts connect the five villages of Verbier, La Tzoumaz, Nendaz, Veysonnaz and Val de Bagnes. But it doesn't stop there – a day pass is also valid at Super St Bernard, which is located just up the road. At Super St Bernard, you can actually ride into Italy.

Although the major connecting lifts at Verbier are gondolas and cable cars, these are few and far between. The majority of the 100 lifts are in fact slow, fixed-grip chairs. However, this is gradually changing. Verbier has plans to begin upgrading some of its lifts.

The base of the resort starts at 1,500 m (4,950 ft) and rises to 3,300 m (10,900 ft) on the mighty Mont-Fort, giving a vertical of some 1.8 km (1.1 miles). The riding in the high alpine regions of Verbier is extreme. There are numerous cliff bands and steep couloirs. It is little wonder that the Red Bull Freeride Extremes are held here every year.

Verbier is a popular and prestigious resort, so be prepared to pay the price. Frequented by the famous, Verbier is definitely a place to be seen. However, if you can avoid all this hype and really experience the terrain, you will be totally

Left: *The team rolls into Verbier on a cloudy winter's day.*

blown away. Often a better option than staying on the mountain is to stay in Le Châble; it's cheaper and more relaxed. Further, there is a gondola that lifts you from Le Châble up into Verbier.

Given the size and prestige of the resort, it is not surprising that Verbier has some great nightlife. Check out the Mont-Fort Pub and Le Garage for some après atmosphere, and Marshall's for late-night dancing.

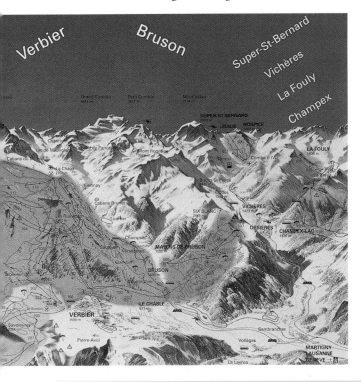

Above: *Damo Liddy styles a stalefish into a foggy Verbier.*

TERRAIN

FREERIDING

The freeriding terrain at Verbier is enormous. But be aware, it is also dangerous, as many of the slopes are prone to avalanche, especially after the warm föhn wind blows up the valley. If you are going off-piste, always wear an avalanche transceiver and speak to the locals before you head out.

Most of the slopes at Verbier face southwest, and so receive a lot of sun. This is good if you want a suntan, but it turns light, dry powder into heavy, clag-like snow in a matter of hours.

Powder Turns: For the best powder, head up onto the Mont-Fort Glacier. Stick to the right-hand side of the glacier, hook right past the Glacier T-bars (5), and ride down into Tortin.

Cliffs: This list could go on forever. Some of the best cliffs are located off L'Olympique, at the top of the Attelas Gondola.

Bad Weather: Definitely stay off the Mont-Fort, as you won't be able to see a thing. Your best bet is to head to the trees off the Siviez Chairlift (61). There is always good visibility here.

Avoiding Crowds: When Verbier gets crowded, it is a good opportunity to go and check out Super St Bernard and Bruson.

Hiking: There is some extreme hiking at Verbier, but you really need to speak to the locals. A relatively easy hike is to traverse straight out behind the Lac des Vaux No. 1 Chairlift (116), circle around the Col des Mines, then drop into the front face. You can actually ride right back into the village.

Beginners: The best beginner runs are located at Thyon.

FREESTYLE

As the freeriding terrain at Verbier is so good, the freestyle scene is not huge. However, Verbier does put a fair bit of effort into having a pipe and park. In fact, the park is sponsored by Swatch. During winter, both park and pipe facilities are located at La Chaux. In summer, they are moved up to the Mont-Fort Glacier.

Halfpipes: The halfpipe is shaped using a Pipe Dragon. Although the transitions can be good, it tends to be maintained irregularly, and is often closed.

Snowboard Parks: The park is located next to the La Chaux No. 1 Chairlift (113). It is a super-long and super-good park. It is basically a huge boardercross track with kickers of differing sizes located all the way through the course. There are a few rails at the bottom. The park is maintained much more regularly than the pipe.

SAAS FEE
SWITZERLAND

STATISTICS

Elevations	(m)	(ft)
Top:	3500	11483
Base:	1800	5905
Vertical Drop:	1700	5577

Lifts	
Surface Lifts:	17
Double Chairs:	0
Triple Chairs:	0
Quad Chairs – Fixed Grip:	2
Quad Chairs – Express:	0
Six Chairs – Express:	0
Gondolas:	3
Cable Cars:	4
Funiculars:	1
Total:	27

Contact Details	
Phone:	+41 27 958 1858
Fax:	+41 27 958 1860
Email Address:	to@saas-fee.ch
Internet Site:	www.saas-fee.ch

RESORT REVIEW

Saas Fee is a unique resort, and is home to some of the world's best riders. The Saas Fee village is located directly below the slopes at 1,800 m (5,940 ft), and is not open to vehicles apart from authorized electric carts owned by the resort and hotels. The village is a winter wonderland, with narrow streets lined with shops, bars and cafes.

Saas Fee offers year-round riding, with amazing snowboard facilities in summer. The terrain at Saas Fee is massive, with 1,700 m (5,610 ft) of vertical. Much of the terrain is covered by glaciers and is out-of-bounds. The best part of the terrain is the length of the runs which, from top to bottom, will take a good, fit rider around 30 minutes. The Metro Alpin is a funicular that takes you to the top of the resort at 3,500 m (11,550 ft). It is the world's highest underground train. The three halfpipes and the terrain park are located up in the high alpine area. The run from the top starts relatively gently, then becomes varied in difficulty, ranging from advanced-level steeps to intermediate-level gullies to beginner cat tracks. From this point down you have about another vertical kilometer (0.6 mile) during which you can choose the terrain that bests suits you and the conditions. The run from top to bottom is exhausting, and one round trip takes about an hour because of the two cable cars and the underground train you need to reach the top. However, it is well worth it, especially on a powder day.

Left: *Deep in the heart of Saas Fee. Photo courtesy of Saas Fee Tourism Office.*

TERRAIN

Above: *With most of the terrain at Saas Fee covered by glaciers, venturing out-of-bounds can be a serious health hazard. Photo courtesy of Saas Fee Tourism Office and Geoff Webb.*

FREERIDING

Ignoring Verbier, when it comes to extreme terrain, Saas Fee is the Swiss capital. The massive glaciers which characterize the landscape have cut some brilliant features into the mountain. However, most of the glacier terrain is out-of-bounds due to the major hazards such as crevices and ice boulders that exist within them. For this reason it is not as good as Verbier for extreme stuff. The steeper runs are a little short or are located in the out-of-bounds glaciers. There is a run through the Saas Fee Glacier which is rideable, but only with a paid guide.

The best feature of the in-bounds riding at Saas Fee is that it has a consistent gradient almost from top to bottom. On a powder day, the terrain from the top to bottom is amazing and rivals the best powder bowls in the world due to the sheer length of the runs. There are no significant flat spots from the 3,000 m (9,900 ft) level down and therefore on a powder day, you wouldn't be required to skate around the mountain to access the steeps. This is what makes the 1,700 m (5,610 ft) vertical a big drawcard at Saas Fee.

Powder Turns: The bowls below the Spielboden Gondola collect some great powder and there is about a vertical kilometer (0.6 mile) of steep riding.

Early Morning: If it has been a few days since a dump and you want to find the leftover pockets of powder in the morning, pretty much the whole mountain is available as it is almost all in the shade.

Bad Weather: If there are high winds and poor visibility, stay off the top of the mountain – it is very exposed and open. The terrain around the Berghaus Plattjen area offers the best tree terrain and protected spots. It is accessed by a cable car – the perfect thing for bad-weather riding.

Avoiding Crowds: The lift capacity at Saas Fee is massive, with seven cable cars/gondolas and an underground train in addition to two chairs and 17 surface lifts. The early morning rush to the top of the mountain is made easier because five cable cars/gondolas begin in the village. Once the crowds are up on the mountain, the queues for lifts are reasonable, but of course it all depends upon the time of year.

FREESTYLE

Saas Fee has shown a great commitment to snowboarding. Rivaled only by Laax and nearby Verbier, Sass Fee offers three halfpipes, a boardercross course and a series of tabletop jumps, all located at about 3,500 m (11,550 ft).

The effort put into maintaining the pipe and park at Saas Fee isn't as great in winter as in summer. Only one of the three halfpipes is maintained in winter and it is often full of snow due to the massive dumps and high winds that the glacier often receives. The pipe is shaped by a Kassbohrer Pipe Master, which does a relatively good job. The main drawback of the pipe is its being so high up on the mountain (about 3,300 m/10,827 ft). This means that it is exposed to the elements (particularly the cold), making it very icy. Also, if you intend to hike it, bring an oxygen tank, as the air is very thin at this altitude!

Saas Fee is almost unrivaled as a snowboard destination in summer and for many visiting pros and campers visit them. The summer program includes three halfpipes, which are shaped regularly, ensuring that they maintain great shape. Saas Fee is investing a lot of resources into the summer snowboarding program and should be strongly considered as a summer snowboard destination.

Above: *Stick to riding the Saas Fee halfpipes in summer when the sun is out and the weather is warmer. Photo courtesy of Saas Fee Tourism Office.*

LAAX
SWITZERLAND

STATISTICS

Elevations	(m)	(ft)
Top:	3018	9902
Base:	1100	3609
Vertical Drop:	1918	6292

Lifts	
Surface Lifts:	11
Double Chairs:	1
Triple Chairs:	0
Quad Chairs – Fixed Grip:	3
Quad Chairs – Express:	2
Six Chairs – Express:	1
Gondolas:	7
Cable Cars:	4
Funiculars:	0
Total:	29

Contact Details

Phone:	+41 81 921 2120
Fax:	+41 81 921 2255
Email Address:	contact@whitearena.ch
Internet Site:	www.laax.ch

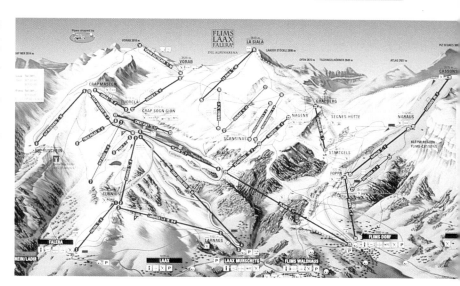

RESORT REVIEW

Above: *Mouse Beuchat stylin' a perfect indy as he plunges 20 feet into Laax.*

Drive into the resort of Laax and the first thing you are confronted with is a large fluorescent sign that says 'Laax Crap'. This is an amazing contradiction. Laax is the most awesome, snowboard-friendly resort you could ever visit. In fact, Laax was recently voted the best snowboard destination in Switzerland in an opinion poll taken by the Swiss 'Sunday-Newspaper' (*Sonntags-Zeitung*), which took a close look at 60 of the most popular winter sport destinations in Switzerland. What makes Laax so amazing is its huge vertical drop, nearly 2 km (1.24 miles), its awesome lift system, its superb snowboard facilities and its radical freeriding terrain. Further, nearly every chairlift is high speed and extremely comfortable. So not only do you get a long ride down but you get a very rapid and pleasant ride back up the mountain. In Romansh, 'crap' means rock. Laax certainly rocks.

The resort management's commitment to snowboarding is impressive. They don't just talk about installing three perfectly shaped halfpipes – they actually do it. In fact, Laax was the first resort in Europe to have a Pipe Dragon. Laax has a permanent park and two in-dirt halfpipes at 2,228 m (7,352 ft) at Crap Sogn Gion and another permanent park and halfpipe on the Vorab

Glacier. Laax is a permanent fixture on the Swatch World Boardercross Tour.

The atmosphere at Laax is very laid back, with the major concern being to enjoy life. This is demonstrated by the huge open air 'Rock-Bar' located next to the Crap Sogn Gion Cable car. On beautiful days it seems that people just travel up to the Rock-Bar, plant their board or skis in the snow, kick back, listen to the music and soak up the sun. It is a very relaxing atmosphere. What's more, everyone at Laax is extremely friendly and helpful.

TERRAIN

FREERIDING

The terrain at Laax is extremely varied, from steep groomed runs to undulating off-piste runs with large rollers and cliffs. Snowboarders of any skill level can find terrain to enjoy at Laax. However, Laax does lack one thing. Unlike Verbier and Saas Fee, Laax does not have much in the way of consistently steep, extreme terrain.

Powder Turns: Some of the best places to find fresh turns are off-piste around the Alp Ruschein Double Chair and directly under the Curnus High-speed Quad. The Alp Ruschein area is the better – it is a rickety old chair, very few people venture down the run, and if they do they usually stick to the pistes.

Early Morning: The great thing about Laax is that the majority of the resort receives sun for most of the day. Any of the runs near the top of the mountain hold the sun for most of the day. The area that only receives sun in the morning is around the Crest da Tiarms and Crappa Spessa. So if you wish to do this area, hit it in the morning.

Bad Weather: The top of Laax is very exposed, with very few trees. There are not a lot of runs cut through the trees at Laax, so in bad weather it may be difficult to find a run with good visibility. The runs to ride in bad weather are under the Curnius Express Quad and down at the base of the resort, where there are some trees. In bad weather it is probably best to find an alternative activity.

Avoiding Crowds: The Laax lift system is huge. It has a capacity of 42,000 people per hour. On the busiest days there are only about 23,000 skiers and snowboarders. This means there are very few problems with lift queues. The worst lift for queues is the Crap Sogn Gion Cablecar. If this is crowded, just walk across to the Larnags Gondola.

Hiking: One of the best backcountry runs is the Cassons Run, which starts from the top of the Cassons Cablecar. It starts off with a nice steep gradient that is awesome in fresh snow, then opens up into a superb bowl with a deep natural gully down the centre. The gully has some great hips and lips. Another great freeriding run begins at the Crap Masegn. Traverse hard to skiers' right, climb over the ridge to the right of the Crest da Tiarms Run, and drop into a wide open bowl that has plenty of small cliffs and rollers. Follow the run all the way back to the Falera Lift.

Above: *With the distinctive Crap Sogn Gion in the background, Damo Liddy exposes his backside in the Laax halfpipe.*

Beginners: The Foppa High-speed Quad is the best place for beginners. There are some nice gentle slopes here.

FREESTYLE

Laax is renowned for its halfpipes and it certainly deserves such a reputation.

Halfpipes: There are three halfpipes, two at Crap Sogn Gion and the other at the Vorab Glacier. All are shaped every few days by a Pipe Dragon and are always in excellent condition. During the winter, the halfpipes at the Crap Sogn Gion are more heavily used; during summer, the halfpipe on the Vorab Glacier is used for summer camps. The major problem with the pipes at the Crap Sogn Gion is that the rope tow that services them does not go all the way to the top. This can become quite frustrating. Above the Crap Sogn Gion halfpipes is a really cool snowboard bar known as the No-Name-Cafe, which pumps out music all day long. Inside the bar you can kick back on the comfortable lounges and let your legs recover. There are snowboard parks next to each of the halfpipes.

Snowboard Parks: A park comprising two kickers is set up next to the halfpipes at Crap Sogn Gion. Unlike the pipes, these are not of superb quality. The landings on the jumps tend to be too short. There is a boardercross track on the Vorab Glacier and it's super fun.

DAVOS
SWITZERLAND

STATISTICS

Elevations	(m)	(ft)
Top:	3146	10322
Base:	1560	5118
Vertical Drop:	1586	5203

Lifts	
Surface Lifts:	36
Chairs:	7
Gondolas:	3
Cable Cars:	8
Funiculars:	3
Total:	57

Contact Details	
Phone:	+41 81 415 2162
Fax:	+41 81 415 2101
Email Address:	davos@davos.ch
Internet Site:	www.davos.ch

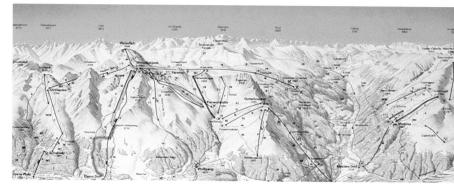

RESORT REVIEW

Davos is well known because it is Europe's highest town (as opposed to village), at 1,540 m (5,082 ft). And it certainly is a town, stretching from Klosters through Davos Dorf and on to the town centre at Davos Platz. It has all the conveniences of a large town – supermarkets, bars, restaurants, sports fields, cinemas, swimming pools and even a golf driving range. And if you feel like a spot of gambling, Davos has its very own casino.

The Davos/Klosters region comprises seven large ski areas – Parsenn, Pischa, Jakobshorn, Strela-Schatzalp, Rinerhorn, Madrisa and Gotschna. There are over 40 lifts, with verticals at most of the areas close to or exceeding 1,000 m (3,333 ft).

The lift systems, especially on Jakobshorn and Parsenn, are modern, fast and efficient. Davos usually hosts some of the major ISF halfpipe competitions. For this reason its freestyle facilities are excellent.

The Davos area operates an excellent 'hands-free' lift ticket system. You pay a deposit of CHF10 to receive a card that automatically scans at the gates of all lifts. When you return your card, your deposit is returned. The system works well and saves you the hassle of always pulling your pass out.

Being a large town, Davos has a very lively nightlife. The best place to head to is the Bolgenshanze. It is located down by the river, below Jakobshorn. It plays music late into the night and often has theme nights. But the best thing about the Bolgenshanze is the game of pflock. To find out what the game is, you'll just have to go there and check it out.

Davos was originally established in the 1860s as a health resort for tuberculosis sufferers. The high-altitude of Davos was supposed to repress the disease. Although tuberculosis is no longer a major disease, Davos still has numerous health clinics that offer treatments and therapies for respiratory illnesses.

Above: *Mouse Beuchat risks his life as he jibs a rail alongside a 1,000-foot cliff! OK, maybe we are exaggerating a little.*

TERRAIN

FREERIDING

With seven mountains, the freeriding terrain at Davos is endless. Each area has its own special characteristics.

PISCHA (2,483 M / 8,193 FT)

Pischa is probably one of the smallest areas in the region. For this reason it tends not to be as crowded as the larger Jakobshorn and Parsenn. There is a good natural halfpipe on the Grat Run. If you know where you are going, you can head off to skier's right of the Flüelameder Lift (b) and ride all the way down to the Davoser Lake. Then it is just a matter of walking out to the road.

JAKOBSHORN

Jakobshorn (2,590 m/8,547 ft) is renowned among snowboarders around Europe as an awesome freeriding mountain. The area directly under the Luftseil Cablecar (e) faces north and has some great rolling terrain as well as medium-sized rock drops. The bottom third of the mountain, particularly around the Carjol-Fuxägufer Double Chair (g), has some nice tree runs. Although the forest is pretty dense in parts, it is still possible to find good lines. Just be aware that there are cliff bands in the trees. A good backcountry run is to head off the bottom of the Jatzhorn Lift (k), through the trees down to the village of Muhle. For some groomers, try the runs around the Clavadel Chairlift (l).

RINERHORN

Like Pischa, Rinerhorn (2,490m/8,217ft) is not large but it holds good powder and is usually not very crowded. One of the best backcountry runs is Run 10, which starts from the top of the Nüllisch Lift (p), heads through an open powder bowl, then down through the trees along a ridge line, finishing up in the village of Glaris.

MADRISA

The big thing at Madrisa (2,602 m/8,586 ft) is hiking. Some awesome terrain can be reached via short hikes. For an excellent run, hike off to skiers' left of the Madrisa Lift (y), then drop into an awesome valley that goes all the way down to the village of Schlappin.

GOTSCHNA

Gotschna (2,285 m/7,540 ft) is home to some of the most extreme terrain in the Davos region. Cliffs and chutes litter the north face of this resort. The on-piste stuff is totally harmless, but anywhere off-piste you could get killed. Check with the locals before trying anything too stupid.

PARSENN

Parsenn (3,102m/10,236 ft) has the highest lifted point in the region – the Weissfluh, at 2,844 m (9,385 ft). Not surprisingly, it also has the longest runs. The Standseil Funicular takes you all the way from the Davos Dorf almost to the peak. It provides access to an amazing array of terrain. There is a small snowboard park off the Meierhofer Tälli Chair (n). The north face of the Parsenn is extreme, so be careful.

Above: *Justin Drerup finds solace in the trees of Jakobshorn.*

SCHATZALP/STRELA

Schatzalp (2,545m/8,398 ft) probably has one of the best freeriding runs in the whole region. There is a gully that runs from the top of the Strelapass all the way down to Davos Platz. Along the way there are rollers, banks and small drops. Just stick in the gully all the way. At the bottom you can ride through the trees and you will eventually hit the sled track. It is probably the most enjoyable run at Davos.

FREESTYLE

Unlike the freeriding, which is spread over the seven regions, the main freestyle facilities are located on Jakobshorn. A park and beginner pipe are located up on the mountain, next to the Jatz-Junior T-bar (j), and a World Cup pipe is located at the base of the mountain just next to the Bolgen T-bar (i).

Halfpipes: The halfpipe next to the Bolgen T-bar is of World Cup standard. It is about 80 m (264 ft) long with good 3.6-4.2 m (12-14 ft) walls. It is on a steep slope, so maintaining speed is not a problem. The transitions and the vert are excellent. It's maintained regularly with a Snow Turbo Grinder. Several nights during the week the lights are turned on and so begins an awesome night expression session. What's more, the Bolgen T-bar (i) is free at night. The great thing about the pipe is that you can do circuits using the Bolgen T-bar (i). The Davos pipe is definitely one of the best in Europe.

Snowboard Parks: The park next to the Jatz-Junior T-bar (j) is small. The jumps are really designed for beginners. If you want some freestyle fun, go to the halfpipe.

ST MORITZ
SWITZERLAND

STATISTICS

Elevations	(m)	(ft)
Top:	3057	10030
Base:	1720	5643
Vertical Drop:	1337	4386

Lifts	
Surface Lifts:	8
Chairs:	3
Gondolas:	0
Cable Cars:	3
Funiculars:	0
Total:	14

Contact Details

Phone:	+41 81 838 7373
Fax:	+41 81 838 7310
Email Address:	kvv@stmoritz.com
Internet Site:	www.stmoritz.com

RESORT REVIEW

St Moritz is the capital of the fur coat and the poodle in a cardigan. There are more people wearing dead animals in this town than anywhere else in the world. Yes, that's right, St Moritz is the ski choice of the rich and famous. With its own airport, they wing in at any time, sporting the latest ski gear and the compulsory fur coat. But the good thing is, the rich and famous hardly ever go off-piste, which means there is always plenty of powder to track.

St Moritz is actually split into two parts, representing the old and the new. St Moritz Dorf is the old town and contains the exclusive shops, hotels and restaurants. It is located up on the hill overlooking the valley. St Moritz Bad is the new but less attractive part of town. It came out of the 1970s building spree so it is not particularly aesthetically pleasing, to say the least. If you want a more relaxed atmosphere, head for the villages of Pontresina or Celerina, 15 minutes down the valley.

St Moritz comprises four resorts – Corviglia-Marguns-Suvretta (shortened to Corviglia), Corvatsch-Furtschellas (shortened to Corvatsch), Pontresina and Diavolezza. The biggest areas are Corviglia and Corvatsch, which together have 38 lifts including two funiculars and four cable cars. Although the major lifts are cable cars, gondolas or high-speed quads, the majority of lifts are in fact t-bars. The lift systems at Corviglia are the largest and most efficient.

St Moritz is home to some of Switzerland's top riders. Michi Albin, Franco Furger, Reto Lamm and Therry Brunner all use St Moritz as a base camp and training ground.

If you're after nightlife, you are better off heading to Davos or Laax. There is some nightlife in St Moritz but it is pretty dull. Check out the Stübli and Müli bars in the Schweizerhoff Hotel.

Above: *The Corviglia Tram rises high above the fur coats and ritzy jewels of St Moritz.*

TERRAIN

FREERIDING

Forget about the prestige and pompousness of St Moritz; the freeriding is totally amazing. The best freeriding exists at Corviglia and Corvatsch. There is good riding at Pontresina and Diavolezza, but the lifts tend to be a little slower.

One of the funnest runs at St Moritz is located in-bounds at Corviglia. At the base of the Murezzan Chair, head off to skiers' left and you will find a large gully. This gully runs half way down the mountain. It is full of small hits, banks and spines. When the gully runs out there are numerous cat tracks to launch off on your way back to the base. It is the perfect run to finish the day.

Powder Turns: The pick of the crop is probably the chute off the Piz Nair at Corviglia. Take the Piz Nair Gondola (d) up to the peak at 3,057 m (10,081 ft) and drop the front-facing chute. This slope is south-facing, so it gets baked pretty quickly – the best time to hit it is early morning. At the base of the chute, head off to skiers' right. You will hit a wide-open gully with rolling terrain. You can ride the gully all the way to the base of the mountain.

The powder at Corvatsch stays a little longer than at Corviglia since most of the slopes are north-facing. The run from the top of Giand Alva (2,643 m/8,721 ft) down through the Hahnensee and into St Moritz Bad is pretty amazing.

Early Morning: Corviglia is the best place to hit in the morning since it receives the sun first. For some high-speed runs, head up to the Marguns area and the Las Trais Fluors Chair.

Bad Weather: Stick to the trees under the Signal Cablecar at Corviglia. Don't even bother with Corvatsch – the runs are too exposed.

Avoiding Crowds: If you want to avoid the crowds, take a trip out to Pontresina and Diavolezza. These resorts have some great terrain to explore.

Above: *Perfect pipe and perfect blue skies. A local gives praise to his parents for raising him in St Moritz. Photo courtesy of Oberengadiner Bergbahnen.*

Hiking: There are some excellent hikes off the Las Trais Fluors peak at Corviglia but you really need to know where to go.

Beginners: The best slopes for beginners are around the Quartas and Tschainas T-bars at the base of Corviglia.

FREESTYLE

Corviglia is the place for freestyle riding. The park, pipe and boardercross track are located under the Signal High-speed Quad.

Halfpipes: The halfpipe at Corviglia is one of the best in the country. It is about 90 m (297 ft) long with 3.6 m (12 ft) walls. It is a fairly narrow pipe, like the one in Laax. It is regularly cut using a Pipe Dragon, which ensures that the transitions and vert are always super smooth. It even has its very own rope tow, although the ride is extremely painful. In fact, you probably use more energy catching the rope tow than riding the halfpipe. On any particular day, some of St Moritz's top riders can be found sessioning the Corviglia pipe.

Snowboard Parks: The park at Corviglia is located next to the Murezzan T-bar (m), right beside the pipe. The park is an excellent affair with a huge quarterpipe and a big gap jump. There are also a few smaller hits to keep the intermediate riders happy. Despite St Moritz's reputation as a place only for the rich and famous, the park facilities at Corviglia are a freestyler's heaven and should not be missed just because you think St Moritz is too snobby.

At Furtschellas (part of Corvatsch) there is a small park and a boardercross track, but you are far better off searching out the natural hits on the mountain or heading over to the Corviglia pipe.

Left: *Classic St Moritz. Blue skies, fresh snow and a beautiful method. Photo courtesy of Oberengadiner Bergbahnen.*

GLOSSARY

Like most other sports, snowboarding has many technical terms whose meanings are not immediately obvious. Here is a glossary of the terms that are most important and are used quite often.

Air As in 'get air' – The act of jumping on a snowboard.

Asymmetrical A board is asymmetrical when the heel-side and toeside sidecuts are offset. This is especially popular on race boards.

Back from center This refers to the position of the bindings relative to the center of the board. If the center of the distance between the bindings (ie the center of the stance width) is in line with the center of the snowboard, then the stance is said to be center. If the center of the stance width is closer to the tail of the snowboard, then the stance is said to be back from center. For all-round riding, back from center is best.

Backside spin When riders spin 'backside', they are turning their upper body backwards so that their first 90 degrees of rotation are blind and their back faces down the hill. For regular footers, a backside spin is clockwise. For goofy footers, a backside spin is anticlockwise.

Base The underside of a snowboard, which is usually made of P-Tex.

Bindings Equipment that is attached to a snowboard and is used to hold the snowboard onto a rider's feet. Bindings can either be straps or step-ins (where the rider's foot is secured by a special latch on the boot).

Above: *Step-in bindings by K2.*   **Above:** *Step-in bindings by Burton.*

Boardercross
Race that involves four to six riders who must negotiate obstacles such as bumps, banks and tabletops. The first two (or three in a heat of six people) riders to cross the line progress to the next round.

Bone To straighten one leg while performing a trick in the air.

Bonk To purposely hit an object with the snowboard whilst in the air.

Cap construction A snowboard has a cap construction when it has no separate sidewalls. Rather, the topsheet is moulded into the sidewalls.

Corduroy After a slope has been freshly groomed, small grooves line the snow. This snow is excellent for carving on.

Corn snow This is the type of snow that exists in spring. The warm weather melts the snow, causing the snow crystals to become very large. This snow is usually very slushy and slow.

Crud Old lumpy snow.

De-tune Method used to reduce the sharpness of the edges at the tip and tail. This aids in turning.

Fakie Riding backwards (same as switch).

Fall-line Refers to the direction of the slope. If you are going directly down the slope, following its contour, then you are snowboarding the fall-line. If you are traversing the slope, you are said to be going across the fall-line.

Fixed-grip lift Refers to a type of chairlift where the chair is permanently attached to the cable. Fixed-grip chairs are much slower than high-speed chairs.

Flat ground tricks Freestyle tricks performed on flat, groomed slopes without using hits. These tricks are performed using the natural spring in the board.

Flex pattern Refers to the flex through the nose, waist and tail of the board. The flex of a board can be either soft or stiff. The flex pattern will affect the turning performance of the board.

Fluorescent one-piece suits Something that should be left to the 1980s.

Foam core The center of the board is made of foam instead of wood. Foam-core boards are lighter but have a shorter life than wood-core boards.

Freeriding This type of riding involves using the whole mountain and incorporates freestyle, carving, extreme, powder and cruising.

Freestyle Halfpipe and kicker riding.

Frontside spin When riders spin 'frontside', they open up their shoulders so that their upper body is facing forwards down the hill during the first 90 degrees of the rotation. For regular footers, a frontside spin is anticlockwise. For goofy footers, a frontside spin is clockwise.

Goofy footers Refers to those who stand on their snowboard with their RIGHT foot FORWARD (as opposed to regular footers).

GS turns Giant Slalom turns – wide, arcing turns performed at high speed.

Halfpipe A mound of snow constructed in a U shape for the purpose of snowboarding. An International Snowboard Federation halfpipe is 100 m (330 ft) long, with walls that are 3.5 m (11.5 ft) high.

Above: *Todd Richards, halfpipe master.*

Highback The piece on the back of a snowboard binding that leans up against the rider's calf muscle.

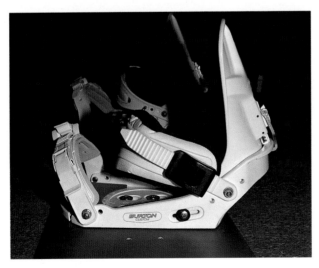

Above: *This photograph illustrates the latest in highback technology.*

High-speed lift Refers to the type of chairlift where the chair detaches from the cable in the loading stations. High-speed chairs are much faster than fixed-grip chairs.

Hit A more general term used for any type of jump or kicker.

Hole pattern Refers to the pattern of the inserts in the snowboard which are used to attach the bindings. There are two standard hole patterns – the Burton 3-D Hole Pattern and the more widely used 4-Hole Pattern.

Hucking Refers to the situation where a rider launches off a huge kicker or cliff. It can be used in both a derogatory or complimentary sense. If a rider is simply throwing him or herself off jumps, it is derogatory. However, where the rider is stomping the landing, it is complimentary.

In-bounds Refers to all areas within the ski area boundary.

Inserts Inserts are made of steel and fixed into the snowboard. Bindings are attached to the snowboard using the inserts.

Invert A freestyle move where the rider gets upside down.

Jibbing This refers to riding on objects such as logs, rocks, rails and benches.

Kicker A mound of snow that is built and shaped for the purpose of jumping off with a snowboard.

Kook Someone who has no idea.

Leash Strap that links the rider to the snowboard.

Lip The very top edge of the halfpipe or end of a kicker. When a snowboarder airs out of a halfpipe or off a kicker, the lip is the last piece of snow touched.

Mitts Fingerless gloves.

Moguls Bumps formed on slopes from people continually skiing the same line. Loved by skiers and hated by snowboarders.

New school Refers to the latest style and tricks in snowboarding. What is and isn't new school changes over time. Jibbing used to be new school, then became old school and is now new school again.

Off-piste Anywhere off the groomed and marked runs.

Ollie This is a technique utilized by a rider to get in the air without using a jump.

Out-of-bounds Refers to all areas outside the ski area boundary.

Park An area set aside at a resort that contains kickers, spines and rail slides.

Pieps Avalanche transceiver. Also a brand name.

Poma A type of lift. A dinner plate-sized disc is attached to a pole, which is attached to the lift cable. The person places the disc between their legs and is dragged up the mountain.

P-Tex Bases of most snowboards are made of this.

Punter Someone who has no idea.

Quarterpipe Half of a halfpipe. It may be natural or man-made. They are the latest thing to session in the backcountry.

Regular footers Refers to those who stand on their snow board with their LEFT foot FORWARD (as opposed to goofy footers).

Rodeo An inverted backside or frontside spin.

Salting When the snow is too soft, specially formulated salt is used to harden it. It is especially useful for hardening a soft halfpipe in spring. The only problem with salting is that the salt continually eats away at the snow.

Shredding the gnar This is a non-serious phrase thought up by the Americans to refer to a situation where a rider is doing some pretty crazy trick.

Side slip Moving down a slope with the edge perpendicular to the fall-line.

Skating The technique used to get across flat sections. The rider pushes with the back foot and places his/her weight on the front foot.

Slam To fall hard after performing a trick.

Slopestyle A competition where a rider is judged on tricks performed over two or more jumps.

Slush In spring, the snow crystals melt and lose their shape. The snow becomes very watery and provides a sensation of water-skiing rather than snowboarding.

Snake When someone jumps the queue and drops into the pipe or a kicker, they have snaked the line.

Stance angles The angles of your bindings measured from the perpendicular position.

Stance width This is the distance from the front binding to the back binding.

Stiffy To straighten both legs whilst in the air. May involve a grab.

Stomp Refers to the situation where the rider lands a jump perfectly. It is said that the rider 'stomped' the landing.

Stomp pad A piece of grippy rubber or plastic that is stuck on the snowboard between the two bindings (usually closer to the back binding). The rider uses the stomp pad to control the snowboard when the back foot is not strapped in.

Switch Riding backwards (same as fakie).

T-bar A surface lift that drags two people up the slope at the same time and is called this because the bar you sit on is actually in the shape of a 'T'.

Topsheet Material that forms the top of the snowboard.

Torsional stiffness This refers to how easy the snowboard can be twisted along its longitudinal plane. Torsional stiffness provides greater stability when turning at high speeds. It eliminates the chattering effect.

Transition (or trannie) In relation to a halfpipe, the transitions are the curved sections on the walls. In relation to a kicker, the transition refers to the curved section between the run-in and the lip of the kicker.

Twin tip A snowboard design where the tip and tail shape and flex are identical. Used for freestyle riding, although they have gone out of fashion.

Vert (halfpipe) The top section of the halfpipe wall, which is vertical.

Vertical rise The vertical distance from the lowest to the highest point on the mountain that is accessed by lifts. If the lowest lifted point is 1,000 m (3,300 ft), and the summit is 1,500 m (4,920 ft), then the vertical rise of the resort is 500 m (1,640 ft). It is used as a general guide of how big a resort is and how long the runs may be. Commonly referred as the vertical at a resort.

Waist The narrowest part of a snowboard.

Winding down the windows This happens when a rider loses it off a jump and begins swinging their arms in an anticlockwise direction in an effort to try to regain balance. It usually indicates an impending slam.

Wood core The wooden center of the board. A small percentage of boards have foam cores.

INDEX